Public Mental Health Today

A handbook

Edited by Isabella Goldie

Mental Health Foundation

Pavilion

Public Mental Health Today

A handbook

Published by:
Pavilion Publishing (Brighton) Ltd.
Richmond House
Richmond Road
Brighton
BN2 3RL

Tel: 01273 623222
Fax: 01273 625526
Email: info@pavpub.com

First published 2010

ISBN: 978-1-84196-285-6

Pavilion is the leading training and development provider and publisher in the health, social care and allied fields, providing a range of innovative training solutions underpinned by sound research and professional values. We aim to put our customers first, through excellent customer service and good value.

Editor: Isabella Goldie, Mental Health Foundation
Production editor: Kerry Boettcher, Pavilion
Cover design: Emma Garbutt, Pavilion
Page layout: Emma Garbutt, Pavilion
Printing: Ashford Press

Public Mental Health Today

A handbook

Edited by Isabella Goldie

Mental Health Foundation

Pavilion

Contents

About the contributors

Jacqueline M Atkinson

Jacqueline Atkinson is a chartered psychologist and professor of mental health policy in the section of public health and health policy at the University of Glasgow where she has worked for more than 30 years. Her earlier research interests included behaviour therapy with people with schizophrenia and the development of psychosocial education and support for people with schizophrenia and their carers. Latterly her research has focused on mental health legislation and policy, advance directives in mental health, capacity and impaired ability and mental health law, the protection of adults at risk and horticultural therapy with veterans. In 2002 she was appointed adviser to the Scottish Parliament Health and Community Care Committee to take a new Mental Health Bill through Parliament. She has a strong interest in research ethics and was a member of a LREC in Glasgow for eight years. She currently convenes the University's Ethics Committee for Non-Clinical Research on Human Subjects. She teaches both undergraduate medical students and postgraduate students studying for a Master's degree in Public Health.

Margaret Barry

Margaret Barry, PhD, is a professor of health promotion and public health and head of the World Health Organization Collaborating Centre for Health Promotion Research at the National University of Ireland, Galway. Professor Barry has published widely in mental health promotion and works closely with policy-makers and practitioners on the development, implementation and evaluation of mental health promotion interventions and policies at national and international level. Elected as Global Vice President for Capacity Building, Education and Training by the International Union for Health Promotion and Education (IUHPE) in 2007, she is co-ordinating international collaborative work on the development of core competencies for health promotion, including a major European Commission funded initiative in the European region. Having completed her primary degree and doctoral studies in psychology at Trinity College, Dublin, she has held previous posts as lecturer in psychology at the University of Birmingham, UK; Trinity College, Dublin, and as deputy director of the Health Services Research Unit at University College, North Wales. She was also visiting fellow at the Victorian Health Foundation, Australia in 2007 and visiting lecturer in 2002 at the World Health Organization Collaborating Centre at the Institute of Psychiatry, King's College, London. She is also co-author of the text *Implementing Mental Health Promotion* (Barry & Jenkins, 2007) published by Elsevier.

Manjit Bola

Manjit Bola has over 20 years of teaching and research experience, and has a special interest in health, race and gender issues. She is the course leader for the MA in Community Leadership and the course leader for all of the community engagement courses offered by the International School for Communities, Rights and Inclusion, which are delivered on a national basis. These leadership roles include the further development of new courses, and delivery of existing programmes of study, which contribute to widening participation in education for often marginalised groups. Her current teaching responsibilities involve teaching research methods to undergraduate and postgraduate students and the supervision of postgraduate dissertation students. Her research interests currently include exploring issues around mental well-being in BME communities, and health information and communication needs among diverse communities.

Lyndal Bond

Lyndal Bond joined the Medical Research Council Social and Public Health Sciences unit in January 2008 as associate director and programme leader for evaluating the health effects of social interventions. Prior to this appointment she was a senior research fellow with the University of Melbourne based at the Centre for Adolescent Health, Royal Children's Hospital, Australia (1997–2007). From 1997, she led the evaluation of the Gatehouse Project, a cluster randomised trial evaluating a multi-level school-based intervention (gatehouseproject.com) and subsequently developed and directed the Adolescent Health and Social Environments Programme. Lyndal is a member of the International Collaboration for Complex Interventions and is an investigator, or adviser, for a number of studies based on the Gatehouse Project approach to school-based interventions in the UK, North America and Australia. Her current research interests include understanding the health effects of social interventions, researching the implementation and sustainability of complex interventions and evaluating the implementation of evidence-based policy into practice. She is one of the principal investigators of GoWell, a 10-year evaluation examining the impact on health and the social determinants of health of housing and neighbourhood change.

Fiona Borrowman

Fiona Borrowman is presently health improvement manager for mental health and well-being in later life and dementia at NHS Health Scotland. Fiona has been in this post since November 2001 and is currently working part-time. She previously worked in health promotion in Lothian for 10 years working in primary care health promotion and managing a programme to promote the health of older people. Her background is primary care and community nursing. The NHS Health Scotland Mental Health and Well-being in Later Life Programme over the last six years has developed a health improvement programme of work including promotion of physical activity, mental health and well-being, falls prevention, osteoporosis awareness and dementia. She is a member of the EU Healthy Ageing Project from the European Union's Public Health Workplan 2003–2008, now Healthy Ageing Programme, Towards a Mentally Flourishing Scotland Reference Group on Mentally Healthy Later Life and on the Scottish Government Dementia Forum.

Dick Churchill

Dr Dick Churchill is a part-time general practitioner in Nottingham and associate professor of primary care at the University of Nottingham Medical School. Dick originally trained as a clinical biochemist and worked in this role for several years before changing career paths and undertaking a medical degree at the University of Nottingham, followed by vocational training in general practice. On completion of training he joined the academic department of general practice at the University of Nottingham where he has remained, working in both research and education combined with clinical practice in primary care. In addition to providing routine primary health care for young people within a general practice setting, Dick has undertaken research into adolescent health and mental health in primary care. He has also contributed to the development of training materials for GPs and practices, and represented the Royal College of General Practitioners (RCGP) on child and young people's health issues at policy level. Dick is chair of the RCGP Adolescent Health Group and was a founder member and trustee of the Association for Young People's Health (AYPH). He is also clinical co-editor of the E-Learning for Healthcare e-learning package on Adolescent Health, and has also contributed to other e-learning programmes in this field.

David Crepaz-Keay

David Crepaz-Keay is head of empowerment and social inclusion for the Mental Health Foundation, a UK charity that undertakes research, develops services, designs training, influences policy and raises public awareness to help people survive, recover from and prevent mental distress. He is leading the development, delivery and evaluation of 60 self-management courses for people with a severe psychiatric diagnosis across Wales. He is also a member of the All Wales Mental Health Promotion Network advisory board. Prior to this he was chief executive of Mental Health Media. David is an eloquent and passionate campaigner against discrimination on the grounds of mental health history. With over 25 years of involvement, first as a user of mental health services and later as a campaigner, he is also an advocate of service user voices being included in mental health service planning and delivery. David was a commissioner for patient and public involvement in health (January 2003– August 2007). The Commission (CPPIH) was created to give the public a voice in decisions that affect their health. He was a founder member of the English National Survivor User Network (NSUN). David is a former civil servant, who wrote economic models at HM Treasury and is currently undertaking a doctorate in promoting effective mental health service-user involvement at Middlesex University.

Elizabeth Corker

Elizabeth Corker is a research worker on the Viewpoint survey, part of the evaluation of the national anti-discrimination campaign, Time to Change, based at the Institute of Psychiatry, King's College London. Elizabeth is also undertaking a PhD determining the effects of self-stigma on self-esteem and empowerment in people with mental illness, after completing an MA (hons) in psychology at the University of St Andrews and an MSc in health psychology at University College London.

Linda de Caestecker

Linda de Caestecker is the joint director of public health for NHS Greater Glasgow and Clyde and Glasgow City Council. NHS Greater Glasgow and Clyde is the largest NHS Board in Scotland with a 1.2 million of population and encompasses the most deprived areas of Scotland. She is leading the implementation of a population-based parenting programme across Glasgow City area. Linda is also an honorary professor of public health with the University of Glasgow. Linda graduated in medicine from the University of Glasgow in 1979 and trained in obstetrics and gynaecology. She had various jobs in obstetrics and gynaecology around the UK and worked for a number of years in a university in Ghana in West Africa. She then returned to London in the late 1980s to start training in public health. She completed her training at the Public Health Research Unit at the University of Glasgow and was then appointed as a consultant in public health with Greater Glasgow Health Board in the mid-1990s. She worked as head of the maternal and child health unit of the then Scottish Executive for two years before returning back to NHS Greater Glasgow and Clyde as director of public health. She has retained an interest in child public health and has also been involved in research with Strathclyde and Glasgow Business Schools on employing lay workers as part of a health visiting team. She chairs the Maternity Services Action Group for the Scottish Government and was a member of the Scottish Government Steering Group for their recently published Early Years Framework.

Public Mental Health Today © Pavilion Publishing (Brighton) Ltd 2010

David Donald

David Donald is visiting research fellow in political economy in the Department of Economic Studies and International Business, Glasgow Caledonian University and a senior fellow at the Stirling Centre for Economic Methodology, University of Stirling. He has taught at Caledonian, Strathclyde and Cambridge Universities and has published in the *Journal of Economic Issues, Economic Journal and Business Studies*. A political scientist, he has special interests in the possibilities of a political economy of citizenship, in the roles and responsibilities of private firms in democratic politics, and in economic ideologies.

Maryanne Freer

Dr Maryanne Freer is a practising psychiatrist, a clinical academic and trains GPs in mental health across England, Northern Ireland, Scotland and Wales. GP education, mental health promotion and young people and mental health are Dr Freer's special interests. Being based in clinical practice and with an academic primary care career, Dr Freer has been working for the last 10 years on ways to engage GPs and teams in mental health in the context of the high patient demand across all clinical areas that GPs and primary care experience. She worked across Northern Ireland over a three-year period engaging with the majority of GPs and teams training on ways to mainstream mental health promotion into the GP consultation. She runs North East (England) Trailblazers programme – a national training programme for GPs and practice teams in mental health, which has been established for over 10 years. She teaches on a regular basis, both GP trainers and GP trainees, on the mainstream GP training programmes in the North East. Dr Freer has recently been appointed as the Charlie Waller Associate for the North East to deliver training to GPs on young people and mental health. Dr Freer is currently a member of the Royal College of GPs (England) mental health forum. She was a member of the Department of Health expert group for the white paper on mental health as well as having input into the Community Mental Health Teams Policy Guidance. She regularly speaks at national conferences. Dr Freer has a clinical background in community mental health teams and currently works clinically in rehabilitation psychiatry. She holds a clinical academic post at Newcastle-Upon-Tyne Medical School teaching and leading the Medicine in Community programme of the undergraduate medical degree. She worked previously in the Primary and Community Care Learning and Development Unit at the University of Northumbria and was a member of the development group for the World Health Organization Emerging Psychosis Declaration. She was also a member of an international mental health expert group visiting Ecuador in 1995.

Isabella Goldie

Isabella Goldie has been head of mental health programmes in Scotland, within the Mental Health Foundation, for six years. During her time within the Foundation, Isabella has developed a number of research and service improvement projects and worked extensively on Scottish mental health policy. Much of this work has focused on later life, equalities, inequality and the arts. She supported the development of VOX, the Scottish mental health service-user organisation and continues to support work ensuring that people with experience of mental health problems have a voice in mental health and public policy and service development, and to support the development of service user-centred research. Prior to her appointment, she worked at Glasgow Association for Mental Health (GAMH) in a range of posts including six years as Scotia Clubhouse director and latterly as an operations manager for GAMH. During her time at GAMH, she sat on the faculty board for the International Centre for Clubhouse Development, a role that involved supporting and accrediting Clubhouses around the world. Within this role she worked closely with Clubhouses in Harlem, New York and Cambridge, England. She has a Master's in Public Mental Health from University of Glasgow and trained and worked as a registered mental health nurse (RMN) early in her career. Isabella worked as a registered nurse for nine years in a range of settings including acute admission and forensic services. She held a number of community posts including later life and adult day services and latterly in the Southern General Psychotherapy Unit. Isabella has worked with colleagues in the Foundation to support the development of the Scottish Mental Health Arts and Film Festival (SMHAFF) and is chair of the festival.

Sandra Grant

Dr Sandra Grant started psychiatric training in Denver, Colorado, returning to Edinburgh to complete this and become a member (later fellow) of the Royal College of Psychiatrists. She qualified in psychoanalytical psychotherapy, subsequently becoming a training analyst. After 10 years as consultant psychotherapist in Glasgow, she moved into management (with an MBA) to help close a large mental hospital and establish 19 community mental health resource centres. As chief executive of the Scottish Health Advisory Service her focus broadened to include older people and people with a learning or physical disability. She worked with the Scottish Government in numerous review and planning groups, including the ministerial committee for Free Personal Care for the Elderly and reviewing services prior to the new Mental Health Act. Parallel to this she was chief executive of a small international NGO working with service users to foster social inclusion and was on the board of Mental Health Europe. Currently, she is on the board of the International Association for Forensic Psychotherapy. She now works independently in the fields of later life and mental health for race equality. Her work with older people has included health promotion work for NHS Health Scotland following the Age Concern/Mental Health Foundation inquiry into Promoting Mental Health and Well-being in Later Life, the National Steering Group for Mental Health in Later Life, the Reference Group for later life in Towards a Mentally Flourishing Scotland and the group on promoting psychological therapies in later life. Her consultancy work includes supporting a peer mentoring project on facilitating social activity for older people and a project to improve access to primary mental health care for Chinese older people. She is a director of Castlemilk Pensioners Action Centre.

Rob Gründemann

Dr Rob Gründemann is based in the Netherlands where he is a senior researcher at TNO, an independent research organisation specialising in business competitiveness, economic issues and quality of life. He is professor in human resources management at HU University of Applied Sciences Utrecht, and involved in numerous international projects on work and workplaces.

Gregor Henderson

Gregor Henderson works as an adviser and consultant in mental health and well-being to government, voluntary, public and private sector agencies in the UK and abroad. Gregor is also currently the national programme lead for the National Mental Health Development Unit's (NMHDU) Well-being and Population Mental Health Programme. NMHDU is the agency charged with supporting the implementation and delivery of mental health policy in England. Previously, the first director of Scotland's innovative and now internationally renowned National Programme for Improving Mental Health and Well-being from April 2003 to March 2008, Gregor has also been the director of the Scottish Development Centre for Mental Health and a senior fellow at the Institute of Psychiatry, King's College London. Gregor writes on mental health and well-being issues and lectures across the UK, Europe and internationally and is interested in exploring how policy, practice, research and people's lived experience can be integrated to help transform and improve how we think and act about mental health.

John Hollingsworth

John Hollingsworth is senior communications manager for NHS Health Scotland, the national health improvement body. Specialising in social marketing, he has promoted mental health improvement in a variety of

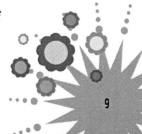

professional and community settings including social marketing strategies focused on peer support and well-being. He has an MBA from Aston Business School and his research interests include the relationship between corporate responsibility, organisational culture and public health outcomes.

Ade Kearns

Ade Kearns is professor of urban studies at the University of Glasgow, which he joined as a research fellow in 1987. He has conducted policy-related research into a wide range of housing and urban issues. His current research interests include community mix; neighbourhood quality and social cohesion; patterns and impacts of ethnic residential segregation; neighbourhood change, health and well-being; the impacts of residential turnover and relocation. Ade was co-director of the ESRC Centre for Neighbourhood Research, which conducted policy-related research and research reviews relevant to processes of neighbourhood change, sustainable communities and community cohesion.

Michael Killoran-Ross

Dr Michael Killoran Ross is deputy team leader of the STEPs Primary Care Mental Health Team in Glasgow, Scotland. A clinical psychologist, he has held posts in primary care in Ayrshire and was formerly the project manager of the Starting Well Health Demonstration Project, a national Scottish child health initiative managed through NHS Greater Glasgow and Clyde. Dr Killoran-Ross has extensive experience in community psychology. In addition to being a board member of the Clifford Beers Foundation (The European Centre for Mental Health Promotion), he is on the editorial boards of *The International Journal of Mental Health Promotion, The Journal of Mental Health Promotion* and *The Journal of Primary Prevention* (USA).

Lee Knifton

Lee Knifton holds several roles including visiting academic in applied social sciences, Strathclyde University, associate head of the Mental Health Foundation programmes in Scotland, health improvement lead in the NHS, director of the Scottish Mental Health Arts and Film Festival (mhfestival.com), co-chair of the UK Public Health Association section on mental health, and editorial board member of the *Journal of Public Mental Health*. His academic and professional interests lie in the areas of health equity, public mental health, stigma and discrimination. His professional remits are varied and span communications, arts, policy, practice and research. He is primarily concerned with research that brings together communities, practitioners and academics to achieve solutions and has published widely on studies undertaken at local, national and international level.

Trevor Lakey

Having originally trained as a biological scientist, Trevor Lakey has worked for over 20 years in the sphere of public health, with a predominant focus on West Central Scotland. Throughout his various roles, the central theme has been tackling health inequalities through partnership and community engagement approaches. For example, during 1992–1997 he established and managed the Greater Glasgow Health Board's Inequalities in Health Initiative. Allied roles have included serving a three-year term as a director of the Scottish Poverty Alliance, membership of the Scottish Executive's Social Inclusion Action Team – Local Anti-Poverty Action Group, acting co-ordinator of the Glasgow Healthy City Partnership, and a wide variety of leadership roles within health promotion and public health. He was also Scottish chair of the Society of Health Education and Promotion Specialists during the late 1990s and spent six years as a member of the Scottish Health Promotion Managers' Group. Some of the health promotion roles undertaken have included establishment and management of a range of child, youth and early years teams and programmes, with a focus on marginalised and disadvantaged groups; senior management team member for the Starting Well Child Health Demonstration Project (with a lead for community development functions); sexual health, men's and women's health programmes; equalities team and policy work (with a particular focus on black and ethnic minority communities and deaf community work); addictions; mental health; primary care and workplace health improvement. Mental health and well-being have been common threads throughout much of this work, including, in more recent years, a focus on suicide prevention activity. Since 2006, Dr Lakey has undertaken the role of health improvement and inequalities manager for the Mental Health Partnership, NHS Greater Glasgow and Clyde. He is responsible for managing a mental health improvement team and alcohol and drugs health improvement team and is also the choose life co-ordinator for Glasgow city and the commissioner of the Glasgow Anti-Stigma Partnership.

Rachel Lart

Rachel Lart is a senior lecturer in social policy in the School for Policy Studies at the University of Bristol. Her research interests include drug misuse policy and the overlap between criminal justice policy and mental health. Recent publications include *Interventions Aimed at Reducing Re-offending in Female Offenders: A rapid evidence assessment* (2008), published by the Ministry of Justice.

Andrew McCulloch

Andrew McCulloch has been chief executive of the Mental Health Foundation since 2003. Prior to his appointment, he was director of policy at the Sainsbury Centre for Mental Health for six years where he established a reputation as a leading authority on mental health policy. He was formerly a senior civil servant at the Department of Health for 16 years and he was responsible for policy on mental health and learning disabilities from 1992 to 1996. He has spoken and published widely on mental health issues. He has a PhD in psychology from the University of Southampton. Andrew's other experience has included being a school governor, the non-executive director of an NHS trust and the chair of Mental Health Media. He has chaired or served on a number of national advisory committees and is mental health adviser to the National Endowment for Science, Technology and the Arts. He has advised the Council of Europe, World Health Organization Europe and a number of major charitable foundations and NHS bodies on mental health and other public policy issues. He served on the independent review of mental health improvement in Scotland chaired by professor David Hunter. He is a trustee of the UK Council for Psychotherapy. He chairs two major national alliances related to mental health. Andrew has advocated for public mental health for many years. Outside of mental health Andrew has a keen interest in the natural environment and in the arts.

David McDaid

David McDaid is senior research fellow in health policy and health economics at the Personal Social Services Research Unit, LSE Health and Social Care and the European Observatory on Health Systems and Policies at the London School of Economics and Political Science. He is co-ordinator of the Mental Health Economics European Network and has published widely on the use of economics in health policy-making generally, and on mental health policy in particular, including the case for investing in promotion and prevention strategies. He has spoken widely to academic and policy orientated audiences and has provided expert advice to a variety of governments, public and voluntary agencies on mental health issues, including the World Health Organization and European Commission.

Karen Newbigging

Karen's current work has a particular focus on equalities and mental well-being. She is currently undertaking research in relation to advocacy and developing commissioning guides for local health and local authorities in England on mental well-being. Karen has over 30 years' experience in mental health including service development and provision, commissioning, consultancy and research. She originally trained and worked as a clinical psychologist in the NHS and was subsequently a lead commissioner for mental health services. Karen's recent research includes examining good practice in social care for asylum seekers and refugees, conceptualisations of mental well-being by BME communities in Scotland, addressing gender inequalities in mental health services and the organisation of mental health advocacy for African-Caribbean men.

Chris O'Sullivan

Chris O'Sullivan graduated from the University of Aberdeen in 2001, and is currently with the Scottish Development Centre for Mental Health (SDC). SDC is a small charity providing research, development and support services for improving mental health and well-being. Chris works across the spectrum of public mental health and mental ill health. Previously to joining SDC, Chris was a campaign development officer with Scotland's award winning anti-stigma campaign 'See Me'. Over the past four years Chris has worked extensively to support the European Commission in developing and delivering its mental health activities. For three years between 2006 and 2009 he led the SUPPORT Project, an EU public health programme providing close policy support to the European Commission in developing the European Pact on Mental Health and Well-being. Chris continues to work on the implementation of the Pact as a member of the IMPACT consortium, a group carrying out a framework contract for the EC to deliver the high level thematic conferences in each of the Pact themes. Chris is the lead scientific expert on social inclusion and stigma. He uses his lived experience of mental ill-health to inform his practice. He was a member of the steering group that developed Voices Of eXperience, the Scottish national service user organisation. He is chair of trustees of Depression Alliance Scotland. Chris uses Twitter (@mentalcapital) to discuss mental health, user involvement and mental health improvement. He is a keen amateur photographer and photo-blogger.

A-La Park

A-La Park is a research officer at the Personal Social Services Research Unit, LSE Health and Social Care at the London School of Economics and Political Science. A health economist by training, her principal research interests include making the economic case for investment in mental health promotion and mental disorder prevention, as well as examining the cost effectiveness of early intervention for individuals at risk of psychosis. She has worked on a number of projects funded by organisations including the European Commission, National Institute for Health and Clinical Excellence and the Department of Health in England. A-La also undertakes work in the area of injury prevention, with a particular interest in the economic case for preventing both suicide and falls.

Jane Parkinson

Jane Parkinson initially trained as an undergraduate in molecular biology at the University of Cambridge, followed by a PhD in molecular virology at the

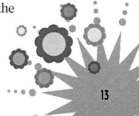

University of Oxford before spending several years as a postdoctoral researcher at the Medical Research Council (MRC) Virology Unit in Glasgow. In 2001, Jane moved into public health as a public health adviser with the newly established Public Health Institute of Scotland (now part of NHS Health Scotland, the national Scottish health improvement organisation). Since then she has worked on projects covering a range of topics from smoking and alcohol to the public health role of pharmacists and completed a Masters in Public Health part-time at the University of Glasgow. More recently, since 2004, her work has focused on developing and establishing national mental health indicators to assess the mental health of the Scottish population and the associated contextual factors. This work has been to support Scottish Government policy, initially contributing to the National Programme for Improving Mental Health and Well-being in Scotland and more recently to *Towards a Mentally Flourishing Scotland: Policy and action plan 2009–2011*. A set of adult mental health indicators was finalised at the end of 2007 with the associated data report in 2009. Jane is now working on a similar set of indicators for children and young people. The work to develop the indicators has involved combining an assessment of current policy, the evidence base, theory and data collection as well as influencing data collection systems in Scotland to gain better mental health data coverage. Jane has been involved in the development of the UK validated Warwick-Edinburgh Mental Well-being Scale (WEMWBS), to assess mental well-being, which is currently being used to collect data for one of the Scottish Government's National Performance Indicators.

Sarah Payne
Sarah Payne is a professor in health policy and gender in the School for Policy Studies at the University of Bristol. Recent research and publications have focused on the relationship between sex, gender and health, and on issues of gender equity in access to health care and in policy making. Publications include *The Health of Men and Women* (2006), *Gender Equity in Health Systems in Europe – Expert briefing for the World Health Organization* (2009) and *Gender and Access to Health Services* (2008), published by the Department of Health. Sarah is currently working on the relationship between mental health and social exclusion, as part of the project, Poverty and Social Exclusion in the United Kingdom being conducted by Bristol University together with colleagues from Heriot-Watt University, the National Centre for Social Research, Northern Ireland Statistics and Research Agency, Open University, Queen's University Belfast, University of Glasgow and the University of York.

David Pilgrim

David Pilgrim PhD is professor of mental health policy in the School of Social Work at the University of Central Lancashire and views himself as a generic social scientist with no particularly strong disciplinary loyalty. He has higher degrees in both psychology and sociology and his career has been divided between working in the British National Health Service in clinical psychology, and research and teaching in academia, with a particular interest in professionalisation, service innovations and service users' views. His book, *A Sociology of Mental Health and Illness* (Open University Press, 2005, with Anne Rogers), was winner of the 2006 British Medical Association's Medical Book of the Year Award. His other books include: *Examining Trust in Health Care: A multidisciplinary perspective* (Palgrave, 2010, with Floris Tomasini and Ivalyo Vassilev); *Key Concepts in Mental Health* (Sage, 2009); *A Straight Talking Introduction to Psychological Treatment* (PCCS Books, 2009); and Mental Health and Inequality (Palgrave, 2003, with Anne Rogers). He is currently writing a book on recovery from a critical sociological perspective with Ann McCranie, Indiana University USA (to be published by Palgrave).

Neil Quinn

Neil Quinn has a background in mental health social work and community development and is an academic within the Glasgow School of Social Work, Universities of Strathclyde and Glasgow. His principal research interest is mental health stigma and discrimination and he has published widely on tackling stigma and mental health inequalities within the media, the arts, low-income communities, work places and has also published work on cultural beliefs about mental health. Much of his research is based at the Mental Health Foundation, in particular focusing on the EU funded ASPEN programme, designed to address the stigma associated with depression across the EU member states. Neil combines his academic role with a practice one, managing an innovative mental health improvement programme within East Glasgow, which tackles inequalities in mental health within schools, workplaces and with asylum seeker and later life groups. He also chairs a range of groups including the Glasgow Anti-Stigma Partnership, the Sanctuary programme working with asylum seekers and refugees and is co-chair of the UK Public Health Association Mental Health Special Interest Group.

Jacquie Reilly

Jacquie Reilly is a sociologist and has been a research fellow at the Section of Public Health and Health Policy, University of Glasgow since 2004. Previous research was carried out at the Department of Sociology, University of Glasgow. Research interests have centred on risk and human behaviour in relation to a variety of health issues as well as in the production, content and reception of mass media messages. More recently in collaboration with Jacqueline Atkinson, she has carried out research centring on mental health legislation and policy, including the use of advance directives in mental health, capacity and impaired ability and mental health law, and horticultural therapy with veterans.

Jenny Secker

Jenny Secker is professor of mental health at Anglia Ruskin University and the South Essex Partnership University NHS Foundation Trust. She trained in Edinburgh, first as a mental health nurse and later as a social worker. After completing her PhD with the Department of Social Work and Social Policy at Edinburgh University she worked as a researcher in a number of academic and practice organisations. Her main research interests are in the area of mental health, employment and social inclusion. Between 2005 and 2007 she led the team commissioned by the Department of Health and Department for Culture, Media and Sport to carry out the study 'Mental Health, Social Inclusion and Arts'. Following publication of that study she has supported the development of Open Arts, a project providing arts participation and wider inclusive opportunities for people with mental health needs in South Essex.

David Shiers

Dr David Shiers, is the primary care adviser for the National Audit of Schizophrenia, Royal College of Psychiatry and the GP adviser to the National Mental Health Development Unit in England. Until March 2010 David was also the joint lead, with Dr Jo Smith, of the National Early Intervention in Psychosis Programme from its commencement in 2004. He has presented and written extensively both nationally and internationally about the issues facing young people and their families with emerging psychosis. David is an active member of the RCGP/RC Psychiatrists Forum for Primary Care Mental Health, contributing several guidance papers for GPs on psychosis. Previously a practising GP in Staffordshire for 20 years, his special interest in mental health stems from personal involvement as carer to a daughter with schizophrenia. This experience convinced David of the need to improve services for young people with early psychosis at a critical time of transition from adolescence to emerging adulthood.

Aideen Silke

Aideen Silke is project manager for Feeling Good About Where You Live, a joint research project led by NHS Greenwich and Greenwich Council which is seeking to understand the nature of factors in the physical and social environment and mental well-being for housing estate residents in deprived areas. She has presented widely on this project. Prior to this, Aideen was health strategy manager at the London Development Agency responsible for building public health into regeneration and supporting the agency to broaden its public health understanding working closely with key partners. At the Medical Schools Council, Dental Schools Council and Association of UK University Hospitals, she was responsible for clinical academic numbers, testing students for blood borne viruses, and admissions to medical and dental school. Her publications include: *A Survey of Clinical Academic Staffing Numbers in UK Medical and Dental Schools*, 2004, 2005 (London, CHMS); *Feeling Good About Where You Live: Improving mental well-being through improving the residential environment in Greenwich* (paper to the Heath Protection Agency Annual Conference, 2009); *Improving Mental Wellbeing Through Building the Community in Greenwich* and *Delivering Health Promotion in Partnership: Case study research on the contribution of a Metropolitan Police Safer Neighbourhood Team to health promotion* (Papers to UK Public Health Association 2010 annual conference). She holds an MPhil in history and philosophy of science and medicine from the University of Cambridge and an MSc in Public Health from the University of London. Her academic research includes an exploration of the role of the police in health promotion; clinical academic numbers in UK medical and dental schools; women and medicine in Cambridge; and an exploration of the role of Arabella Buckley as a populariser of science in 19th century Britain.

Carol Tannahill

Carol Tannahill grew up in Glasgow, graduated with a BA in Human Sciences from Oxford University, and MPH and PhD in Public Health from the University of Glasgow. She is currently director of the Glasgow Centre for Population Health, having been involved in establishing the organisation and leading its development since 2004. Prior to this, Carol held the posts of director of health promotion and executive board member of Greater Glasgow Health Board, and then senior adviser in health development in the Public Health Institute of Scotland. She is a fellow of the Faculty of Public Health, honorary professor with the University of Glasgow, and honorary visiting professor in the School of Health and Social Care at Glasgow Caledonian University.

Graham Thornicroft

Graham Thornicroft is professor of community psychiatry, and head of the multidisciplinary Health Service and Population Research Department at the Institute of Psychiatry, King's College London. He is a consultant psychiatrist and is director of research and development at the South London and Maudsley

NHS Foundation Trust. He chaired the External Reference Group for the National Service Framework for Mental Health in setting the mental health policy for England for the decade from 1999. His areas of research expertise include stigma and discrimination; mental health needs assessment, the development of outcome scales; service user involvement in mental health research; cost-effectiveness evaluation of mental health treatments; and mental health services in low income countries. He has authored and co-authored 23 books and over 205 papers in peer reviewed journals. His recent book *Shunned: Discrimination against people with mental illness* (2006) was named by the British Medical Association as Mental Health Book of the Year in 2007.

Katherine Weare

Katherine Weare is Emeritus professor of education at the University of Southampton and the University of Exeter. Her field is mental, emotional and social well-being and emotional and social learning, areas on which she has researched and written extensively. Her publications include *Developing the Emotionally Literate School* and *Promoting Mental, Emotional and Social Health: A whole school approach*, which are among the leading books in the area. She advised the Department for Children, Schools and Families (DCSF) on policy in the area of social and emotional learning and mental health in schools. Her report to the Department for Education and Skills (DfES) on What Works in Promoting Children's Emotional and Social Competence formed the research basis for primary and secondary SEAL, national projects now found across the UK. She is currently acting as a consultant to various national and international agencies to help them develop their education and mental health services, including the World Health Organization, the European Union, the Scottish Executive and the Welsh Assembly. She is a fellow of the Society of Public Health, editor of the journal *Health Education* and board member for Intercamhs (International Network for Child and Adolescent Mental Health and Schools).

Chapter 1

Introduction

Andrew McCulloch and Isabella Goldie

Public mental health is a relatively new concept that draws on the tradition of public health established in Victorian times. The idea of applying the public health model to mental health is on the face of it an obvious, and necessary, one. After all, mental illness is a massive 'disease group' with heavy mortality, morbidity and social and personal cost. Equally, poor mental health across society contributes to wider socio-economic and health problems such as higher levels of physical morbidity and mortality, lower levels of educational achievement and work performance/productivity, greater incidence of addictions, higher crime rates and poor community and societal cohesion. Anything that can be done to improve mental health at a population level will be of enormous benefit to society.

This much is apparently straightforward but as the subject is unpacked, difficulties and confusions can arise. Some of the key questions people ask about public mental health include the following.

▶ How is it different to public health? Is there any difference in the factors that support good physical health and those that support good mental health? What is distinctive about public mental health?

▶ What is the relationship between public mental health, mental health promotion, the prevention of mental illness and its treatment? Consequently do mental health services have a role?

▶ Given the determinants of mental health (eg. poverty, lifestyle),   is public mental health not just progressive social policy?

▶ What is the hard evidence that you can improve population mental health? What are the equivalents to clean water and air in mental health terms?

▶ Can investment in mental health promotion be prioritised within an economic environment where we have finite resources? Isn't it more ethical to focus limited resources on developing effective treatments for mental illness?

These are difficult questions, but we believe that they are worth grappling with in order to reach a better understanding of population approaches to mental health. They are threads that will run right through this book, but this introduction attempts to set the scene and introduce some basic concepts and arguments.

Public health

Great figures in health care have long understood that wider determinants of disease and recovery must be addressed as part of health care. Florence Nightingale expressed this well:

> 'I use the word nursing for want of a better. It has been limited to signify little more than the administration of medicines...(but) It ought to signify the proper use of fresh air, light, warmth, cleanliness, quiet, and the proper selection and administration of diet...'
> (Nightingale,1859; reprinted 1969).

These principles apply equally in public health as in treatment: in Victorian times improvements in sanitation, housing and the discovery of vaccination were much more important to population health than individual health care.

However, McKeown (1979) and others have argued that during the 20th century, wider determinants of disease and health were downplayed amidst a wave of technological health care advancements. This has taken place in mental health as much as physical health. While the bio-medical model of disease is relatively weak in relation to most mental illnesses, with crucial exceptions such as the dementias, little has been done until recently to develop a wider approach to mental health. Although there has been much criticism of the bio-medical model, not least from anti-psychiatry, this has tended to divert debate from public health and mental illness rather than focus on it, perhaps because it presents mental illness as a myth or a by-product of family dysfunction rather than a legitimate focus for health policy, which it absolutely must be (see McCulloch, 2006). In other words, we have been missing the point that whatever the precise nature of mental illness it is desirable both to prevent it and to promote good mental health.

With this in mind a useful definition of public health and one that makes sense in understanding public mental health is the one used in The Acheson Report (1998). That public health is:

> *'the science and art of promoting health and preventing disease through the organised efforts of society.'*
> (Acheson, 1998)

Mental health and mental illness

The World Health Organization's constitution defines health as:

> *'... a state of complete physical, mental and social well-being and not merely the absence of disease and infirmity.'*
> (WHO, 1946)

This definition indicates an early appreciation of the central role that mental health plays in overall health. Since then there have been many attempts to describe what we mean by mental health with the Health Education Authority describing it as:

> *'the emotional and spiritual resilience which enables us to survive pain, disappointment and sadness. It is a fundamental belief in our own and others' dignity and worth.'*
> (Health Education Authority, 1997)

and the World Health Organization as:

> *'...a state of well-being in which the individual realises his or her abilities, can cope with the normal stresses of life, can work productively and fruitfully and is able to make a contribution to his or her community.'*
> (WHO, 1986)

However, over recent years many have come to agree that achieving positive mental health is determined by more than just individual factors such as resilience and coping skills, and that it is also determined by environmental and social factors (eg. Secker, 1998; Rogers & Pilgrim, 2003; Friedli, 2009; Marmot, 2010).

Modern definitions of mental health stem from the idea that there is a state of positive health that is more than just the absence of illness, and that can indeed co-exist with illness. In other words, a mentally healthy person can develop a mental illness under certain circumstances, just as a physically healthy person can acquire an injury or infection.

Many people working in public mental health use a two dimensional model of mental health and mental illness (Tudor,1996; Keyes, 2002). This is often called the two continua concept as illustrated in table 1.

Table 1: Mental illness and mental health as different dimensions	
High mental illness	
Functional survivors Irrelevant diagnoses	Mentally ill and struggling
High mental health	**Low mental health**
Happy and healthy Functional and healthy	Struggling with life
Low mental illness	

In practice, of course, the quadrants in table 1 will not contain the same numbers of people. Most people at any one time will be situated in the bottom half of this diagram and will swing between struggling and functioning well. Similarly, many people with a mental illness will also struggle with their general mental health, but some people retain a specific mental illness diagnosis while coping very well. This model, like all models, is imperfect because there is, of course, a correlation between mental illness and poor mental health, just as there is between physical illness and poor physical health. Although the main intent of this two continua concept is to differentiate between health and illness it can be problematic when considering common mental health problems such as depression and anxiety, and the counter argument for using this model is that there is a risk of 'pathologising' what may be responses to difficult lives. Equally, this model has developed from work with western populations and may have less meaning within different cultural settings. However, despite these limitations, which are explored in greater detail within later chapters, the two continua concept does provide a useful tool from which further discussion can flow.

In public mental health we are usually aiming to improve population mental health generally ie. to draw people towards the bottom left hand quadrant of this diagram, but attempts to prevent mental illness are, of course, a perfectly legitimate part of public mental health.

Determinants of mental health

While we do not have a precise understanding of the determinants of many individual mental health problems, probably because mental health problems are ill defined and overlap anyway (McCulloch, 2006) and also because they are inadequately researched, we do have a general understanding of the conditions that promote mental health at social, community, family and individual level. Table 2 provides some key examples.

Table 2: Some determinants of good mental health			
Society	**Community**	**Family**	**Individual**
Equality	Personal safety	Family structure	Lifestyle (diet, exercise, alcohol)
Unemployment levels	Housing and open spaces	Family dynamics (eg. high/low expressed emotion)	Attributional style (ie. how events are understood)
Social coherence	Economic status of the community	Genetic makeup	Debt/lack of debt
Education	Isolation	Inter-generational contact	Physical health
Health care provision	Neighbourliness	Parenting	Relationships

It is very difficult to weight determinants as we lack the data and anyway, many determinants themselves are inter-related. However, it is likely that parenting, genetics, life events (and how they are interpreted) and inequality/ poverty are all major determinants of many mental illnesses as well as general mental health. It is not, however, easy to talk about individual 'causes' of mental illness as the determinants interact right through the individual's life history and have a cumulative effect. Sometimes though, there is an immediate 'cause' or determinant such as bereavement that will stand out clinically and practically.

What is public mental health?

Building on Acheson's definition of public health as outlined earlier, the term public mental health has been coined in order to underline the necessity for public health to take account of mental health (and mental illness). As such it refers to all or some of the following:

▶ actions taken to improve the mental health of a population – in national policy terms this is usually a country – but it could be a sub-population/ community

▶ the current mental health status of that population

▶ the knowledge base underpinning mental health improvement and the resulting professional practice

▶ policies to achieve the above such as the document *Confident Communities, Brighter Futures in England* (Department of Health, 2010) and *Towards a Mentally Flourishing Scotland* (Scottish Government, 2009).

The essential features are that we are seeking to improve or promote the population's mental health using a public health perspective, often with secondary aims such as reducing the prevalence of mental illness or specific negative outcomes such as suicide.

Public mental health is key to public health as a whole as many effects on health are impacted or mediated by mental health, for example, the impact of low self-esteem on risk behaviour or the links between depression, stress and heart disease.

Applying a socio-ecological model

Socio-ecological models are applied widely in public health, as it enables us to take account of the environment in which people live their lives alongside individual factors, which influence health status. This model provides an explanatory framework, which can also help us make sense of the broad range of factors that contribute to mental health. In other words it takes account of biological, psychological and social elements of mental health, whilst also recognising structural influences such as health care systems and the interactions between all these factors. A socio-ecological model also allows for a life course perspective and a consideration of how these factors combine and accumulate over time to promote or undermine mental health (for example, see Evans & Stoddart (1990) and Dahlberg & Krug (2002)).

What is different and distinctive about public mental health?

We would argue that public mental health is not fundamentally different or distinct to public health, it is simply a neglected element of it that needs to be emphasised, researched, and put into practice. The determinants of mental health are crucially similar to the determinants of physical health. This is especially true of cardiovascular health, which is intimately linked with a range of mental illnesses including dementias and depression, but there is strong evidence linking other body systems such as the endocrine and immune systems with mental health. These relationships are dynamic because mind and body are linked – or to put it another way the brain and central nervous system are organs supported by other body systems and receive oxygen, nutrients etc from them. It is not surprising that mental health and physical health are linked, indeed they are fully integrated and co-dependent. For historical reasons they have become disconnected within the health care industry but this has no real intellectual basis and much current thinking is about re-integrating conceptions of mind and body.

However, there is a range of issues that require special emphasis when considering mental health within a public health framework.

1. Epidemiological perspectives have allowed us to understand many public health issues, such as the link between tobacco and lung cancer, and there is much to be gained by considering their application in helping us

to understand the impact of socio-ecological factors on mental health (eg. factors which contribute to the development of dementias or the impact of racism on mental health within minority ethnic communities). However, mental health does require its own research agenda and although much can be learned from health research it is important to acknowledge that sometimes different and mixed methodologies need to be applied.

2. Psycho-social aspects are very important, in other words, how people think, behave and construct society.

3. Because most mental illnesses are poorly differentiated especially as regards causation, targeted preventative programmes may be impossible to construct. Actions taken to prevent depression may, for instance, be the same as to prevent generalised anxiety disorder.

4. Mental health improvement work needs to be truly multidisciplinary and inter-sectoral because no one discipline has all the required models and knowledge. Equally, no discipline (eg. medicine or social work) should be denigrated as regards its contribution.

5. A systems approach is needed as the evidence and theory suggest that whole systems interventions are likely to be much more effective.

Of course, all these arguments can be applied to public health as a whole and we hope the emergence of public mental health can enrich the public health movement.

What are the components of public mental health?

Public mental health is probably most usefully viewed as an over-arching concept, which covers all that a society does to promote and protect the mental health of its citizens. This will include structural and institutional change directed at improving mental health such as parenting programmes, health promoting schools and workplaces and the reduction of inequalities, but it will also include the following.

▶ The prevention of mental illness. As mentioned above, because most determinants of mental illness are more general determinants of poor mental health, there is a massive overlap between prevention and health promotion. However, there are mental illnesses that have some known determinants (eg. dementia and post-traumatic stress disorder) that could be appropriate for specific preventative action.

▶ The effective treatment of mental illness. Although a much misunderstood point, it is crucial to note that treatment programmes do form part of an over-arching approach to public mental health because they can ameliorate the illness and improve health or help to keep people with severe mental illness physically and mentally well. It is important for mental health providers to focus on the overall health of their clients as well as the reduction of psychiatric symptoms and there is much that they can do in this regard.

Is a public mental health programme realistic?

An important criticism of public mental health is simply that the agenda is too big. In others words, the determinants of public mental health cover pretty much social goods and ills and therefore the concept simply equates to good government. As such, it can be further criticised as being value laden or being based on neo-Marxist philosophy if it is seen to focus exclusively on structural factors such as inequality.

The counter argument is two-fold. First, that structural factors are demonstrably important to mental health. The correlation between position on the social gradient and mental health is well evidenced: the lower one is on the social gradient, the poorer the mental health outcomes. However, how one chooses to address those factors is partly determined by the evidence but legitimately partly by political choice. There is no reason why public mental health strategies cannot co-exist with social democratic or liberal public policies within a free market economy.

Second, the legitimacy of public mental health comes from the importance placed on good mental health, which does relate to how we order our society but also to what tools it can offer that can practically improve mental health. In the latter area there is a rapidly increasing evidence base about the effectiveness of all sorts of interventions such as mental health promotion in schools and parenting programmes, and these interventions are suited to a range of societies, cultures and political systems. Indeed the consequences of not investing in the mental health of our society would be challenging within any political structure.

This would be felt in terms of the prevalence of mental illnesses and the economic costs of treating these, but also the indirect socio-economic costs of poor mental health across society, such as crime levels, educational attainment and productivity within workplaces. In showing that a public mental health agenda can be successful it is important to focus on what is achievable and what the evidence says can work, as well as to tailor the strategy to local, regional or national need. Much of the rest of this book is concerned with some of these issues.

What is the evidence?

While there is no direct equivalent to clean air and water in mental health there are many parallels. Some of the structural issues that determine physical health are the same for mental health such as housing, welfare benefits and employment. Others are more generally associated with mental rather than physical health (although they affect both) such as parenting and freedom from abuse and bullying. In general, it is true to say the evidence for good public mental health interventions is building rapidly and in some cases it is of the same standard as required for treatment interventions.

Recently Barry *et al* (2009) reviewed the evidence base for mental health promotion and primary and secondary prevention, and in 2010 the Department of Health's document *Confident Communities, Brighter Futures* listed 58 separate public mental health interventions achieving the highest levels of evidence (ie. systematic review), while many others have high quality evidence falling short of this level. Although much more research is required, it is a myth to say that evidence for public mental health interventions is lacking.

Conclusion

We believe that applying the concept of public mental health has many benefits. It is:

1. designed to bring mental health properly into public health by providing a framework for action that acknowledges the central role that mental health plays in mediating wider health and social outcomes

2. de-stigmatising as it is primarily health focused, but it does not neglect those with a diagnosable illness

3. able to bring together key agencies that can improve population mental health that go well beyond the health care system

4. a focus for policy, research and practice on building resilience at individual, community and societal levels rather than waiting for problems to develop. It can therefore be cost-effective although much more economic analysis is required.

The need to focus on mental health will undoubtedly grow over the coming years and the field of public mental health will also develop as a result, despite resource constraints. In time it should be explicitly subsumed within public health as a whole. In England, for example, this may be aided by the re-creation of a public health service in local authorities coupled with explicit government commitment to a public mental health agenda. The latter, of course, has existed in Scotland for some time. The emerging evidence base and the very early stages of economic analysis of public mental health interventions led by institutions such as the London School of Economics (LSE), New Economics Foundation and the Institute of Psychiatry will help. Indeed, a research strategy for public mental health forms an essential subcomponent of both public health and mental health research, which UK research institutions are relatively well placed to pick up.

Delivery needs to be supported by better mental health awareness and training among public health staff and wider awareness across key agencies. Some local authorities and indeed larger businesses are already getting there, where a focus on well-being has been adopted, but much of the public sector and small and medium-sized businesses still lag behind. Education has already made good advances and we can expect more as the importance of well-being to learning becomes better understood.

All this is cautiously optimistic and could easily be thrown off course as UK governments struggle to restore our national budget deficit. But it is in some ways more general and long-term changes to our society that create the biggest threats (and opportunities) for public mental health, such as: increasing socio-economic inequalities, poverty and debt; changing demographics; environmental changes; changes in population-related health behaviour; population movement; the impact of conflict; and anxieties resulting from economic shocks or other disasters.

Much of the rest of this book is concerned with these issues and we hope that the discussions that follow will stimulate debate and prompt consideration of where 'mental health' sits within a public health framework. It is a difficult task to do justice to all of these issues within one book. However, in the chapters that follow we hope to:

► consider a range of perspectives and explore some of the theoretical and conceptual frameworks underpinning work within public mental health (as well as to provide some support to navigate the complexity and often contested terminology associated with mental health)

► provide a focus on some of the issues that pose significant challenges for society, such as the mental health of veterans returning from active combat and our ageing population

► consider mental health across the life course (ie. the role for public mental health in early years, work with children and young people and through to later life)

► reflect the diversity within our society by exploring mental health and gender and mental health within minority ethnic communities

► discuss settings in which mental health can be promoted or damaged, such as communities and neighbourhoods, the workplace, and schools

► provide some insights into the practicalities and challenges of making it happen through the experience of GPs and from within mental health improvement partnerships

► consider innovative and participatory ways to approach mental health improvement such as through participatory arts and community development work

► explore ways in which mental health can be measured, and the associated challenges.

There are threads running throughout much of this book, however, one central theme is the relationship between socio-economic inequalities and mental health. This challenge can best be summed up by Wilkinson and Marmot:

'Disadvantage has many forms and may be absolute or relative. It can include having few family assets, having a poorer education during adolescence, having insecure employment, becoming stuck in a hazardous or dead-end job, living in poor housing, trying to bring up a family in difficult circumstances and living on an inadequate retirement pension. These disadvantages tend to concentrate among the same people, and their effects on health accumulate during life.

The longer people live in stressful economic and social circumstances, the greater the physiological wear and tear they suffer, and the less likely they are to enjoy a healthy old age. If policy fails to address these facts, it not only ignores the most powerful determinants of health standards in modern societies, it also ignores one of the most important social justice issues facing modern societies.'
(Wilkinson & Marmot, 2003)

Although Wilkinson and Marmot were referring to health inequalities, these are the same social justice issues that the mental health field must grapple with. In response to these issues the authors within this book have sought to consider ways forward and key points that have emerged are:

▶ the need to take an inter-sectoral approach to achieve an impact on the wider determinants of mental health

▶ the importance of taking account of the context in which people live their lives, by adopting a facilitative approach to supporting communities to identify solutions that make sense to them

▶ the importance of linking research, policy and practice to ensure that policy and practice are informed by evidence but also that research agendas are informed by the priorities of communities

▶ the increasing opportunities to share learning across European and international stages

▶ the recognition that achieving public mental health gain will not address inequalities in mental health; we need to focus our energies instead on achieving greater mental health equity.

The authors in this book make a compelling case for prioritising public mental health. This is a long-term agenda, which requires long-term investment. This does not sit well with short-term approaches to funding mental health programmes. After reading this book no one should be in doubt of the need to continue and further develop work to improve public mental health; given the costs and losses associated with poor mental health, can we really afford not to?

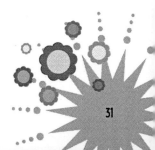

References

Acheson D (1998) *Independent Inquiry into Inequalities and Health* (Acheson Report). London: The Stationery Office.

Barry MM, Canavan R, Clarke A, Dempsey C & O'Sullivan M (2009) *Review of Evidence-based Mental Health Promotion and Primary/Secondary Prevention*. Report prepared for the Department of Health, London: Health Promotion Research.

Dahlberg LL & Krug EG (2002) Violence – a global public health problem. In: E Krug, LL Dahlberg, JA Mercy, AB Zwi & R Lozano (Eds) *World Report on Violence and Health*. Geneva: WHO.

Department of Health (2010) *Confident Communities, Brighter Futures: A framework for developing well-being*. London: DH.

Evans RG & Stoddart GL (1990) Producing health, consuming health care. *Social Science and Medicine* **31** 1359.

Friedli L (2009) *Mental Health, Resilience and Inequalities*. Copenhagen: WHO Europe.

Health Education Authority (2007) *Mental Health Promotion: A quality framework*. London: HEA.

Keyes CLM (2002) The mental health continuum: from languishing to flourishing in life. *Journal of Health and Social Behaviour* **43** 207–222.

Marmot M (2010) *Fair Society: Healthy lives – Strategic review of health inequalities in England post-2010* [online]. Available at: http://www.ucl.ac.uk/marmotreview (accessed August 2010).

McCulloch A (2006) Understanding Mental Health and Mental Illness. In: C Jackson & K Hill (Eds) *Mental Health Today: A handbook*. Brighton: Pavilion.

McKeown T (1979) *The Role of Medicine: Dream, mirage or nemesis?* Oxford: Blackwell.

Nightingale N (1969) *Notes on Nursing*. New York: Dover.

Rogers A & Pilgrim D (2003) *Mental Health and Inequality*. Basingstoke: Palgrave/Macmillan.

Scottish Government (2009) *Towards a Mentally Flourishing Scotland: Policy and action plan 2008–2011* [online]. Available at: http://www.scotland.gov.uk/Publications/2009/05/06154655/0 (accessed August 2010).

Secker J (1998) Current conceptualisations of mental health and mental health promotion. *Health Education Research* **13** (1) 57–66.

Tudor K (1996) *Mental Health Promotion: Paradigms and practice*. London: Routledge.

Wilkinson R & Marmot M (Eds) (2003) *Social Determinants of Health: The solid facts*. (2nd ed). Copenhagen: WHO.

World Health Organization (1946) *Constitution*. Geneva: WHO.

World Health Organization (1986) *Ottowa Charter for Health Promotion*. Ottowa: WHO.

Further reading

Cattan M & Tilford S (Ed) (2006) *Mental Health Promotion: A lifespan approach*. Maidenhead: Open University Press.

McCulloch A, Ryrie I, Williamson T & St John T (2005) The medical model: has it a future? *The Mental Health Review* **10** (1) 7–15.

Mental Health Foundation (2005) *Choosing Mental Health*. London: Mental Health Foundation.

Wilkinson R & Pickett K (2009) *The Spirit Level: Why more equal societies almost always do better*. London: Allen Lane.

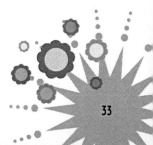

Chapter 2

Understanding mental health

Gregor Henderson

Introduction

Understanding mental health is complex. Anyone picking up this book will know that either before or certainly after reading it. So it's a daunting task to deal with this complexity in a single chapter. However, this chapter aims to give an outline and basic introduction into some of the current thinking on understanding mental health from which further questions, lines of inquiry, debate and discussion, can flow, as well as to provide some context for the chapters that follow.

This chapter concentrates on understanding mental 'health' as part of public or population mental health and is therefore not about understanding 'mental illness, mental disorders or mental health problems'. There are of course links and connections, and I will allude to these in the chapter. The understanding of mental illness is also a complex and dynamic area that has changed and developed significantly over the last 50 years or so and deserves a separate body of work in itself. But that work is not contained here.

This chapter is naturally selective, but aims to cover some of the key areas for consideration in understanding mental health. A summary of the key points in the chapter is included. References and other helpful resource materials are also provided.

Any omissions, inaccuracies or unhelpful interpretations are mine alone for which I take full responsibility. As it is my own mental health, my genetic inheritance, upbringing, background, family, economic and material circumstances, social, educational and working experiences that have shaped my views and opinions and these may be evident in the words I have chosen for this chapter.

Key summary points:
1. Mental health is culturally determined.

2. We are essentially social beings and mental health can be socially created and socially destroyed.

3. Mental health can be located in people individually, in families, neighbourhoods, communities and in wider populations.

4. Mental health is more than the absence of mental illness.

5. A focus on addressing mental health at a population level brings benefits for those living with and recovering from mental illness.

6. We are improving our understanding of what influences mental health individually and collectively.

The search for a unifying definition?

I think it's best to be honest and clear about this from the outset: there is no one universal definition of mental health, rather there is what seems like a bewildering array of definitions depending on different cultural, social, political, professional and even economic factors and considerations. Some regard this as a 'poverty of clarity', which can impede work in policy, practice and research. Others find it liberating and one of the attractions of constantly searching for meaning and definitions in ways that open up new possibilities. The history of 'mental health' shows the use of many different definitions, which have had relevance at a certain time and in a certain context. It is fair to say that defining mental health will continue to be dynamic and fluid and will grow and change as context and cultural influences change.

In understanding mental health, one also needs to be aware of the different and often conflicting uses of the term 'mental health', where, even today, it is too often accepted as a euphemism for mental illness, mental disorder or mental health problems. The term 'mental' is also used in a variety of ways in everyday language, though mostly with negative connotations; the term 'health' itself is also used very loosely in everyday language to mean anything from a state of wellness and health to illness.

However, while there is no clear and universally applicable definition of 'mental health', real progress is being made in developing a wider, richer and more helpful understanding of what we mean by mental health, and what the consequences and possibilities might be for us as individuals, families, neighbourhoods, societies, cultures and populations. There seems to be a realisation that such a complex and challenging issue is likely to be better understood by embracing a wide range of insights, contributions, experiences and disciplines of study in a much more integrated way.

With this welcome integration of ideas and perspectives, we now seem to be moving to the next stage of understanding by building on our previous knowledge and insights. Concepts of mental health over the last 50–150 years have been most influenced by an individualistic, scientific, biological and medical model of understanding. More recently this has been significantly added to by insights from psychology, sociology, anthropology, neurosciences, economics, community development, public health and so on. In this widening and expanding mix some helpful new insights are emerging which bring with them the prospect of a deeper and more helpful way to think about mental health.

Some of these insights seem to be encapsulated by the following definitions, albeit within the cultural context of western market economies:

> 'Mental health is an integral component of health, it is a state of well-being in which the individual realises his or her own abilities, can cope with the normal stresses of life, can work productively and fruitfully, and is able to make a contribution to his or her community.'
> (WHO, 2001)

> 'Mental health is not simply the absence of mental illness, but the foundation for well-being and effective functioning of individuals and communities.'
> (WHO, 2005)

> 'For citizens, mental health is a resource which enables them to realise their intellectual and emotional potential and to find and fulfil their roles in social, school and working life. For societies, good mental health of citizens contributes to prosperity, solidarity and social justice.'
> (European Commission, 2005)

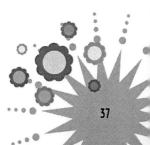

'A dynamic state, in which the individual is able to develop
their potential, work productively and creatively, build strong
and positive relationships with others, and contribute to their
community. It is enhanced when an individual is able to fulfil their
personal and social goals and achieve a sense of purpose in society…
Mental health (and well-being) are fundamental to flourishing
individuals, families and communities and to national economic
productivity and social cohesion.'
(Foresight Project, 2008)

One helpful aspect of applying these broader definitions is that it enables us to
see work on addressing wider mental health as being complementary to work
that concentrates on responding to the needs of people living and recovering
from mental illness. Any focus on mental health at a population level includes
people living and recovering from a mental illness. Therefore, actions in this
wider population arena will complement and underpin work that aims to both
prevent mental illness and respond to the needs of people living with and
recovering from a mental illness.

'The significance of mental health and its role in our survival
confirms the importance of humans as social beings: levels
of social interaction are universal determinants of well-being
across all cultures. But the unique nature of each person's mental
character also reminds us of the power of the individual: "no one
survives without community and no community thrives without
the individual". Progress in improving public mental health will
also mean drawing on lessons from the user/survivor and recovery
movements, with their emphasis on empowerment and respect for
what each individual needs to hold on to or regain a life that has
meaning for them.'
(Friedli, 2009)

Multiple terminology

Here, it is worth saying that there is a large variety of terms in use covering
mental health such as 'positive mental health', 'good mental health', 'mental
well-being', 'well-being' etc. These tend to be used interchangeably and also
used to give emphasis to language and terms that are more familiar in one
context than another. For example, those working in education and schools

may tend to favour the use of the term 'emotional health' or 'emotional well-being' to the word 'mental', which may be more commonly used by those from a clinical or social work practice background. This use of multiple terms is a feature of work in both mental health and in mental illness where terms such as 'mental disorder', 'mental health difficulties', 'mental distress' etc. are used. This can also add to the existing confusion around concepts of mental health. However, this is such an inherent part of the landscape of mental health, that there seems no prospect of universal agreement of terms and definitions. This can be seen as enriching as it means that there is a variety of concepts, definitions and terms that can be used in the search for greater understanding and can prompt discussion and debate from a wide range of perspectives.

Mental health continua

One of the central messages from these expanding definitions is that mental health is now seen as much more than the absence of mental illness. It was previously thought that there was a continuum from mental wellness or good mental health to mental illness along which all mental health 'states' could be plotted. Recent research and insights are showing that mental health and mental illness (mental disorders or mental health problems) can be thought of as being on a 'dual continuum', from optimal mental health/mental well-being on one end and from minimal mental illness to maximal mental illness on the other. There have been a number of attempts to put some of this thinking into models or frameworks. One of the earlier attempts is from Canada (Canadian Ministry of National Health and Welfare, 1988).

This has been expanded on recently drawing on the work of Tudor (1996) and Keyes (2002). Figure 1, on page 40, was used in the consultation for *Towards a Mentally Flourishing Scotland* (Scottish Government, 2007).

What figure 1 attempts to show is that a person can have an identifiable and diagnosable mental illness and at the same time still have a high level of mental well-being. Conversely, someone with no diagnosable mental illness can have a low level of mental well-being. This two continua model is proving to be helpful in understanding the two different, but linked concepts of mental health and mental illness.

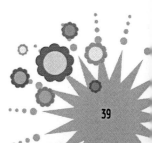

Figure 1: A model of mental health	
Optimal mental well-being (flourishing)	
eg. a person who experiences a high level of mental well-being despite being diagnosed with a mental illness	eg. a person who has high level of mental well-being and who has no mental illness
Maximal mental illness	**Minimal mental illness**
eg. a person experiencing mental illness who has a low level of mental well-being	eg. a person who has no diagnosable mental illness who has a low level of mental well-being
Minimal mental well-being (languishing)	

Mental well-being

The key question that follows is what makes up mental well-being? This is an area that has been significantly enriched in recent years with an expansion of research and study. For a good insight into this emerging science see Huppert (2005).

There is a variety of concepts of well-being in circulation and many more being developed. One concept that has attracted a lot of attention has been developed by Keyes (1998, 2002, 2007). Keyes conceptualises well-being in terms of complete mental health. He argues that mental health or well-being is made up of three main components: emotional well-being (positive feelings or subjective well-being); psychological well-being and social well-being (Keyes *et al*, 2002). Also see Carlisle *et al* (2010) for a broader review of 'understanding well-being'.

These three components interact with each other and along with wider determinants such as socio-economic status, gender, race, age, education and personality characteristics are all determinants of complete mental health. There are other conceptualisations of well-being or mental well-being and these incorporate a range of plausible components and determinants of well-being. For a good overview of different concepts of well-being see Carlisle *et al* (2010). Some rely on more individually located characteristics and traits such as in concepts developed by positive psychologists involving separate components of positive emotions, engagement and meaning and purpose (see Seligman, 2000, 2002).

Others rely on 'capability'. Where the focus is on what an individual has the ability to do or be, rather than what they achieve, possess or consume. Where the desirable functions for well-being are dependent on the socio-cultural and environmental setting (Sen, 1985, 1993).

Others are based on having control over political and material aspects of life and freedom to exercise choice as fundamental components of a good life (Nussbaum, 2000).

Another concept of well-being comes from modern economics, pioneered by the New Economics Foundation (http://www.neweconomics.org/). Here well-being is based on conceptualising people's subjective experience and feelings, where it is the interaction between one's circumstances, activities, and psychological resources (sometimes also called 'mental capital') that matter.

The New Economics Foundation's concepts of well-being, include:

▶ personal well-being = positive functioning, vitality, resilience and self-esteem, life satisfaction and emotional well-being

▶ social well-being = supportive relationships, trust and belonging

▶ well-being at work = job security, job satisfaction, work-life balance satisfaction, working conditions and emotional experience at work.

All these and other attempts to conceptualise well-being also need to be understood in the context of wider cultural influences. In western countries there is a paradox where economic growth has been accompanied by a rise of individual and social problems such as increased rates of depression and other mental illnesses, higher rates of suicide, increasing rates of violence, addictions and family breakdown, and widening health and social inequalities. Recent public health research suggests that the required determinants of good mental health and well-being have been significantly eroded by particular aspects of contemporary culture, such as economism, individualism, materialism and consumerism (Eckersley, 2005). These erode our ability as a culture to live life in ways that support our individual and collective well-being and in ways that also help ensure the sustainability of our natural resources and environment. This is indeed macro level analysis, but one that is gaining significant ground and shaping how we see mental health.

Measuring mental health and well-being

So how do we measure mental health and well-being? In the UK, the Scottish Government led the development of a population-based measure of mental well-being. Between 2005 and 2008 work was undertaken by Warwick University and Edinburgh University, through NHS Health Scotland, to develop the Warwick-Edinburgh Mental Well-being Scale. This has become affectionately known as WEMWBS (NHS Health Scotland, 2006). The scale is made up of a 14-point questionnaire designed to capture the social, emotional and psychological factors that make up well-being. The scale is only usable at a population level and has proven to be a popular way of measuring population's mental well-being (eg. in Scotland and North West England).

The WEMWBS scale was developed in Scotland as part of wider work on developing a set of national indicators for mental health and well-being. Over a period of three years a series of key constructs and indicators were developed. This was and still remains an impressive body of work which attempts to bring a wider scope of understanding to mental health by including not just individual contextual constructs but also community/social and structural/ policy constructs. Work on these national indicators continues in Scotland and a set of indicators for children's well-being is also now being developed (NHS Health Scotland, 2010).

Social determinants and inequality

Other authors include wider social determinants in their construction of mental health and this is a conceptualisation that aims to understand mental health as more than a collection of 'individual attributes'.

Friedli (2009), in her influential report for World Health Organization Europe, argues powerfully for an understanding of mental health that is located more within the social context of our lives and world. By incorporating a more socially determined view of mental health, Friedli argues that we are better able to address those factors that most significantly determine our individual and collective mental well-being. For Friedli and others this is crucial if we are to address the social, economic and material inequalities we see today.

'For this reason, levels of mental distress among communities need to be understood less in terms of individual pathology and more as a response to relative deprivation and social injustice, which erode the emotional, spiritual and intellectual resources essential to psychological well-being. While psycho-social stress is not the only route through which disadvantage affects outcomes, it does appear to be pivotal.'
(Friedli, 2009)

In the UK recently there has been a greater focus on addressing inequalities. Some of the most persuasive arguments for the need to significantly impact on the social determinants of mental health have been put forward by Wilkinson and Pickett (2009) in their book *The Spirit Level*.

One of the key emerging considerations in understanding mental health is that it is not equally distributed and any policies and actions developed will need to ensure that they address inequalities.

Understanding what needs to be done to improve mental health

The above selected definitions, concepts, terms, frameworks, measures and indicators are helpful in demonstrating a developing and wider understanding of mental health. They also help to frame what policy, evidence and practical actions may be helpful in improving individual, family, community and population mental health.

One area that has recently received a lot of attention is the collection and presentation of the evidence for improving mental health and well-being. A helpful summary review of a selection of the evidence was published in March 2010 (Marmot, 2010). This provides a good overview of where there is the most compelling evidence for action in addressing population mental health, though the majority of the examples of interventions cited are more related to prevention of mental illness rather than the promotion of mental health. This presents a significant challenge to the future direction of research and points to the need to ensure that research resources are better balanced by targeting work on the promotion of mental health and not just on the alleviation and prevention of mental illness.

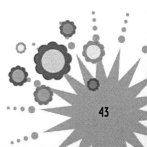

Within the modern mental health policy arena, two specific themes are emerging: first, the need for public mental health work to sit alongside work on supporting people experiencing mental health problems; and second, the need to take a life course approach to mental health (from birth to later life). This life course framework is looking promising and along with a concentration on activities in a range of settings (eg. schools, workplaces, communities) looks like being a helpful way of organising and implementing the required actions to improve our understanding of and outcomes in mental health. Recent examples of policies include the National Programme for Improving Mental Health and Well-being in Scotland (Scottish Government, 2003) and New Horizons in England (Department of Health, 2009).

The emerging areas for action that the evidence indicates will have positive benefit (including not just social benefit, but also economic benefit) are being identified with ever more increasing confidence. The chapters that follow pick up on some of this work and show the importance of not just the prevention of mental illness but the promotion of good mental health.

One of the exciting features of current work on mental health is the expansion into other areas of public policy, social, health and community life and is one of the significant gains of the last few years. This means that mental health (as well as mental illness) is now increasing in visibility in wider public, social and political agendas. Mental health seems to be moving helpfully beyond being an area of specialist interest, too often marginalised and ignored, into something much broader and more mainstream. This move beyond mental health 'exceptionalism' and into the mainstream is to be welcomed. Increasing the rigour and widening our understanding is going to be an important part of this continuing journey.

Future challenges

The search for improved definitions of mental health will continue. This search has already taken us way beyond the traditional definitions of mental health as being more defined around mental illness. The ability to further refine and differentiate between mental health and mental illness will continue. Part of the challenge for the future will be to do this in ways that prove complementary to both the improvement of public mental health and the improvement of the lives and recovery of people living with and or experiencing mental illness. Future work will have a greater focus on achieving a much more integrated understanding of mental health.

By improving population-wide mental health, or as it is often referred to in the UK, improving public mental health, the ability to improve the lives of people living with mental illness is also enhanced. This also helps to open up the opportunity for an improved understanding of mental illness and mental health problems as being one part of the human condition and as such, to be understood within a more social and human context. This brings with it challenges for ensuring that responses to mental health and mental illness are more socially located in families and communities and are part of a complementary and holistic approach to overall health and well-being.

As understanding of mental health continues, the notion that there may be a separate set of definitions for mental well-being and one for well-being will become less evident. Any overall understanding of well-being includes within it dimensions that are emotional, social and psychological. In the future, the challenge will be to improve our ability to use these definitions interchangeably and to ensure that any focus on health and well-being includes an understanding of the social, emotional and psychological.

By improving our understanding of mental health in terms of theory, definitions and concepts we also become more able to identify the practical actions that can be taken to make a difference to the lives and opportunities of people, families and communities. These actions in turn also help us to expand and refine our understanding of the mind, how we function, how we adapt and how we continue to learn and develop as individuals, as communities and societies in ways that are sustainable and in tune with what enables us to be mentally healthy and achieve well-being. This truly is a 21st century challenge.

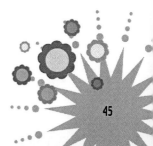

References

Canadian Ministry of National Health and Welfare (1988) In: K Tudor (1996) *Mental Health Promotion: Paradigms and practice*. London: Routledge.

Carlisle S, Hanlon P, Hannah M, Lyon A & Reilly M (2010) Enabling well-being in a time of radical change: integrative public health for the 21st century. *Public Health* (in press).

Department of Health (2009) *New Horizons: Towards a shared vision for mental health*. London: DH.

Eckersley R (2005) *Well and Good: Morality, meaning and happiness* (2nd ed). Melbourne: Text Publishing.

European Commission (2005) *Green Paper – Improving the Mental Health of the Population: Towards a strategy on mental health for the European Union*. Brussels: Health and Consumer Protection Directorate, European Commission.

Foresight Project on Mental Capital & Well-being (2008) *Final Project Report* [online]. London: Government Office for Science, London. Available at: www.foresight.gov.uk (accessed August 2010).

Friedli L (2009) *Mental Health, Resilience and Inequalities*. Copenhagan: World Health Organization Regional Office for Europe.

Huppert FA (2005) Positive mental health in individuals and populations. In: F Huppert, N Bayliss & B Keverne (Eds) *The Science of Well-being*. Oxford: Oxford University Press.

Keyes CLM (1998) Social well-being. *Social Psychology Quarterly* **61** 121–140.

Keyes CLM (2002) The mental health continuum: from languishing to flourishing in life. *Journal of Health and Social Behaviour* **43** 207–222.

Keyes CLM (2007) Promoting and protecting mental health as flourishing. *American Psychologist* **62** (2) 1–14.

Keyes CLM, Shmotkin D & Ryff CD (2002) Optimizing well-being: the empirical encounter of two traditions. *Journal of Personality and Social Psychology* **82** 1077–1022.

Marmot M (2010) *Strategic Review of Health Inequalities in England Post-2010: Fair society, healthy lives – the Marmot Review final report*. London: The Marmot Review.

New Economics Foundation website. Available at: http://www.neweconomics.org (accessed August 2010).

NHS Health Scotland (2006) *Warwick-Edinburgh Mental Well-Being Scale (WEMWBS)*. Edinburgh: University of Warwick and University of Edinburgh.

NHS Health Scotland (2010) *Children's Well-being Indicators* [online]. Available at: http://www.healthscotland.com/scotlands-health/population/mental-health-indicators.aspx (accessed August 2010).

Nussbaum M (2000) *Women and Human Development: The capabilities approach*. New York: Cambridge University Press.

Scottish Government (2003) National Programme for Improving Mental Health and Well-being: Action plan 2003–2006 [online]. Available at: http://www.scotland.gov.uk/Publications/2003/09/18193/26509 (accessed August 2010).

Scottish Government (2007) *Towards a Mentally Flourishing Scotland: Discussion paper on mental health improvement 2008–2011*. Edinburgh: Scottish Government.

Seligman MEP (2000) The positive perspective. *The Gallup Review* **3** (1) 2–7.

Seligman MEP (2002) *Authentic Happiness: Using the new positive psychology to realize your potential for lasting fulfillment*. New York: Free Press.

Sen AK (1985) *Commodities and Capabilities*. Oxford: Oxford University Press.

Sen AK (1993) Capability and well-being. In: Nussbaum & Sen (Eds) *The Quality of Life*. Oxford: Clarendon Press, pp30–53.

Tennant R, Hiller L, Fishwick R, Platt S, Joseph S, Weich S, Parkinson J, Secker J & Stewart-Brown S (2007) The Warwick-Edinburgh Mental Well-being Scale (WEMWBS): development and UK validation. *Health and Quality of Life Outcomes* **5** 63.

Tudor K (1996) *Mental Health Promotion: Paradigms and practice*. London: Routledge.

Wilkinson R & Pickett K (2009) *The Spirit Level: Why more equal societies almost always do better*. London: Allen Lane.

World Health Organization (2001) *Mental Health: New understanding, new hope*. The World Health Report. Geneva: WHO.

World Health Organization (2005) *Mental Health Action Plan for Europe: Facing the challenges, building solutions*. Copenhagen: WHO.

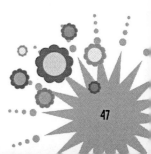

Further reading

NMHDU Factfile 4 public mental health and well-being. Available at:
www.nmhdu.org.uk

WellScotland website. Available at: http://www.wellscotland.info

Afternow website. Available at: http://www.afternow.co.uk/

The Warwick-Edinburgh Mental Well-being Scale (WEMWBS)

Below are some statements about feelings and thoughts. Please tick the box
that best describes your experience of each over the last two weeks

Statements

None of the time 1, Rarely 2,   Some of the time 3, Often 4, All of the time 5.

I've been feeling optimistic about the future	1	2	3	4	5
I've been feeling useful	1	2	3	4	5
I've been feeling relaxed	1	2	3	4	5
I've been feeling interested in other people	1	2	3	4	5
I've had energy to spare	1	2	3	4	5
I've been dealing with problems well	1	2	3	4	5
I've been thinking clearly	1	2	3	4	5
I've been feeling good about myself	1	2	3	4	5
I've been feeling close to other people	1	2	3	4	5
I've been feeling confident	1	2	3	4	5
I've been able to make up my own mind about things	1	2	3	4	5
I've been feeling loved	1	2	3	4	5
I've been interested in new things	1	2	3	4	5
I've been feeling cheerful	1	2	3	4	5

Chapter 3

Adopting a mental health promotion approach to public mental health

Margaret Barry

Introduction

This chapter outlines current concepts and principles of mental health promotion and examines the conceptual frameworks and models for promoting positive mental health. An overview of international developments in terms of research, policy and practice developments is given, including the evidence concerning the effectiveness of mental health promotion interventions. The application of the growing knowledge and evidence base to current practice and policy is discussed. The chapter also considers the key requirements for advancing effective policy and practice for promoting public mental health.

Mental health promotion

Mental health promotion is concerned with promoting positive mental health among the general population, strengthening protective factors and enhancing well-being and quality of life. Mental health is conceptualised as a positive resource for living, which is embedded in the social, economic and cultural life of the individual and community. Therefore, mental health promotion brings a shift in focus from the modification of individualistic risk factors for mental disorders to the promotion of protective and competence enhancing factors that keep individuals and populations mentally healthy. The implementation of mental health promotion requires the development of programme and policy interventions, which extend beyond the clinical and treatment focus of current mental health service delivery, to address the influence of broader social, economic, and environmental determinants of mental health.

The strength of evidence from systematic reviews and effectiveness studies supports the value of programmes promoting positive mental health as effective initiatives capable of impacting positively across multiple domains of functioning (Durlak & Wells, 1997; Hosman & Jané-Llopis, 1999; Friedli, 2003; Herrman et al, 2005; Jané-Llopis et al, 2005; Barry et al, 2009). Mental health promotion interventions have been found to impact on a range of positive health and social outcomes and the reduction of social problems such as delinquency, child abuse, school drop-out, lost days from work and social inequity (Hosman & Jané-Llopis, 1999; Jané-Llopis et al, 2005). The accumulating evidence base demonstrates the feasibility of implementing effective mental health promotion programmes across a range of diverse population groups and settings (Barry & Jenkins, 2007).

Positioning its core focus on the 'health' end of the mental health–disease continuum, mental health promotion has relevance for the whole population, including those at risk from, or experiencing mental health problems. This includes creating supportive environments, reducing stigmatisation and discrimination, and supporting the social and emotional well-being of service users and their families. The underlying principle of this approach is that mental health is an integral part of overall health and is, therefore, of relevance to all.

The importance of positive mental health

Positive mental health is fundamental to good health and is a resource for everyday life, which enables us to manage our lives successfully. As a resource, mental health contributes to the functioning of individuals, families, communities and society. The need to address mental health as an integral part of improving overall health and well-being is increasingly recognised at the international level (WHO, 2001, 2002, 2004; US Department of Health and Human Services, 1999). The concept of mental health cannot be separated from that of overall health, which was defined in the World Health Organization Constitution of 1946 as a state of complete physical, mental and social well-being and not merely the absence of disease or injury. More recent definitions have gone on to describe health as a resource for living and as a positive concept emphasising social and personal resources, as well as physical capacities (WHO, 1986). Positive mental health has been conceptualised as encompassing the dimensions of both subjective emotional well-being and positive psychological and social functioning (Keyes, 2007; Kovess-Masfety *et al*, 2005). Empirical findings support the independence of positive and negative mental health showing that the absence of mental disorder does not equal the presence of mental health (Keyes, 2005, 2007; Huppert, 2005). As a positive resource, mental health contributes to the social, human and economic capital of society (Lehtinen *et al*, 2005). The promotion of positive mental health is, therefore, important in its own right. The phrase 'there is no health without mental health', conveys clearly this positive sense of mental health. Mental health is intrinsic to good health and quality of life and as such, needs to be firmly placed within the broader public health and health promotion fields of practice.

The World Health Organization report in 2001 (WHO, 2001) was devoted exclusively to mental health and advocated a comprehensive public health approach, including mental health promotion and prevention, in order to reduce the burden of mental health problems at a population level. The *Prevention and Promotion in Mental Health* report (WHO, 2002) further prioritised the role of prevention and promotion in the field of mental health in order to reduce stigma, increase cost-effectiveness and provide multiple positive outcomes. Both reports acknowledged that policies focused on curing or preventing mental ill-health alone will not necessarily deliver on improved mental health at a population level. The World Health Organization reports *Promoting Mental Health: Concepts evidence, practice* (WHO, 2004; Herrman *et al*, 2005) and the International Union of Health Promotion and Education (IUHPE) special issue on the evidence of mental health promotion effectiveness (Jané-Llopis *et al*, 2005), clarified further the main concepts relating to the promotion of mental health, the emerging evidence for the effectiveness of interventions, and the public health policy and practice implications. Through such publications the rationale for mental health promotion, an understanding of its distinctive approach, and the feasibility of implementing effective mental health promotion strategies are becoming more clearly established internationally.

Alongside the development of a public health perspective on mental health, there is also an increasing emphasis on the importance of positive mental health for population well-being and social and economic development. For example, the World Health Organization *Mental Health Declaration and Action Plan for Europe* (WHO, 2005a) and the European Commission Mental Health Green Paper and Strategy (European Commission, 2005) clearly state that the social and economic prosperity of Europe depends on improving mental health and well-being, which are regarded as essential for social cohesion and active citizenship. The Foresight Project on Mental Capital and Well-being (2008) also endorsed this perspective and highlighted, as one of its main messages, that mental health and well-being are critical to future prosperity and development in a changing, increasingly connected and competing world.

Mental health policies, which embrace a public health perspective and advocate for a flourishing society based on positive well-being are being introduced and strengthened in a number of countries. For example, mental health policy development in Australia, Canada, England, Ireland, Scotland, and New Zealand (GermAnn & Ardiles, 2009) has incorporated the promotion of public mental health into both population health and mental health policies. Many of these policies also acknowledge the role that mental health promotion plays in reducing health inequities as poor mental health is seen to both reflect socio-economic deprivation and to contribute to it (Social Exclusion Unit, 2004; Melzer *et al*, 2004; Rogers & Pilgrim, 2005; Pickett *et al*, 2006; Friedli, 2009).

Good mental health is a key asset and resource for population well-being and the long-term social and economic prosperity of society. Promoting mental health and well-being will deliver improved outcomes for the general population and for people with mental health problems. To promote and enhance positive mental health effectively requires an understanding of appropriate frameworks for practice at a population level informed by a multidisciplinary knowledge base of theory, values and evidence.

Promoting positive mental health: theoretical frameworks for practice

As a multidisciplinary area, mental health promotion derives its theoretical and research base from a number of diverse disciplines. The practice of mental health promotion needs to be underpinned by sound conceptual and theoretical frameworks which provide coherent models for designing, conducting and evaluating interventions. In considering these frameworks, it is useful to make a distinction between the practice of mental health promotion and the prevention of mental disorders. These two areas, while clearly related and overlapping, tend to operate within different conceptual frameworks. Mental health promotion focuses on positive mental health and its main aim is the building of psychosocial strengths, competencies and resources. In contrast, the area of prevention concerns itself primarily with specific disorders and aims to reduce the incidences, prevalence or seriousness of targeted problems, ie. mortality, morbidity and risk behaviour outcomes. Articulated as such, these two fields have different starting points and seek to impact on different outcomes. In practice, however, there is much common ground between the two areas, particularly with regard to primary prevention and mental health promotion interventions.

Mental health promotion and prevention frameworks

The most widely used prevention framework in mental health was put forward by Mrazek and Haggerty (1994) in the Institute of Medicine (IOM) report entitled *Reducing Risks for Mental Disorders: Frontiers for preventive intervention*. This prevention framework, originally depicted as a half circle, places prevention activities in the wider mental health intervention spectrum of treatment, maintenance and rehabilitation. Three main categories of prevention activities are identified:

▶ universal – targeting the general population

▶ selected – targeting high-risk groups

▶ indicated – targeting high-risk individuals or groups with minimal but detectable signs or symptoms of mental disorder.

While clearly articulating the different types of prevention, this framework does not include interventions focusing on promoting positive mental health, nor does it explicitly identify links across the different areas of prevention, treatment and rehabilitation. However, it would appear that at least conceptually, there is quite an overlap between universal prevention activities, as outlined in the framework, and those of mental health promotion. Barry (2001) adapted the framework to include mental health promotion (see figure 1 on page 54) indicating some core concepts by way of example (by no means meant to be exhaustive or exclusive). This amended figure depicts mental health promotion as the largest part of the circle, given its universal relevance, and indicates the unifying central area between the different interventions as that centred on strategies for promoting well-being and quality of life. It is interesting to note that the 2009 report by

the US Committee on Prevention of Mental Disorders and Substance Abuse of Children, Youth and Young Adults (O'Connell *et al*, 2009) strongly recommends the inclusion of mental health promotion in the spectrum of mental health interventions. This report endorses the view that mental health is more than the absence of disorder and that a focus on wellness and the promotion of mental health will have far-reaching benefits that extend beyond a specific disorder.

Figure 1: Modified Mental Health Intervention Spectrum

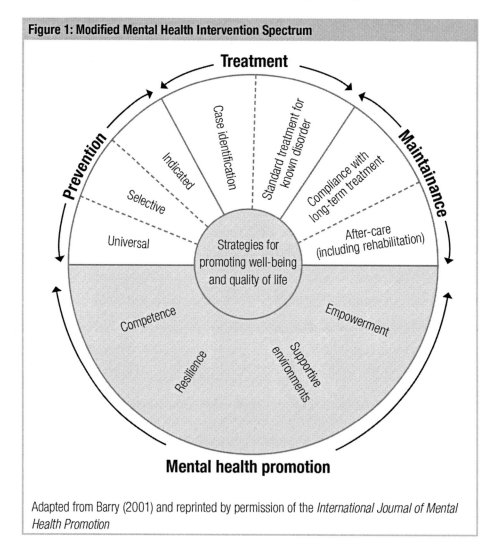

Adapted from Barry (2001) and reprinted by permission of the *International Journal of Mental Health Promotion*

Adopting a mental health promotion approach

A population approach to mental health focuses on improving the mental health status of the entire population, or sub-population, rather than individuals. A population perspective underscores the relevance of mental health promotion across all population groups and identifies strategies that can be applied, ranging from building resilience and promoting mental health for healthy populations, to reducing risk for those at higher risk of developing mental health problems, and promoting recovery and well-being for people with mental disorders.

Adopting a population mental health promotion approach builds on the basic tenets and socio-ecological model of health as outlined in the *Ottawa Charter for Health Promotion* (WHO, 1986) and subsequent World Health Organization directives (WHO, 2005b, 2009). The principles of health promotion practice, as articulated in the *Ottawa Charter* (WHO, 1986), are based on an empowering, participative and collaborative process, which aims to enable people to increase control over their health and its determinants. *The Ottawa Charter* (WHO, 1986) outlined five key areas for action to promote health, each of which can be applied to mental health promotion as follows.

▶ Building healthy public policy places mental health promotion on the agenda of all policy makers and calls for co-ordinated action across health, economic and social policies for improved mental health. For example, workplaces supported by health and safety policies which embrace the importance of mental health at work; educational policies which promote integrated social and emotional learning in schools; poverty reduction policies which reduce health inequities.

▶ Creating supportive environments moves mental health beyond an individualistic focus to consider the influence of broader social, physical, cultural and economic environments and highlights the importance of mediating structures, such as the home, school, workplace and community settings as key contexts for creating and promoting good mental health.

▶ Strengthening community action focuses on the empowerment of communities through their active engagement and participation in identifying their needs, setting priorities, planning and implementing action to achieve better mental health at the community level.

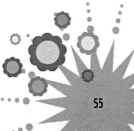

▶ Developing personal skills involves enabling personal and social development through providing information, education and enhancing life skills for improving mental health. Interventions include life skills development, enhancing coping skills, personal development and building resilience.

▶ Reorientating health services requires that they embrace the importance of mental health to overall health and well-being and that mental health services embrace promotion and prevention strategies as well as treatment and rehabilitation. A shift in orientation to mental health promotion in primary care, mental health services and population health interventions are included in this action area.

A socio-ecological model of mental health, based on the *Ottawa Charter* (WHO, 1986), conceptualises mental health as being embedded in, and influenced by, a wider social, economic and cultural ecology (Zubrick & Kovess-Masfety, 2005). This perspective stresses the interdependence of the individual, family, community and society and moves the concept of mental health beyond an individualistic focus to consider the broader social, economic and environmental determinants. Mental health promotion emphasises that mental health is created within the settings where people live their lives and it is in the everyday contexts or settings, such as the home, school, workplace and community, where mental health can be promoted and protected. Mental health promotion interventions, therefore, seek to promote behavioural, socio-environmental and policy change, addressing the broader social and economic environments that determine the mental health of populations and individuals.

The socio-ecological model of mental health promotion underscores the need for integrated action at the level of the individual, community, supportive environments and policies, in order to bring about sustainable change that will create and promote positive mental health (Herrman *et al*, 2005; Barry, 2007). A number of international policies have embraced the *Ottawa Charter* as a basis for mental health promotion (see for example, Commonwealth Department of Health and Aged Care, Australia 2000; Health Education Authority, 1997; VicHealth, 1999, 2009; Ministry of Health New Zealand, 2005). The health promotion framework usefully informs the conceptualisation and principles of mental health promotion, which have been articulated by Barry (2007) based on the *Ottawa Charter* (WHO, 1986).

Mental health promotion: involves the population as a whole in the context of their everyday life, rather than focusing on people at risk from specific mental disorders

► focuses on protective factors for enhancing well-being and quality of life

► addresses the social, physical and economic environments that determine the mental health of populations and individuals

► adopts complementary approaches and integrated strategies, operating from the individual to socio-environmental levels

► involves intersectoral action extending beyond the health sector

► is based on effective public participation, engagement and empowerment.

Addressing the determinants of mental health

Mental health is determined by biological, psychological, social, economic and environmental factors, which interact in complex ways (Mrazek & Haggerty 1994; Rogers & Pilgrim 2005). Demographics such as age, gender and ethnicity are important determinants, influencing exposure to risk and protective factors across the life course. The complex interaction or 'web of causation' among the determinants of mental health affects how individuals and communities exercise a sense of control over their lives and seek to maximise their well-being. Improved knowledge of the relative impact of determinants operating at the structural, community and individual level, and the synergistic impacts and outcomes that are likely to arise from comprehensive interventions operating across levels, is critical to understanding the key drivers of mental health (Barry, 2009).

Recognition of the broader determinants of mental health has led to a growing emphasis on models of mental health promotion that seek to intervene at the level of strengthening individuals, strengthening communities and removing the structural barriers to mental health through initiatives to reduce poverty, discrimination and inequities (Herrman *et al*, 2005; Barry & Friedli, 2008; Friedli, 2009). The findings of the World Health Organization Commission on the Social Determinants of Health (WHO, 2008) point to a considerable body of evidence on the impact of daily living conditions on our health and the effects of the inequitable distribution of power, money and resources, which act as structural drivers of inequality. Friedli (2009) argues that mental health is directly and indirectly related at every level to how people experience and respond to social inequities influencing their sense of control over their lives, efficacy, self-esteem and connectedness, and their ability to deal with chronic stress and adversity. Improved standards of living, access to education and employment, freedom from discrimination and poverty, fewer adverse life events and good physical health and social support, enhance and protect positive mental health. An integrated policy approach is, therefore, required to address these factors and underlines the need for cross-sectoral policy implementation. The existence of review level evidence of the effectiveness of mental health promotion interventions strengthens the case for action (WHO, 2004; Herrman *et al*, 2005; Jané-Llopis *et al*, 2005; Keleher & Armstrong, 2005; Barry *et al*, 2009). The wider health and social benefits that will accrue from mental health promotion are evident in the international evidence base.

The effectiveness of mental health promotion

Good progress has been made over the last 20 years in establishing a sound theoretical and evidence base for mental health promotion practice. There is consensus that there are clusters of known risk and protective factors for mental health (Mrazek & Haggerty, 1994); there is a growing body of evidence that interventions exist which can modify these factors; and a number of intervention programmes evaluated in efficacy and effectiveness trials have been established and disseminated (Hosman & Jané-Llopis, 1999; Jané-Llopis *et al*, 2005; Herrman *et al*, 2005; Keleher & Armstrong, 2005; Barry & Jenkins, 2007). There is compelling evidence from high quality studies that mental health promotion interventions, when implemented effectively, can lead to lasting positive effects on a range of health and social outcomes (Durlak & Wells, 1997; Friedli, 2003; Keleher & Armstrong, 2005; Herrman *et al*, 2005; Barry & Jenkins, 2007; Barry *et al*, 2009). Findings from systematic reviews indicate that there is sufficient knowledge to move evidence into practice (Jané-Llopis *et al*, 2005).

Box 1: Key advances in the mental health promotion evidence base (from Barry *et al*, 2009)

Mental health promotion for children and families:

▶ High quality comprehensive programmes carried out in collaboration with families, schools and communities can produce lasting positive benefits for young people and their parents.

▶ Early childhood interventions (eg. home visiting and parenting programmes) and high quality pre-school education programmes lead to improved mental health of children and their parents, reduced behavioural problems, improved social functioning, academic and work performance and general health behaviours.

▶ The effects of early years interventions are especially evident for the most vulnerable families, including those living in disadvantaged communities.

▶ Economic analyses of several childhood interventions demonstrate that effective interventions can repay their initial investment with savings to the government and benefits to society, with those at risk making the most gains.

Mental health promotion in schools:

▶ There is substantial evidence that mental health promotion interventions in schools, when implemented effectively, can produce long-term benefits for young people, including emotional and social functioning and improved academic performance.

▶ Comprehensive programmes that target multiple health outcomes in the context of a co-ordinated whole school approach are the most consistently effective strategy.

Mental health promotion in the workplace:

▶ Comprehensive approaches to mental health promotion in the workplace, which combine individual and organisational level interventions, are more likely to be effective in improving and maintaining mental health at work.

▶ Effective workplace interventions address the physical, environmental and psychosocial factors influencing mental health; they strengthen modifying factors such as support from staff, enhanced job control, increased staff involvement, workload assessment, effort-reward balance, role clarity and policies to tackle bullying, harassment and discrimination.

▶ Supported employment schemes will improve employment for people with severe mental health problems.

Community-based mental health promotion:

▶ Mental health stigma and discrimination reduction campaigns including mass media interventions, particularly when supported by local community action, can have a significant impact on public understanding of mental health, reducing stigma, and increasing knowledge of coping and sources of support.

▶ There is a growing evidence base on the relationship between physical and mental health and the role of mental health promotion in health care.

▶ There is some limited evidence that policy interventions, such as improved neighbourhoods, housing, social cohesion, antidiscrimination, and social participation including life long educational opportunities, can directly or indirectly impact positively on mental health and well-being.

The available evidence supports the view that competence-enhancing programmes carried out in collaboration with families, schools, workplaces and the wider community, have the potential to impact on multiple positive outcomes across social and personal health domains (Jané-Llopis & Barry, 2005). Most interventions have been found to have the dual effect of reducing problems and increasing competencies. Mental health promotion interventions that can be implemented and sustained at a reasonable cost, while generating clear health and social gains in the population, represent a cost-effective use of resources and a strong case for policy investment (WHO, 2002, 2004; Friedli & Parsonage, 2007; Zechmeister *et al*, 2008; Barry & Friedli, 2008).

Best available evidence needs to be translated into practice and policy and the necessary conditions and resources put in place to ensure the implementation of successful interventions. Effective interventions need to be brought to scale so that they are at a coverage, scope and intensity that can make a critical difference at a population level. On the basis of the evidence and a review of successful programmes, a number of cross-cutting principles that guide the implementation of effective interventions have been identified (Barry & Jenkins, 2007; Barry, 2007). These include:

▶ a socio-ecological approach to programme conceptualisation in order that interventions will seek to bring about positive change at the level of the individual, the family, social group or community and broader society

▶ competence enhancement approach emphasising the promotion of resourcefulness, generic coping skills and life competence

▶ theory-based interventions grounded on established theories of human functioning and social organisation

▶ comprehensive and sustained interventions that are not once-off but are designed to produce long-term effects

▶ high quality programme delivery based on a supportive implementation system

▶ sytematic evaluation methods of programme process, impact, outcomes and costs, that will contribute to the ongoing improvement and sustainability of effective interventions

▶ intervention sustainability built on organisational and system-level practices and policies that will ensure the long-term impact of effective, high-quality interventions.

Advancing best practice: connecting research, practice and policy

Evidence informed practice plays a critical role in demonstrating the success and added value of promoting public mental health and is vital to justifying funding for sustaining initiatives in the longer-term. In advancing best practice, there is a need to focus efforts and resources on interventions and initiatives that are cost effective, feasible and sustainable in local settings. The best available evidence needs to be applied systematically so that what is known to work will guide the implementation of effective strategies and approaches that are responsive to local needs and priorities (Barry *et al*, 2005). New and improved interventions will also need to be developed where there are gaps in the evidence base and where existing interventions need to be adapted to specific contexts. This requires a clearer focus on programme implementation and sustainability.

The integration of evidence-based interventions into established practice and policy is far from automatic. Few interventions are sustained over time regardless of their impact. Demonstrating that interventions can be implemented successfully as part of routine service delivery is an important challenge. A number of evaluation studies have pointed to the variable quality of programme implementation across sites and the need for staff training and organisational support to ensure a structured approach to high quality delivery (Durlak, 1998; Domitrovich & Greenberg, 2000; Mihalic *et al*, 2002). The assessment of the quality and quantity of implementation is an absolute necessity in programme evaluations (Durlak & DuPre, 2008). However, the inclusion of these data is not common, even in the majority of systematic evaluations. Durlak and DuPre (2008) report clear evidence from a series of meta-analyses of over 500 studies on prevention and promotion for children and adolescents that the level of implementation affects outcomes and that mean effect sizes for positive outcomes are two to three times higher when interventions are carefully implemented.

Implementing programmes in complex multi-level systems such as schools, workplaces and communities, requires a focus on the complex interaction of characteristics of the intervention, the implementer, the participants, the organisational capacity and support of the delivery system (both general and intervention-specific capacity) and the specific contexts in which the intervention is being implemented (Chen, 1998; Fixsen *et al*, 2005; Greenberg *et al*, 2006). The recognition of implementation complexity and the importance of relevance to the local context and community are important considerations in advancing quality implementation and the development of practice-based evidence.

A recent study evaluating the implementation of an international emotional well-being programme for primary school children in disadvantaged schools in Ireland revealed a number of interesting findings regarding programme adoption and the influence of the local context on implementation. The findings from a randomised controlled design involving 730 pupils and 42 teachers in 30 schools indicated that the programme, Zippy's Friends, was successfully adopted and implemented in the Irish school context and led to a number of significant positive effects for the pupils, including improved emotional literacy and coping skills, reduced hyperactivity levels and improved relationships in the classroom (Clarke & Barry, 2010). More detailed case studies of implementation in two of the schools provided some useful insights into how factors operating at the local level impacted on how the programme was adopted in the school and implemented in the classroom. In particular, the case studies revealed that the individual school ethos and culture, the extent of parental involvement and engagement with the school, the profile of the local community and the degree of connection between the school and the community, were all important contextual factors influencing implementation (Clarke *et al*, 2010). These findings indicate that contextual factors operating in the whole school environment can impact and influence programme implementation and ultimately programme outcomes. The evaluation study also highlighted the need for supportive organisational and system-level practices and policies to ensure the sustainable integration of effective interventions at the local level.

Building capacity for mental health promotion

The task of translating policy and research into effective action needs to be supported by building capacity for effective implementation at the national, regional and local levels. This requires an increased focus on developing the infrastructures for effective mental health promotion practice. The required technical skills need to be put in place in order to build the capacity for the effective implementation of evidence-informed interventions.

While a policy framework gives a clear mandate for action, in itself it is not sufficient to guarantee translation into effective practice. Policy documents need to be accompanied by a realistic plan for effecting the translation of the policies into action at the local level and the provision of the necessary resources, mechanisms and skills required to make this happen. Similarly, while good progress is being made in building the evidence base for mental health promotion, evidence on its own is not enough. The evidence base needs to be translated and disseminated so that it serves the needs of practitioners concerned with the practicality of implementing successful interventions that are relevant to the needs of the populations they serve.

A skilled and trained workforce with the necessary competencies to work at the level of population groups, communities and individuals, is recognised as being critical to effective implementation. Partnership working and the implementation of cross-sectoral strategies call for high-level expertise in order to engage and facilitate the participation of diverse sectors. The leadership required for effective translation of plans into action needs to be developed and facilitated all the way from the level of macro policy to local implementation. While public mental health is indeed everybody's business, as we all have mental health needs, dedicated time, resources and competencies are required to guide, direct, and be accountable for, the process of effective implementation.

Building the capacity of the workforce in developing, implementing and evaluating mental health promotion interventions is fundamental to mainstreaming and sustaining action in this area. Continuing professional development and training is required to enhance the quality of practice and update the skill set required to work within changing social and political contexts.

Making knowledge work for improved public mental health

The development of effective interventions is only the first step in promoting mental health. Transferring interventions to real world settings and sustaining them is a long-term process that is necessary for maximising population impact. The effective scaling up of interventions in standard service delivery is critical to achieving large-scale impacts at a population level. Building capacity for the adoption and sustainability of effective interventions across diverse cultural and economic settings is fundamental to future practice developments in this field. Determining the transferability of implementation evidence and practice knowledge across cultures, systems, structures and contexts is an important focus for future development (Barry *et al*, 2007).

There is a need for researchers, practitioner and policy-makers to work collaboratively to bridge the gaps between science, practice and policy. By building on the empirical and experiential knowledge base accumulated to date, public mental health will benefit from the adoption of a collaborative and systematic approach to the implementation of effective and sustainable mental health promotion interventions in different contexts. Further systematic studies of programme implementation, adoption and adaptation across cultures are needed so that evidence-informed practice and practice-based theory may be generated and developed. The commitment of policy-makers to this translational focus needs to be mobilised so that mental health promotion practice and effective implementation is given greater priority in policy development.

References

Barry MM (2001) Promoting positive mental health: theoretical frameworks for Practice. *International Journal of Mental Health Promotion* **3** (1) 25–34.

Barry MM (2007) Generic principles of effective mental health promotion. *International Journal of Mental Health Promotion* **9** (2) 4–16.

Barry MM (2009) Addressing the determinants of positive mental health: concepts, evidence and practice. *International Journal of Mental Health Promotion* **11**(3) 4–17.

Barry MM, Canavan R, Clarke A, Dempsey C & O'Sullivan M (2009) *Review of Evidence-based Mental Health Promotion and Primary/Secondary Prevention* [online]. Report prepared for the Department of Health, London. Health Promotion Research Centre, National University of Ireland Galway. Available at: www.nuigalway.ie/hprc (accessed July 2010).

Barry MM, Domitrovich C & Lara A (2005) The implementation of mental health promotion programs. In: E Jané-Llopis, MM Barry, C Hosman & V Patel (Eds). The evidence of mental health promotion effectiveness: strategies for action. *Promotion and Education IUHPE Special Issue* **2** 30–35.

Barry MM & Jenkins R (2007) *Implementing Mental Health Promotion*. Oxford: Churchill Livingstone Elsevier.

Barry MM, Patel V, Jané-Llopis E, Raeburn J & Mittlemark M (2007) Strengthening the evidence base for mental health promotion. In: DC McQueen & CM Jones (Eds). *Global Perspectives on Health Promotion*, pp67–86. New York: Springer.

Barry MM & Friedli L (2008) *The Influence of Social, Demographic and Physical Factors on Positive Mental Health in Children, Adults and Older People*. Foresight Mental Capital and Wellbeing Project. State-of-Science Review: SR-B3. London: Government Office of Science and Innovation, UK.

Chen H (1998) Theory-driven evaluations. *Advances in Educational Productivity* **7** 15–34.

Clarke AM & Barry MM (2010) *An Evaluation of the Zippy's Friends Emotional Wellbeing Programme for Primary Schools in Ireland* [online]. Health Promotion Research Centre, National University of Ireland Galway. Available at: http: www.nuigalway.ie/hprc (accessed July 2010).

Clarke AM, O'Sullivan M & Barry MM (2010) Context matters in programme implementation. *Health Education* **110** (4) (current issue in press).

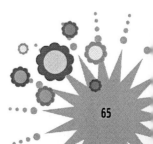

Commonwealth Department of Health and Aged Care (2000) *National Action Plan for Promotion, Prevention and Early Intervention for Mental Health 2000* [online]. Canberra: Mental Health and Special Programs Branch, Cw. Department of Health and Aged Care. Available at: www.health.gov.au/internet/main/publishing.nsf/Content/mental-pubs-n-promote (accessed July 2010).

Domitrovich CE & Greenberg MT (2000) The study of implementation: current findings from effective programs that prevent mental disorders in school-aged children. *Journal of Educational and Psychological Consultation* **11** (2) 193–221.

Durlak JA (1998) Why program implementation is important. *Journal of Prevention and Intervention in the Community* **17** (2) 5–18.

Durlak JA & Wells AM (1997) Primary prevention mental health programs for children and adolescents: a meta-analytic review. *American Journal of Community Psychology* **25** (2) 115–152.

Durlak JA & DuPre EP (2008) Implementation matters: a review of research on the influence of implementation on program outcomes and the factors affecting implementation. *American Journal of Community Psychology* **41** (3–4) 327–350.

European Commission (2005) *Green Paper – Improving the mental health of the population: towards a strategy on mental health for the European Union*. Brussels: Health and Consumer Protection Directorate, European Commission.

Fixsen DL, Naoom SF, Blasé KA, Friedman RM & Wallace F (2005) *Implementation Research: A synthesis of the literature*. Tampa, Fl: Louis de la Parte Florida Mental Health Institute, The National Implementation Research Network, University of South Florida.

Foresight Project on Mental Capital and Wellbeing (2008) *Final Project Report* [online]. London: Government Office for Science. Available at: www.foresight.gov.uk (accessed July 2010).

Friedli L (2003) *Making it Effective: A guide to evidence based mental health promotion*. London: Mentality.

Friedli L & Parsonage M (2007) *Mental Health Promotion: Building an economic case*. Belfast: Northern Ireland Association for Mental Health.

Friedli L (2009) *Mental Health, Resilience and Inequalities*. Copenhagen: World Health Organization Regional Office for Europe.

Public Mental Health Today © Pavilion Publishing (Brighton) Ltd 2010

Greenberg MT, Domitrovich CE, Graczyk PA & Zins JE (2006) *The Study of Implementation in School-based Prevention Research: Implications for theory, research, and practice*. Rockville, MD: Centre for Mental Health Services, Substance Abuse and Mental Health Services Administration.

GermAnn K & Ardiles P (2009) *Toward Flourishing for All: Mental health promotion and mental illness prevention policy background paper* [online]. Canada: Commissioned by the Pan Canadian Steering Committee for Mental Health Promotion and Mental Illness Prevention. Available at: http://www.utoronto.ca/chp/mentalhealthpdffinal/Toward%20Flourishing%20for%20All%20Companion%20Document%20%20Final%20Version%20April%202009.pdf (accessed July 2010).

Health Education Authority (1997) *Mental Health Promotion: A quality framework*. London: Health Education Authority.

Herrman H, Saxena S & Moodie R (Eds) (2005) *Promoting Mental Health: Concepts, emerging evidence, practice*. A report of the World Health Organization, Department of Mental Health and Substance Abuse in collaboration with the Victorian Health Promotion Foundation and University of Melbourne. Geneva: WHO.

Hosman C & Jané-Llopis E (1999) Political challenges 2: mental health. In: *The Evidence of Health Promotion Effectiveness: Shaping public health in a new Europe*. A report for the European Commission. International Union for Health Promotion and Education. Paris: Jouve Composition & Impression.

Huppert FA (2005) Positive mental health in individuals and populations. In: F Huppert, N Bayliss & B Keverne (Eds) *The Science of Well-being*. Oxford: Oxford University Press.

Jané-Llopis E & Barry MM (2005) What makes mental health promotion effective? In: E Jané-Llopis, MM Barry, C Hosman & V Patel (Eds) The evidence of mental health promotion effectiveness: strategies for action. *Promotion and Education IUHPE Special Issue* **2** 47–55.

Jané-Llopis E, Barry MM, Hosman C & Patel V (2005) Mental health promotion works: a review. In: E Jané-Llopis, MM Barry, C Hosman & V Patel (Eds) The evidence of mental health promotion effectiveness: strategies for action. *Promotion and Education IUHPE Special Issue* **2** 9–25.

Keleher H & Armstrong R (2005) *Evidence-based Mental Health Promotion Resource*. Melbourne: Department of Human Services.

Keyes CLM (2005) Mental illness and/or mental health? Investigating axioms of the complete state model of health. *Journal of Consulting and Clinical Psychology* **73** 539–548.

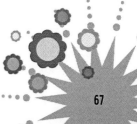

Keyes CLM (2007) Promoting and protecting mental health as flourishing. *American Psychologist* **62** (2) 1–14.

Kovess-Masfety M, Murray M & Gureje O (2005) Positive mental health. In: H Herrman, S Saxena & R Moodie (Eds) *Promoting Mental Health: Concepts, emerging evidence, practice* (pp35–45). A report of the World Health Organization, Department of Mental Health and Substance Abuse in collaboration with the Victorian Health Promotion Foundation and University of Melbourne. Geneva: WHO.

Lehtinen V, Ozamiz A, Underwood L & Weiss M (2005) The intrinsic value of mental health. In: Herrman H, Saxena S & Moodie R (Eds) *Promoting Mental Health: Concepts, emerging evidence, practice* (pp46–58). A report of the World Health Organization, Department of Mental Health and Substance Abuse in collaboration with the Victorian Health Promotion Foundation and University of Melbourne. Geneva: WHO.

Melzer D, Fryers T & Jenkins R (2004) *Social Inequalities and the Distribution of Common Mental Disorders*. Maudsley Monographs. Hove: Psychology Press.

Mihalic S, Fagan A, Irwin K, Ballard D & Elliott D (2002) *Blueprints for Violence Prevention Replications: Factors for implementation success*. Boulder, CO: Center for the Study of Prevention of Violence, Institute of Behavioral Science, University of Colorado.

Ministry of Health, New Zealand (2005) *Te Tahuhu: Improving mental health 2005–2015* [online]. Wellington: Ministry of Health. Available at: www.moh.govt.nz/moh.nsf/0/F2907744575A9DA9CC25702C007E8411/$File/tetahuhu-improvingmentalhealth.pdf (accessed July 2010).

Mrazek PJ & Haggerty RJ (Eds) (1994) *Reducing Risks for Mental Disorders: Frontiers for preventive intervention research*. Washington DC: National Academy Press.

O'Connell MA, Boat T & Warner K (2009) *Preventing Mental, Emotional, and Behavioral Disorders Among Young People: Progress and possibilities*. Washington, DC: National Academies Press.

Pickett KE, James OW & Wilkinson RG (2006) Income inequality and the prevalence of mental illness: a preliminary international analysis. *Journal of Epidemiology and Community Health* **60** 646–647.

Rogers A & Pilgrim D (2005) *A Sociology of Mental Health and Illness*. Maidenhead: Open University Press.

Social Exclusion Unit (2004) *Mental Health and Social Exclusion: Social Exclusion Unit report*. London: Office of the Deputy Prime Minister.

US Department of Health and Human Services (1999) *Mental Health: A report of the Surgeon General*. Rockville, MD: US Department of Health and Human Services, Substance Abuse and Mental Health Services Administration, Centre for Mental Health Services, National Institutes of Health, National Institute of Mental Health.

VicHealth (1999) *Mental Health Promotion Plan Foundation Document 1999–2002*. Victoria: The Victorian Health Promotion Foundation.

VicHealth (2009) *The Melbourne Charter for Promoting Mental Health and Preventing Mental and Behavioral Disorders* [online]. Available at: http://www.vichealth.vic.gov.au/en/Resource-Centre/Publications-and-Resources/Mental-health-promotion/Melbourne-Charter.aspx (accessed July 2010).

World Health Organization (1986) *Ottawa Charter for Health Promotion*. Geneva: WHO.

World Health Organization (2001) *Mental Health: New understanding, new hope*. The World Health Report. Geneva: WHO.

World Health Organization (2002) *Prevention and Promotion in Mental Health*. Geneva: WHO.

World Health Organization (2004) *Promoting Mental Health: Concepts, emerging evidence, practice*. Summary Report. A report of the World Health Organization, Department of Mental Health and Substance Abuse in collaboration with the Victorian Health Promotion Foundation and the University of Melbourne [online]. Geneva: WHO. Available at: www.who.int/mental_health/evidence/en/promoting_mhh.pdf (accessed July 2010).

World Health Organization (2005a) *Mental Health Action Plan for Europe: Facing the challenges, building solutions*. Geneva: WHO.

World Health Organization (2005b) *The Bangkok Charter for Health Promotion in a Globalized World*. Geneva: WHO.

World Health Organization Commission on the Social Determinants of Health (2008) *Closing the Gap in a Generation: Health equity through action on the social determinants of health. Final report of the Commission on the Social Determinants of Health*. Geneva: WHO.

World Health Organization (2009) *Nairobi Call to Action for Closing the Implementation Gap in Health Promotion. 7th Global Conference on Health Promotion* [online]. Geneva: WHO. Available online at: http://www.gesundheitsfoerderung.ch/pdf_doc_xls/e/GFPstaerken/Netzwerke/Nairobi-Call-to-Action-Nov09.pdf (accessed July 2010).

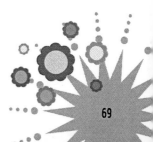

Zechmeister I, Kilian R, McDaid D & the MHEEN Group (2008) Is it worth investing in mental health promotion and prevention of mental illness? A systematic review of the evidence from economic evaluations. *BMC Public Health* [online] **8** (20). Available at: http://www.ncbi.nlm.nih.gov/pmc/articles/PMC2245925/ (accessed July 2010).

Zubrick S & Kovess-Masfety M (2005) Indicators of mental health. In: H Herrman, S Saxena & R Moodie (Eds) *Promoting Mental Health: Concepts, emerging evidence, practice* (pp148–168). A report of the World Health Organization, Department of Mental Health and Substance Abuse in collaboration with the Victorian Health Promotion Foundation and University of Melbourne. Geneva: WHO.

Chapter 4

Some sociological aspects of public mental health

David Pilgrim

Introduction

The relationship between mental health and its social context has been
explored in a number of ways by sociologists. Two main trends have been
evident. First, for those interested predominantly or wholly in causal
arguments, there is an overwhelming case that past and present social
conditions are strong determinants of mental health status (eg. Brown &
Harris, 1978). Age, gender, sexuality, race and social class all predict mental
health status (Rogers & Pilgrim, 2003). Of these variables, social class is the
most robust predictor, with the fewest mixed findings and caveats about data
interpretation. Moreover, in all social groups childhood neglect and abuse
predict diagnosed mental disorder and so may, in large part, account for intra-
social group variation (Pilgrim, Rogers & Bentall, 2009; Spataro *et al*, 2004).
These arguments about social determination can be located strongly in the
structuralist and materialist traditions of sociology (especially derived from
Marx and Durkheim).

Second, for those more interested in constructivist arguments, the social is
also important because of the emergence and ubiquity of context-specific
meanings in human social organisation (compared to that of other species).
The social implications of complex language use are extensive and profound

in human affairs. Beginning with symbolic interactionism, rooted in the work of Weber, and influenced in the past 30 years by French poststructuralist philosophy, mental health research has increasingly attended to critical deconstruction (Miller & Rose, 1985; Parker *et al*, 1995).

This position asserts that we can only know reality via the various ways that humans represent it and these ways are saturated with 'interest work', related to economic inequalities and political, secular and religious ideologies. Those with more power have the power to define and discuss reality on, and in, their own terms. The powerless are silenced relatively or absolutely. For example, if psychiatrists study and promote the reversal of stigma, they will tend to do it on their terms, which are predicated on the assumption of the centrality and validity of their preferred diagnostic labels (Pilgrim & Rogers, 2005). It is in this sort of sociological work about competing discourses that we encounter meaning and values being privileged for consideration over causation.

This chapter summarises a case for taking both of these views seriously because they are both illuminating, though space does not permit a discussion of their points of incompatibility. Tolerating, and learning from, both viewpoints in co-existence allows us to consider mental health as a public health matter. To illustrate this advantage, this chapter will examine two major topics: the prevention of mental disorder and the promotion of mental health, and the challenge of lowering the incidence of misery in society.

Preventing mental disorder and promoting mental health

Mental health promotion has been defined in a variety of ways but tends to include: happiness, the right to freedom and productivity, the absence of mental illness, and the fulfilment of an individual's emotional, intellectual and spiritual potential. Conceptually, the promotion of psychological well-being and the primary prevention of mental health problems are close. However, in the former case, positive mental health is defined, as one or more desired outcomes. By contrast, in the latter case, there is a demonstration that the probability of diagnosed mental illness is reduced. Tudor (1996) warns of the danger of conflating mental health promotion with the primary prevention of mental illness, as it may maintain a medical focus on a limited clinical population and eschew the population's needs as a whole (also see Herrman *et al* (2005) and Barry and Jenkins (2007) on this caution).

The World Health Organization (1986) advocates mental health promotion in terms of the ability of individuals to 'have the basic opportunity to develop and use their health potential to live socially and economically productive lives'. Later, the Organization went on to argue that 'the concept of health potential encompasses both physical and mental health and must be viewed in the context of persona development throughout the life span' (WHO, 1991). Note that even at this stage of definition, the arguments are normative – they include some notion of what it is to be a healthy human being in society. This is a value judgment and so must be considered in terms of meaning, not just causation.

The primary prevention of mental illness can be distinguished from secondary and tertiary forms. Secondary prevention refers to 'nipping mental health problems in the bud' following early diagnosis or when symptoms have been clearly manifested (eg. a first episode of psychosis or early indications of phobic anxiety). Tertiary prevention refers to lowering the probability of relapse in those with chronic mental health problems and so is close to ongoing treatment. All three are affected by social conditions.

The distinction, but also the relationship, between promotion and primary prevention was conceived as the differing permutation of common factors thus:

$$\text{Incidence of mental illness} = \frac{\text{stress} + \text{exploitation} + \text{organic factors}}{\text{support} + \text{self-esteem building} + \text{coping skills}}$$

$$\text{Promotion of mental health} = \frac{\text{coping skills} + \text{environment} + \text{self-esteem}}{\text{stress} + \text{exploitation} + \text{organic factors}}$$

(Albee, 1993)

Some aspects of the factors noted are considered here:

▶ **Stress** – Both poor and rich people suffer stress in their lives but the rich have far more buffering positive experiences to ward off symptom formation and to maintain their morale. Also, those exposed to lower levels of personal and environmental stress are more likely to remain mentally healthy. For example, stable employment is less stressful than insecure short-term contracts. Thus we can think of any social context as providing a range of types and quantities of 'stressors', which impinge on those in its midst (Rogers & Pilgrim, 2003).

▶ **Exploitation** – The exploitation of individuals, whether it is economic or related to physical, sexual or emotional abuse or oppression, increases the risk of mental health problems. Conversely, a person not exposed to these versions of exploitation is more likely to remain mentally healthy. This notion of exploitation disrupts the more traditional 'scientific' or 'disinterested' approach to mental health research typically found in psychiatry and psychology (Sartorius & Henderson, 1992). It implies that political measures to protect children, reduce inequalities and prevent starvation and warfare are important and that all citizens are well housed and educated and protected from the prejudicial actions of others (Sartorius, 2001).

▶ **Organic factors** – These refer to environmental toxins and stressors and to biological susceptibility. These are not merely 'environmental' factors – they are also social because our environment is shaped by human action, which creates a differential exposure of some social groups to pathogenic impacts. For example, the stress of job insecurity and exploitation are mediated by physiological mechanisms to produce brain damage: prolonged raised blood pressure increases the risk of vascular dementia.

▶ **Social support and social capital** – Chronic personal isolation increases the risk of symptoms and these are reduced in probability in those people who are part of a supportive social network or primary group (be it close friends or family) (Sarason *et al*, 1990).

▶ **Self-esteem building** – Family and school life can enable or undermine confidence in the growing child. Self-esteem is also maintained by the presence of benign and affirming current relationships in the family and at work and so links back to the previous point about social support (eg. Sinnoki *et al*, 2009).

▶ **Coping skills** – People vary in their ability to cope with adversity and this is probably a function of personal styles learned in the family and at school. Much of the work of psychological therapists is devoted to enabling patients who lack these coping skills normally to develop them. Therapy thus provides an offer of remediation at the individual level for group or social adversity. A risk then is that this factor is over-valued by mental health workers and the other factors on the list above are ignored and their causal significance marginalised (the risk of 'individualism' or 'psychological reductionism').

Thus, positive mental health and the primary prevention of mental illness implicate a wide range of factors, which are political, social, psychological and biological. Mental health promotion implicates both public policies and public education (Tones & Tilford, 1994). Accordingly, a number of apparently separate policies can affect mental health related to, among other things: environmental pollution, child protection, employment, leisure, street cleaning, traffic levels, parenting, schooling, diet and exercise.

Well-being and happiness

There has been an increasing political consensus that a true mental health policy should be directed towards maximising happiness in the population and minimising misery. Miserable people make poor workers and they impede socio-economic efficiency. Layard (2005) has argued that it is cost-effective for governments to treat mental illness in order to remove the burden it creates in lost productivity, poor fitness for work and the costs of long-term health care access. As Teghtsoonian (2009) has pointed out, this response has been part of a recent neo-liberal pattern of policies in North America and Europe. These policies individualise mental health, especially 'common mental health problems' such as depression. This shifts the focus from the social determinants of unhappiness to unhappy individuals, although Layard, a champion of downstream rescuing (using cognitive-behaviour therapy or CBT), also argues in his model about upstream determinants.

Layard's work and others argue that these upstream factors largely implicate the corrosive impact of consumerism in late modernity. Layard talks of the 'Hedonic Treadmill' (Layard, 2005) and James (2008) writes about 'affluenza', when material possessions and consumption have taken precedence in modern societies over low cost and low striving forms of social affiliation. When kith and kin are relegated in importance, compared to the role of consumption, then distress is generally not far behind.

This form of critique is confirmed by the longitudinal study of happiness worldwide, which has found that the happiest countries are those in which 'post-materialist values' predominate (Inglehart *et al*, 2008). The authors note that the relationship between gross domestic product and happiness is not linear but curvilinear. That is, poverty causes misery; however, once any society reaches a point where the great bulk of its population is not in a state of absolute poverty, then increasing wealth does not increase happiness. Rich, consumer orientated societies develop norms of status envy and competitiveness. This societal ethos demoralises all citizens but especially those who are the least successful and, accordingly, the richest country in the world, the USA, is not the happiest.

By contrast, the happiest developed countries and sub-cultures within each are associated with 'post-materialist' values, which emphasise mutuality and have high levels of social capital. The latter predicts morbidity of most kinds and it is also correlated with rates of recovery from illness. Social isolation and status envy are similarly predictive, which is confirmed by evidence on social support (eg. Cassel, 1976; Cobb, 1976). Some studying social support go further and point out that the mere absence of relationships is the reason people are depressed, even without other evidence of past or current social adversity (Henderson, 1992).

The chances of a person enjoying the mental health advantages of social support increase with their marital status and their socio-economic status, suggesting a virtuous circle, in which the rich get richer in two senses. Those with an intimate partner enjoy more social contact than single people and those with more disposable income have richer social networks (Ross & Mirowsky, 1995). Lower levels of income provide fewer opportunity structures for people to develop social contact and thereby experience personal support (House *et al*, 1988). These opportunity structures include access to paid social events, as well as the increased confidence to interact with others.

Thus economic inequality sets up relative disadvantage in developed societies, where very few are starving from absolute poverty, in a number of ways based around consumption, self-confidence and social status. Relative disadvantage creates envy and insecurity (Wilkinson, 2005). When we combine this point with Layard's one noted above about the 'Hedonic Treadmill' of consumerism, it becomes obvious why materialism, especially conspicuous consumption is a pathogenic force in society. As a consequence, it is the quality of relationships, not buying power, which predicts well-being.

Studies of happy people suggest that domestic intimacy, religious affiliation and employed status are all important causal influences (Myers, 2000). All three domains are potential sources of social support and they give meaning to people's lives, reminding us that meanings, not just causes, are social phenomena to consider. Wilkinson (2005) adds that low socio-economic status brings with it shame and insecurity and makes the low status person more disinclined to make social contact.

Low levels of social support ipso facto bring increasing social isolation. Social isolation predicts the emergence of mental health problems and relapse in those who have had them in the past.

Early studies by the Chicago School of Sociology confirmed that the incidence of mental health problems is correlated directly with social integration. This ecological picture has been confirmed more recently in relation to the incidence of psychosis, suicide and psychiatric admissions in ethnic minority patients living in areas with low levels, of those from their background (Boydell *et al*,

2001). While this point about 'ethnic density' specifically helps us to understand mediating processes about ethnic disadvantage, it also helps more generally to understand the importance of 'social belonging' for mental health. Thus, the social integration findings suggest that people have a need for group belonging. A lack of group membership predicts the emergence of mental health problems and relapse. Moreover, embedded in-group belonging is the opportunity for particular intimate relationships (some of which are expressed in long-term sexual bonding). These intimate and 'close confiding' relationships provide conditions of stable existential security – they are meaningful to the actors involved, not just impersonal stressors impacting upon them.

Discussion

In the light of the arguments above, any holistic sociological account of mental health must take account of both causes and meanings. This implies some reflection about ontology (what is deemed to exist) and epistemology (what form of knowledge it is legitimate to generate). Broadly, three positions are evident about these questions of ontology and epistemology (Pilgrim, 2009).

1. Naïve realists (a few sociologists and most psychiatrists) take the current naming of causes and outcomes of 'mental illness' for granted (the 'neo-Kraepelinian' approach). Thus in this scheme of things, madness is a category called 'schizophrenia' or maybe 'bipolar disorder' and misery a category called 'depression' or 'anxiety disorder' or 'common mental health problem'. Madness is deemed to be largely genetically determined, with stressors acting as triggers. Common mental health problems are largely deemed to be environmentally generated with some influences of genetic vulnerability. These patients then embody, in the tautological minds of naïve realists, living proof of the existence of the putative mental illnesses described so earnestly by them. But these diagnostic labels are merely the currently preferred constructs of professionals, who confuse reality with what they currently call reality. 'Schizophrenia', say, does not exist 'out there' waiting to be discovered. People are diagnosed with schizophrenia – a social transaction.

2. In the opposite direction, radical constructivists consider that reality is always socially constructed and so we can never get beyond representations to understand reality in, and of, itself. If naïve realists are uncritical about their preferred terms then radical constructivists are nihilistic and run the risk of denying likely causes of social inequalities (because causes and reality are problematised so strongly). If 'everything is socially constructed' then we can never say anything for certain about reality.

3. Critical realists (including the author of this chapter) adopt the third and middle position and argue that reality exists and is forceful in its impact on mental health. However, social interests shape and constrain how we can come to know reality, so we must approach knowledge claims sceptically and expect the meaning of any behaviour or experience to be context-dependent. For critical realists it is not reality that is socially constructed (contra 2 above) but our understanding of reality. Moreover, contra 1 above, because of this we should approach the findings of research on mental health sceptically. Who finances it? Whose interests are maintained or extended by asking this sort of question rather than another? Why do we want to call a psychological difference a 'problem' and why do we adopt particular labels in the process?

By adopting this third sceptical, questioning, position the following become important points to consider.

▶ Distress, madness and dysfunction have occurred in all societies and are determined by many factors, some known and some still mysterious, but what they are called and how they are valued varies over time and place.

▶ Distress (fear and sadness) is easier to understand than madness because it has many stable elements across contexts and even species. Fear, in particular, has predictable and measurable physical signs in all mammalian species. Most of us know what it is to feel sad in the face of loss and can even spot it with some confidence in other animals. This regularity of observation is not the case with madness or 'personality disorder'. These arise from context-specific norms about rationality, mutual recognition and obligations and intelligibility. These forms of deviance are peculiarly human and so must be understood in the normative contexts of our forms of social organisation.

▶ Any notion of positive mental health necessarily subsumes hedonic and eudemonic aspects (about positive feelings and social competence respectively). Thus it cannot be studied 'objectively' and as merely a matter of causal argument. Those studying mental health are part of their own context – they cannot stand outside it. The constructs they use in their research are socially derived.

▶ Judgements about illness or health are inherently social. Ultimately, they are value judgments about what it is to act, or be capable of acting, in a good way (connoting implicitly or explicitly some version of Aristotle's 'eudemonia' or 'good life'). Put differently, terms like 'mental disorder' or 'mental abnormality' always imply other forms of action and emotion, which

 Public Mental Health Today © Pavilion Publishing (Brighton) Ltd 2010

are mentally 'ordered' or 'normal'; the way that people ought to think, feel and act as part of an ideal moral order (Wakefield, 1992). Disease and health can and do then become socially contested. For example, the 'happiness' agenda, especially when it offers the technological fix of CBT, is essentially a socio-political one generating its own rhetoric of justification and provoking a competing rhetoric in its critics. It appeals to economists and politicians because it implicates such matters as productivity, fiscal burden and even voting behaviour and it also has an ideological commitment to the notion that there is a therapeutic fix. It turns unhappy people embedded in unique social contexts into de-contextualised patients to be cured on a therapeutic production line of 'stepped care'. It assumes that unhappiness is an illness and that suffering should be cured, not endured. Many psychological therapists have been keen to support and reinforce this discourse because it raises their status and expands their jurisdiction. This position is defensible but it is also open to legitimate challenge for a variety of ethical and ideological reasons (Pilgrim, 2010).

In conclusion, this chapter has emphasised the need to consider sociological investigations of mental health that hold on to causes and meanings, rather than one or the other. Madness, misery and personal dysfunction have occurred in all societies. They are generated unevenly by social forces, which affect some social groups more than others. At the same time, how we codify these phenomena is shaped as well by social forces (for example, related to the sorts of professional interests just noted). When a person is mad or miserable, or for that matter happy or content, these experiences are infused with personal meanings in particular social situations and they reflect contemporary and local normative concerns. An emphasis on meanings alone fails to respect the palpable impact of social inequalities. An emphasis on causes alone fails to respect human beings as social sense-makers existing in a variety of times and places. Both are required.

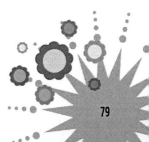

References

Albee G (1993) The fourth revolution. In: D Trent & C Reed (Eds) *Promotion of Mental Health* (Volume III). London: Avebury.

Barry M & Jenkins R (2007) *Implementing Mental Health Promotion*. London: Churchill Livingstone Elsevier.

Boydell J, van Os J, McKenzie K, Allardyce J, Goel R, McCreadie RG & Murray M (2001) Incidence of schizophrenia in ethnic minorities in London: ecological study into interactions with environment. *British Medical Journal* **323** 1336.

Brown G & Harris T (1978) *Social Origins of Depression*. London: Tavistock.

Cassel J (1976) The contribution of host environment to host resistance. *American Journal of Epidemiology* **14** 107–123.

Cobb S (1976) Social support as a moderator of life stress. *Psychosomatic Medicine* **38** 300–314.

Henderson AS (1992) Social support and depression. In: HOF Veil & U Baumann (Eds) *The Meaning and Measurement of Social Support*. New York: Hemisphere.

Hermann H, Saxena S & Moodie R (2005) *Promoting Mental Health: Concepts, emerging evidence and practice*. Geneva: WHO.

House JS, Umberson D & Landis KR (1988) Structures and processes of social support. *Annual Review of Sociology* **14** 293–318.

Inglehart R, Welz C, & Foa R (2008) *Happiness Trends in 24 countries (1946–2006) World Values Survey* [online]. Available at: www.worldvaluessurvey.org (accessed July2010).

James O (2008) *Affluenza*. London: Vermillion.

Layard R (2005) *Happiness: Lessons from a new science*. London: Penguin.

Miller P & Rose N (Eds) (1985) *The Power of Psychiatry*. Oxford: Polity.

Myers DG (2000) The faith, friends and funds of happy people. *American Psychologist* **55** 56–67.

Parker I, Georgaca E, Harper D, McLaughlin T & Stowell-Smith M (1995) *Deconstructing Psychopathology*. London: SAGE Publications.

Pilgrim D (2009) Abnormal psychology: unresolved ontological and epistemological contestation. *History and Philosophy of Psychology* **10** (2) 11–21.

Pilgrim D (2010) The hegemony of cognitive-behaviour therapy in modern mental health care. *Health Sociology Review* (in press).

Pilgrim D & Rogers A (2005) Psychiatrists as social engineers: a study of an anti-stigma campaign. *Social Science and Medicine* **61** (12) 2546–2556.

Pilgrim D, Rogers A & Bentall RP (2009) The centrality of personal relationships in the creation and amelioration of mental health problems: the current interdisciplinary case. *Health* **13** 235–254.

Rogers A & Pilgrim D (2003) *Mental Health and Inequality*. Basingstoke: Palgrave/Macmillan.

Rogers A & Pilgrim D (2009) *A Sociology of Mental Health and Illness* (4th ed). Buckingham: Open University Press.

Ross CE & Mirowsky J (1995) Does employment affect health? *Journal of Health and Social Behavior* **36** 230–243.

Sarason BR, Pierce GR & Sarason IG (1990) Social support: the sense of acceptance and the role of relationships. In: BR Sarason, IG Sarason & GR Pierce (Eds) *Social Support: An interactional view*. New York: Wiley.

Sartorius N (2001) Primary prevention of mental disorders. In: G Thornicroft & G Szmukler (Eds) *Textbook of Community Psychiatry*. Oxford: Oxford University Press.

Sartorius N & Henderson AS (1992) The neglect of prevention in psychiatry. *Australian and New Zealand Journal of Psychiatry* **26** 550–553.

Sinokki M, Hinkka K, Ahola K, Koskinen S, Klaukka T, Kivimaki M, Puukka P, Lonnqvist J & Virtanen M (2009) The association between team climate at work and mental health in the Finnish Health 2000 study. *Occupational and Environmental Medicine* **66** 523–528.

Spataro J, Mullen PE, Burgess PM, Wells DL & Moss SA (2004) Impact of child sexual abuse on mental health: prospective study in males and females. *British Journal of Psychiatry* **184** 416–421.

Teghtsoonian K (2009) Depression and mental health in neoliberal times: a critical analysis of policy and discourse. *Social Science and Medicine* **69** 28–35.

Tones K & Tilford S (1994) *Health Education: Effectiveness, efficiency and equity*. London: Chapman Hall.

Tudor K (1996) *Mental Health Promotion: Paradigms and practice*. London: Routledge.

Wakefield JC (1992) The concept of mental disorder: on the boundary between biological facts and social values. *American Psychologist* **4** (3) 373–388.

Wilkinson RG (2005) *The Impact of Inequality: How to make sick societies healthier*. London: Routledge.

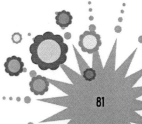

World Health Organization (1986) *Health Promotion: Concepts and principles in action.* Geneva: WHO.

World Health Organization (1991) *Implications for the Field of Mental Health of the European Targets for Attaining Health for All.* Copenhagen: WHO European Regional Office.

Chapter 5

Improving public mental health: the European context

Chris O'Sullivan

Introduction

Active international collaboration provides an opportunity for development and for nurturing of ideas and practice across a range of policy and practice environments. There is a natural affinity between English speaking nations, and an 'active transfer market' exists between the countries of the UK, Australia, New Zealand, Canada, the United States and Ireland. Examples of this include initiatives such as mental health first aid, applied suicide intervention skills training (ASIST), and peer support in recovery, which have been adapted for a UK practice and policy environment from these countries. In turn, UK initiatives have been exported to other countries. With the International Initiative for Mental Health Leadership (IIMHL) providing a forum for the exchange of knowledge and experience across these nations.

Of less immediate currency are the opportunities for transfer of practice and policy initiatives between European nations, many of whom have a fundamental connection to the UK, to the extent that their health and social protection systems are similarly constructed or are facing similar challenges. In turn, there are European nations that have provided examples of good practice, which have been of interest to the UK.

There are many opportunities for European researchers, policy-makers and practitioners to access an almost constant stream of information from peers in other European countries. Public mental health extends across multiple policy and practice areas, which further diversifies the potential information sources for people interested in accessing European initiatives. In some quarters in Europe there is a reticence to consider transferability of policy or practice examples from a non-European context into Europe, and to that end the UK has found itself playing an important bridging role in importing programmes from elsewhere and once their applicability has been evidenced, transferring them to other European countries. One example of this approach is mental health first aid, which originated in Australia, was transferred to Scotland, and was subsequently transferred from there to England, Wales, Ireland and Finland.

The objective of this chapter is to introduce some of the areas of public mental health that are currently being explored at a European or trans-national level in Europe. Within the chapter the roles of the relevant activities of European and international bodies, most notably the European Communities (EC) and the World Health Organization (WHO) will be introduced. Likewise the chapter will aim to introduce some of the key stakeholders in public mental health in Europe, including the non-governmental organisations, networks and lobbying groups via which many practitioners access and influence European initiatives.

The role of mental health in the EU

The European Union is founded on the Treaty on European Union (The 'Treaty'/TEU), a document developed from the original Treaty of Rome and amended by successive treaties. The most recent of these amending treaties is the Lisbon Treaty, signed in 2007.

The Treaty of Amsterdam (1997) was signed in October 1997, and came into force on the 1 May 1999. It substantially amended the Treaty on European Union signed in Maastricht in 1992. The Treaty of Amsterdam added for the first time a specific clause on public health to the treaty. This had the effect of raising public health to the level of EC ('Community') objective. Informal co-operation between Member States had taken place since 1997, but the new article 152 in the Treaty of Amsterdam enabled the European Union to adopt measures aimed at ensuring (rather than merely contributing to) a high level of human health protection.

The article 152 inserted in the Treaty of Amsterdam relates to co-operation on some disease areas and to the protection of human health more widely, but it is fundamentally important to note that responsibility for the organisation of health systems remains with Member States. The role of the 'Community' is subsidiary and mainly involves supporting the efforts of the Member States and helping them formulate and implement co-ordinated objectives and strategies.

The EU Green Paper *Improving the Mental Health of the Population: Towards a strategy on mental health for the European Union* (European Commission, 2005) defined the role of the European Community in mental health as based on the then TEU as being:

'mental health is an issue for the European Community through:
1. *the contribution that good mental health of the population can make to some of the EU's strategic policy objectives*

2. *the role of the Community to encourage and support co-operation between Member States and to address inequalities between them*

3. *the obligation for the Community to contribute to a high level of human health protection through all its policies and activities.'*

(European Commission, 2005, p5)

The Treaty of Lisbon was signed in 2007 and substantially amended the TEU. It came into force in December 2009 following a politically charged process of ratification, including two referenda in the Republic of Ireland. The treaty was ratified in the UK Parliament.

The Lisbon Treaty extends and develops the responsibility of the 'Community' in the field of health. It maintains the subsidiarity of the EU on health systems, and does not seek to harmonise legislation in Member States regarding health. It does, however, have interesting ramifications for the potential of public mental health to be integrated into both EU health policy, and into other policy areas.

An important and immediate change is that 'well-being' becomes a new objective of the EU, in fact part of the first objective. This is significant in that it permits well-being to be raised in assessing and developing policy options in non-health fields.

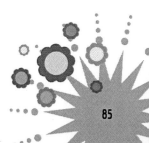

*'The Union's aim is to promote peace, its values and the well-being of
its peoples.'*
(Article 3, Treaty of European Union, 2007)

Article 6 of the Treaty on the Functioning of the European Union (TFEU)
lists 'protection and improvement of human health' as an area where 'the
Union shall have competence to carry out actions to support, co-ordinate or
supplement the actions of the Member States'.

Article 9 of the Treaty on the Functioning of the European Union takes well-
being into a range of other EU policy areas, many of which correspond to
social determinants of mental health:

*'In defining and implementing its policies and activities, the Union
shall take into account requirements linked to the promotion
of a high level of employment, the guarantee of adequate social
protection, the fight against social exclusion, and a high level of
education, training and protection of human health.'*
(Article 9 Treaty on the Functioning of the European Union, 2007)

Mental health is explicitly referenced in article 168 of TFEU, which outlines in
detail the health responsibilities of the EU.

*'Union action, which shall complement national policies, shall be
directed towards improving public health, preventing physical
and mental illness and diseases, and obviating sources of danger
to physical and mental health. Such action shall cover the fight
against the major health scourges, by promoting research into their
causes, their transmission and their prevention, as well as health
information and education, and monitoring, early warning of and
combating serious cross-border threats to health.'*
(Article 168, Treaty on the Functioning of the European Union, 2007)

This clause is extremely important to efforts to increase the profile of public
mental health on an EU level, because it calls for health, including mental
health to be considered in the formulation of all Union policies and activities.
It considers mental and physical health explicitly, and equally in this regard.

A final consideration for public mental health is that the Lisbon Treaty makes
the Charter of Fundamental Rights legally binding on the 25 Member States that
have not secured an opt-out from it. This Charter is a statement of the basic

human rights of European Citizens. Poland and the Czech Republic negotiated opt-outs from the Charter. The UK has a written guarantee that the Charter will not be used by the European Court to alter British social and labour laws.

The mental health of its citizens is a vital but under-valued resource within the EU. There is a close interrelationship between the EU's policy objectives of prosperity, social inclusion and security and public health on the one hand, and mental health on the other. Mental health is affected by policies and practices across many different sectors, notably policy that influences early years and family life, education, employment, working conditions, migration, household income, housing and the built and natural environment. Therefore, a better understanding of mental health and of actions that can be taken to achieve improved mental health can be of considerable added value in addressing a range of social and economic priorities that are of direct concern to the EU and its Member States.

Historical actions on mental health by the European Commission

Mental health has been a component of 'Community' (EU) action since 1997. The EU health policy initiatives have worked to support work in mental health via the funding of projects and through policy events during presidencies and other initiatives. A summary of these projects and activities are given by the EC document *Action for Mental Health*. Activities co-funded from European Community Public Health Programmes 1997–2004 (European Commission, 2004) and in Annexe Five of the Green Paper *Improving the Mental Health of the Population: Towards a strategy on mental health for the European Union* (European Commission, 2005).

The European Union takes forward health policy through its Health Strategy and a co-ordinated EU Public Health Programme 2003–2008 provided the legal basis for action in public health. This programme supported mental health via a range of project and activity grants. It considered health in terms of health determinants, health information, and health risks with mental health referenced in each of these.

The EU launched a new health strategy, *Together for Health: A strategic approach for the EU 2008–2013* (European Commission, 2007), which develops the outcomes of the 2003–2008 Public Health Programme, and sets clear objectives to guide European level action on health, in partnership with Member States. It adopts a value driven approach, and seeks to recognise and illustrate both the links between health and economic development, and the need for health to be a consideration in all policies (Ståhl *et al*, 2006). The Public Health Programme 2008–13 is the legal instrument for taking forward work under the Health Strategy. This programme publishes an annual work plan outlining the tasks for the year under the health strategy, and calls for projects, activities, and tenders that are issued by the European Agency for Health and Consumers. This programme also provides core funding for European level NGOs in the field of public health.

Health is not the only area in which the EU has taken an interest in mental health. One of the objectives of co-ordinated activity in mental health at an EU level has been to bring together existing programmes and the outcomes of previous activities under a common banner of public mental health. Activities in justice, youth, education and culture, and information society have touched on mental health, but the two major supporting policy areas are research and employment, social affairs and equal opportunities and these are summarised in table 1 below.

Table 1: Key European Union policy initiatives supporting public mental health	
Employment, social affairs, and equal opportunities	The social and employment policies of the EU have included several pieces of legislation and programmes relating to public mental health. The European Year for People with Disabilities in 2003 and activities to develop a Disability Strategy have complemented actions on social inclusion and social protection, which include addressing poverty and inequity, both key determinants of public mental health.
	Relevant legislative instruments have included:
	▶ the adoption of directive 2000/78/EC, which prohibits inter alia discrimination on grounds of disability in the field of employment (European Council, 2000)
	▶ the adoption of a European Framework Agreement on work-related stress between social partners in 2004.
	The implementation of these actions is via the Open Method of Co-ordination, which provides a framework for the collection and comparison of activities in Member States.

Research	Research in the European Union is funded and encouraged by Framework Programmes for Research. There have been successive programmes, all of which have supported research in neuroscience, clinical mental health, and in recent years public mental health. In 2007 the sixth research framework funded a series of projects to provide scientific support to policy. Several projects were funded in the field of public mental health. DataPrev was intended to provide summaries of evidence-based interventions for mental health improvement in youth, employment and in later life. ProMenPol collected a wide database of tools for mental health improvement in these areas, and produced implementation support guides to enable better relationships between policy, research and practitioners. The outcomes of both projects are of outstanding relevance to mental health improvement practice.
	The current framework is Framework 7 (FP7). Health research is given a prominent position in the programme, which included funding streams for basic science as well as in health improvement. Projects in the fields of suicide prevention and children's mental health have already been approved.

Co-ordinated action on mental health by the European Commission

In September 2005 the European Commission published the Green Paper *Improving the Mental Health of the Population: Towards a strategy on mental health for the European Union* (European Commission, 2005). This document outlined the relevance of mental health for some of the EU's strategic policy objectives (prosperity, solidarity and social justice, and quality of life of citizens) and was accompanied by a consultation process that engaged stakeholders at all levels.

A key objective of the Green Paper and subsequent discussions was the desire to shift the paradigm of mental health at an EU level from one that looked at the management and consequences of mental illness to one that included consideration of the impact of population mental health on the ability of the EU and the Member States to meet their objectives in other policy areas. The consultation revealed an interest from civil society and other stakeholders for a formal strategy relating to mental health at an EU level. The added value was less clear for Member States, particularly at a time where there was concern about subsidiarity around health care provision. Discussion with stakeholders and Member States took place throughout 2006 and early 2007, with the aim of exploring common ground, and utilising the outcomes of EC funded projects. In addition, there was a need to ensure that EC actions complemented joint work undertaken with international organisations such as The World Health Organization.

By 2007 there was a gathering impetus to ensure that the opportunities presented by the Green Paper and the consultations since were mobilised in a method of co-ordination that would ensure capacity building and knowledge exchange continued at an EU level without a legislative instrument. A new vehicle for co-ordination was developed based on 'consensus statements' in five key domains of public mental health. For each of these subjects, with the exception of combating stigma and social exclusion, an expert group of researchers and policy-makers were drawn together to produce a consensus paper to present alongside the *European Pact for Mental Health and Well-being* (The Pact) (European Commission, 2008). The consensus papers for each area, and the research paper presented on stigma and discrimination are excellent introductory readers for the European context of each of the topics, which are:

1. Mental health in youth and education (Jané-Llopis & Braddick, 2008)

2. Preventing suicide and depression (Wahlbeck & Mäkinen, 2008)

3. Mental health and older people (Jané-Llopis & Gabilondo, 2008)

4. Mental health in workplace settings (McDaid, 2008a)

5. Combating stigma and social exclusion (McDaid, 2008b)

The Pact was launched at a high level conference on mental health and well-being held in June 2008, with the involvement of the Commissioners for Health and Consumer Affairs, and for Employment and Social Affairs, The European Parliament and a range of stakeholders. The Pact is a symbol of the wish to exchange and work together on mental health opportunities and challenges at an EU level. The Pact made some key suggestions for action in each of the five themes, which are summarised in table 2.

Public Mental Health Today © Pavilion Publishing (Brighton) Ltd 2010

Table 2: Actions suggested for the five priority themes of the European Pact for Mental Health and Well-being (European Commission, 2008)	
Prevention of depression and suicide	1. Improve the training of health professionals and key actors within the social sector on mental health. 2. Restrict access to potential means for suicide. 3. Take measures to raise mental health awareness in the general public, among health professionals and other relevant sectors. 4. Take measures to reduce risk factors for suicide such as excessive drinking, drug abuse and social exclusion, depression and stress. 5. Provide support mechanisms after suicide attempts and for those bereaved by suicide, such as emotional support helplines.
Mental health in youth and education	1. Ensure schemes for early intervention throughout the educational system. 2. Provide programmes to promote parenting skills. 3. Promote training of professionals involved in the health, education, youth and other relevant sectors in mental health and well-being. 4. Promote the integration of socio-emotional learning into the curricular and extracurricular activities and the cultures of pre-schools and schools. 5. Programmes to prevent abuse, bullying, violence against young people and their exposure to social exclusion. 6. Promote the participation of young people in education, culture, sport and employment.
Mental health in workplace settings	1. Improve work organisation, organisational cultures and leadership practices to promote mental well-being at work, including the reconciliation of work and family life. 2. Implement mental health and well-being programmes with risk assessment and prevention programmes for situations that can cause adverse effects on the mental health of workers (stress, abusive behaviour such as violence or harassment at work, alcohol, drugs) and early intervention schemes at workplaces. 3. Provide measures to support the recruitment, retention or rehabilitation and return to work of people with mental health problems or disorders.

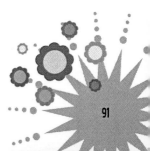

Table 2: Actions suggested for the five priority themes of the European Pact for Mental Health and Well-being (European Commission, 2008) cont.

Mental health of older people	1. Promote the active participation of older people in community life, including the promotion of their physical activity and educational opportunities.
	2. Develop flexible retirement schemes that allow older people to remain at work longer on a full-time or part-time basis.
	3. Provide measures to promote mental health and well-being among older people receiving care (medical and/or social) in both community and institutional settings.
	4. Take measures to support carers.
Combating stigma and social exclusion	1. Support anti-stigma campaigns and activities such as in media, schools and at the workplace to promote the integration of people with mental disorders.
	2. Develop mental health services that are well integrated in the society, put the individual at the centre and operate in a way which avoids stigmatisation and exclusion.
	3. Promote active inclusion of people with mental health problems in society, including improvement of their access to appropriate employment, training and educational opportunities.
	4. Involve people with mental health problems and their families and carers in relevant policy and decision-making processes.

The Pact is, at the time of writing, in the implementation phase. A thematic conference will be held in each of the five thematic areas, in collaboration with Member State governments, European agencies and the presidencies of Sweden, Slovenia, Spain and Belgium. The European Parliament has taken an interest in the development of co-ordinated EU action on mental health. During the Green Paper consultations the Parliament passed a resolution (2006/2058(INI)) supporting action in this field. In 2009 it passed a further resolution (2008/2209(INI)) in which it developed its position on co-ordinated action at an EU level, in the priority areas of the Pact.

The events are being used to gather policy, practice and research practice from across Member States and these will be used to compile an online 'Compass' database of initiatives, and to generate comprehensive background documentation. Like the background papers for the Pact launch, these concise explanations of the problems and potential solutions will be of great use to policy-makers and practitioners on a local and regional level, as well as for people wishing to get an up-to-date précis of the subject. It is anticipated that in 2011 the process of implementation of the Pact will culminate in a conclusion, or resolution at a strategic level (Wahlbeck *et al*, 2010)

The changing events in the global economy over the lifespan of the Pact have seen changes in both the European Union and the stance of the Member States. There have been both risks and opportunities for public mental health at the EU level in this time. In April 2009 the European Commission called an expert 'round table' meeting on managing the psychosocial risks of the financial and economic crisis at which data from a brief survey of member states, and from emerging work on mental health, inequality and resilience (Friedli, 2009) were presented to member states and stakeholder interests. The clear message from the meeting was that public mental health should remain a priority during times of recession. A further review of literature relating to depression and suicide during times of recession was prepared for the Thematic Conference on Suicide and Depression (Wahlbeck & Awolin, 2009).

The Europe 2020 strategy was approved in 2010, to provide an action framework to enable Europe to return to sustainable growth. The strategy calls for 'the exit of the crisis to be a point of entry into a new economy', and it is clear that in addressing the priorities and targets of Europe 2020, mental health and well-being initiatives can play a useful role.

The World Health Organization

The World Health Organization (WHO) is the directing and co-ordinating authority for health in the United Nations systems. It takes a global interest in mental health and public mental health with activities co-ordinated from the Geneva Head Office. There are also complementary areas of work, which WHO has originated, which are of interest to public mental health, particularly on the social determinants of health. The principle activity here has been the Commission on the Social Determinants of Health led by Sir Michael Marmot (WHO, 2008b).

The WHO Regional Office for Europe, based in Copenhagen, is responsible for WHO mental health initiatives in the European Region, which encompasses some 56 states across Europe, including eastern and south eastern Europe and Israel. WHO has been active for several years in the development of co-ordinated action in mental health at the European level. In 2004, two policy documents, *Promoting Mental Health: Concepts, emerging evidence and practice* and *Prevention of Mental Disorders: Effective interventions and policy options* (WHO, 2004a; 2004b) laid the foundations for the development of co-ordinated action by WHO on public mental health. In 2005 WHO held a ministerial conference on mental health: Facing the Challenges, Building Solutions. The ministerial conference resulted in a declaration, and action plan for mental health in Europe (WHO, 2005a; 2005b), which in turn stimulated the European Union to prepare the Green Paper and subsequent activities. The process of policy making during the preparation and implementation of the WHO Action Plan has been studied by the KnowandPol project, and an in-depth report of WHO activities in mental health developed (Freeman *et al*, 2009; Smith-Merry *et al*, 2010, in press).

The WHO regional office works collaboratively with Member States, and via a network of collaborating centres, where groups of researchers, practitioners and policy-makers conduct research on behalf of WHO. WHO Europe has also entered into collaboration with the European Commission on directly funded projects, for example, in the empowerment of people with mental health problems, and on systematic collection of information on mental health policies and practices across Europe. This report, *Policies and Practices for Mental Health in Europe: Meeting the challenges* was published in 2008 and provides an overview of policy and practice in mental health across the European region. It highlights the progress made by most countries over the past years, but also raises some key challenges (WHO, 2008a).

The Council of Europe

The Council of Europe is an international organisation founded in 1949 by 10 nations and now includes 49 nations across the European region. It seeks to develop Europe-wide common and democratic principles based on key documents on 'rights' including the European Convention on Human Rights. The Council of Europe works on social cohesion, public health and the prevention of disability discrimination.

At the European level, NGOs and civil society groups play a significant role in the development of policy. NGOs often provide a bridge between initiatives, projects and political activities, and in this context, they can do much to build a stable base for action. NGOs and their member organisations have access to a range of examples of action that highlight the policy objectives, and that can be used in evidence to support calls for action by other actors.

In mental health and related areas European NGOs fall into three main groups, all of which are relevant to public mental health.

▶ **Representative groups** – Representing a group, population or interest with a stake in mental health. In mental health it is crucial that the voice of people affected by mental ill health is heard, and also that groups representing other sections of society recognise and embrace mental health concepts. At a European level the European Network of Survivors of Psychiatry (ENUSP) represents a range of user-led organisations. In addition, the perspectives of family member organisations are provided by the European Federation of Associations of Families of People with Mental Illness (EUFAMI). Several organisations representing population groups are active in the field of mental health and well-being, including The European Youth Forum and the International Lesbian, Gay, Bisexual, Intersex and Transgender Association (ILGA).

▶ **Umbrella organisations** – Representing member organisations with an interest in mental health. Many NGOs operating at a European level draw their membership from regional, national and local NGOs who look to their European umbrella body to advocate for their interests and cascade relevant information back to them, involving them in discussion and consultation. Often, these umbrella groups are coalitions or federations of representative groups. Mental Health Europe is the leading European NGO working on mental health policy and project work and draws its membership and experience from a broad base of member organisations. EuroHealthNet is a not-for-profit network of regional and national agencies responsible and accountable for health promotion, public health and disease prevention in Europe.

▶ **Professional organisations** – Representing a professional group interested in mental health. Across the workforce groups with a stake in public mental health there are numerous professions that have a role to play in creating and implementing policy action. There are the practitioners who work with mental ill health, including the Network of Psychologists in the Education Sector (NEPES) and HORATIO (psychiatric nurses) as well as medical perspectives from organisations such as the European Psychiatric Association and the Standing Committee of European Doctors. Also active in the field are professional groups representing interests of groups that have a vital part to play, including European Association of Community Pharmacists (PGEU) and the European School Heads Association (ESHA).

Conclusion

The information stream presented by Europe is not dissimilar to a waterfall. There is a constant and powerful deluge of information that has the potential to be useful to many different stakeholders. Like a powerful waterfall there is a temptation to be drawn close to the information flowing from Europe, with similar dangers of being overwhelmed, confused or discouraged by the volume or complexity of the material. As with many complex or large tasks, the key to engaging with European opportunities in public mental health is to be aware of the kinds of information available and to approach the waterfall 'one cup at a time'. It is impossible to discuss every initiative of relevance in one short chapter but it is hoped that this resource will act as a springboard to further reading for those interested. It is certain that opportunities exist to use European evidence, practice, and outputs to enrich practice locally, and to make the case for action when required.

References

European Commission (2004) *Action for Mental Health. Activities co-funded from European Community Public Health Programmes 1997–2004* [online]. Luxembourg: European Commission. Available at: http://ec.europa.eu/health/archive/ph_determinants/life_style/mental/docs/action_1997_2004_en.pdf (accessed July 2010).

European Commission (2007) *White Paper – Together for Health: A strategic approach for the EU 2008–2013*. COM(2007) 630 final [online]. Brussels: European Commission. Available in EU languages at: http://ec.europa.eu/health/ph_overview/strategy/health_strategy_en.htm (accessed July 2010).

European Commission (2008) *European Pact for Mental Health and Well-being* [online]. Available in several languages at: http://ec.europa.eu/health/mental_health/policy/index_en.htm (accessed August 2010).

European Commission, Health & Consumer Protection Directorate-General (2005) *Green Paper – Improving the Mental Health of the Population: Towards a strategy on mental health for the European Union* [online]. Luxembourg: European Commission. Available in EU languages at: http://ec.europa.eu/health/ph_determinants/life_style/mental/keydo_mental_health_en.htm (accessed July 2010).

European Council (2000) Council Directive 2000/78/EC of 27 November 2000 establishing a general framework for equal treatment in employment and occupation. *Official Journal L303 of 2.12.2000*, 16–22 [online]. Available at: http://eur-lex.europa.eu/LexUriServ/LexUriServ.do?uri=CELEX:32000L0078:en:HTML (accessed July 2010).

Freeman R, Smith-Merry J & Sturdy S (2009) *WHO, Mental Health, Europe* [online]. Edinburgh: KnowandPol Project. Available at: http://www.knowandpol.eu/fileadmin/KaP/content/Scientific_reports/Orientation3/WHO.WP11.Production.pdf (accessed July 2010).

Friedli L (2009) *Mental Health, Resilience and Inequalities* [online]. London: WHO Europe/Mental Health Foundation. Available at: http://www.euro.who.int/__data/assets/pdf_file/0012/100821/E92227.pdf (accessed July 2010).

Jané-Llopis E & Braddick F (Eds) (2008) *Mental Health in Youth and Education. EC consensus paper* [online]. Luxembourg: European Commission. Available at: http://ec.europa.eu/health/archive/ph_determinants/life_style/mental/docs/consensus_youth_en.pdf (accessed July 2010).

Jané-Llopis E & Gabilondo A (Eds) (2008) *Mental Health in Older People*. EC consensus paper [online]. Luxembourg: European Commission. Available at: http://ec.europa.eu/health/archive/ph_determinants/life_style/mental/docs/consensus_older_en.pdf (accessed July 2010).

McDaid D (Ed) (2008a) *Mental Health in Workplace Settings* [online]. Luxembourg: European Commission. Available at: http://ec.europa.eu/health/archive/ph_determinants/life_style/mental/docs/consensus_workplace_en.pdf (accessed July 2010).

McDaid D (2008b) *Countering the Stigmatisation and Discrimination of People with Mental Health Problems in Europe* [online]. Luxembourg: European Commission. Available at: http://ec.europa.eu/health/archive/ph_determinants/life_style/mental/docs/stigma_paper_en.pdf (accessed July 2010).

Smith-Merry J, Freeman R & Sturdy S (2010) Reciprocal instrumentalism: Scotland, WHO Europe, and mental health. *International Journal of Public Policy* (in press).

Ståhl T, Wismar M, Ollila E, Lahtinen E & Leppo K (Eds) (2006) *Health in All Policies. Prospects and potentials* [online]. Helsinki: Ministry of Social Affairs and Health. Available at: http://www.euro.who.int/document/E89260.pdf (accessed July 2010).

Wahlbeck K *et al* (2010) European Pact for Mental Health and Well-being: Collating forces to put mental health on the EU political agenda. *Der Psychiatrie* (in press).

Wahlbeck K & Awolin (2009) *The Impact of Economic Crises on the Risk of Depression and Suicide: A literature review* [online]. Luxembourg: European Communities. Available at: http://ec.europa.eu/health/ph_determinants/life_style/mental/docs/depression_factsheets_en.pdf (accessed July 2010).

Wahlbeck K & Mäkinen M (Eds) (2008) *Prevention of Depression and Suicide. EC consensus paper* [online]. Luxembourg: European Commission. Available at: http://ec.europa.eu/health/archive/ph_determinants/life_style/mental/docs/consensus_depression_en.pdf (accessed July 2010).

World Health Organization (2004a) *Promoting Mental Health: Concepts, emerging evidence, practice*. A report from the World Health Organization, Department of Mental Health and Substance Abuse in collaboration with the Victorian Health Promotion Foundation and the University of Melbourne [online]. Geneva: WHO. Available at: http://www.who.int/mental_health/evidence/en/promoting_mhh.pdf (accessed July 2010).

World Health Organization (2004b) *Prevention of Mental Disorders: Effective interventions and policy options*. A report of the World Health Organization Department of Mental Health and Substance Abuse in collaboration with the Prevention Research Centre of the Universities of Nijmegen and Maastricht [online]. Geneva: WHO. Available at: http://www.who.int/mental_health/evidence/en/prevention_of_mental_disorders_sr.pdf (accessed July 2010).

World Health Organization (2005a) *Mental Health Declaration for Europe: Facing challenges, building solutions* [online]. Copenhagen: WHO Regional Office for Europe. Available at: http://www.euro.who.int/__data/assets/pdf_file/0008/96452/E87301.pdf (accessed July 2010).

World Health Organization (2005b) *Mental Health Action Plan for Europe: Facing challenges, building solutions* [online]. Copenhagen: WHO Regional Office for Europe. Available at: http://www.euro.who.int/__data/assets/pdf_file/0008/96452/E87301.pdf (accessed July 2010).

World Health Organization (2008a) *Policies and Practices for Mental Health in Europe – Meeting the challenges* [online]. Copenhagen: WHO Regional Office for Europe. Available at: http://www.euro.who.int/__data/assets/pdf_file/0006/96450/E91732.pdf (accessed July 2010).

World Health Organization (2008b) *Closing the Gap in a Generation: Health equity through action on the social determinants of health: Report of the Commission on Social Determinants of Health Chaired by Sir Michael Marmot* [online]. Geneva: WHO. Available at: http://www.who.int/social_determinants/thecommission/finalreport/en/index.html with further information on the subject at http://www.who.int/social_determinants/en/ (accessed July 2010).

Further reading

ETUC (2004) *Framework Agreement on Work Related Stress* [online]. ETUC. Available at: http://www.etuc.org/IMG/pdf_Framework_agreement_on_work-related_stress_EN.pdf (accessed July 2010).

European Commission (2006) *Responses to the Green Paper. Promoting the mental health of the population. Towards strategy on mental health for the European Union* [online]. Luxembourg: European Commission. Available at: http://ec.europa.eu/health/ph_determinants/life_style/mental/green_paper/mentalgp_report.pdf (accessed July 2010).

European Commission (2009) *Background Document for the Thematic Conference: Promotion of mental health and well-being of children and young people – making it happen* [online]. Luxembourg: European Commission. Available at http://ec.europa.eu/health/ph_determinants/life_style/mental/docs/background_young.pdf (accessed July 2010).

European Commission (2009) *Background Document for the EU Thematic Conference: Preventing of depression and suicide – making it happen* [online]. Luxembourg: European Commission. Available at http://ec.europa.eu/health/ph_determinants/life_style/mental/docs/depression_background_en.pdf (accessed July 2010).

European Parliament (2006) *Improving the Mental Health of the Population – Towards a strategy on mental health for the EU. European Parliament resolution on improving the mental health of the population: Towards a strategy on mental health for the European Union* (2006/2058(INI)) [online]. Available at: http://www.europarl.europa.eu/sides/getDoc.do?pubRef=-//EP// NONSGML+TA+P6-TA-2006-0341+0+DOC+PDF+V0//EN (accessed July 2010).

European Parliament (2009) *European Parliament resolution of 19 February 2009 on Mental Health* (2008/2209(INI)) [online]. Available at: http://www. europarl.europa.eu/sides/getDoc.do?pubRef=-//EP//TEXT+TA+P6-TA-2009- 0063+0+DOC+XML+V0//EN (accessed July 2010).

European Commission (2010) *The Mental Health Compass* [online]. Online database available at: http://ec.europa.eu/health/mental_health/eu_compass/ index_en.htm (accessed July 2010).

Jané-Llopis E & Anderson P (2005) *Mental Health Promotion and Mental Disorder Prevention. A policy for Europe* [online]. Nijmegen: Radboud University Nijmegen. Available at: http://ec.europa.eu/health/archive/ph_projects/2002/ promotion/fp_promotion_2002_a01_16_en.pdf (accessed July 2010).

Jané-Llopis E & Anderson P (2007) A policy framework for the promotion of mental health and the prevention of mental disorders. In: M Knapp, D McDaid, E Mossialos & G Thornicroft (Eds) *Mental Health Policy and Practice across Europe: The future direction of mental health care* (pp188–215) [online]. London: OU Press. Available at: http://www.euro.who.int/__data/assets/pdf_ file/0007/96451/E89814.pdf (accessed July 2010).

Knapp M, McDaid D, Mossialos E & Thornicroft G (Eds) (2007) *Mental Health Policy and Practice across Europe: The future direction of mental health care* [online]. London: OU Press Available at: http://www.euro.who.int/__data/ assets/pdf_file/0007/96451/E89814.pdf (accessed July 2010).

Lahtinen E, Lehtinen V, Riikonen E & Ahonen J (Eds) (1999) *Framework for Promoting Mental Health in Europe* [online]. Helsinki: STAKES. Available at: http://groups.stakes.fi/NR/rdonlyres/1A881D11-03FA-4558-AC75- D213C740E588/0/Framework.pdf (accessed July 2010).

Lavikainen J, Lahtinen E, Lehtinen V (2001) *Public Health Approach on Mental Health in Europe* [online]. Helsinki: Ministry of Social Affairs and Health, European Commission, STAKES. Available at: http://groups.stakes. fi/NR/rdonlyres/1EB54ED4-EC61-405A-8DF5-5B7829917069/0/public2.pdf (accessed July.2010).

Wahlbeck K & Taipale V (2006) Europe's mental health strategy. Responsibility extends beyond health authorities. *British Medical Journal* **330** 210–211.

WHO Regional Office for Europe (2005) *Mental Health: Facing the challenges, building solutions* [online]. Copenhagen: WHO Regional Office for Europe. Available at: http://www.euro.who.int/__data/assets/pdf_file/0008/96452/E87301.pdf (accessed July 2010).

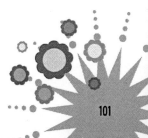

Chapter 6

Measuring success: developing mental health indicators

Jane Parkinson

Introduction: why is this work important?

The past few years have seen a significant shift in policy and practice from a predominant concern with mental health problems (mental illness) to an interest in public mental health (the mental health of the whole population), including mental well-being (positive mental health). This is evident in a range of UK and European mental health and public health policy, as well as in broader debates about well-being, happiness and life satisfaction, and recognises that mental health is more than the absence of mental health problems (Department of Health, 2005; Department of the Environment, Food and Rural Affairs, 2005; Eckersley, 2005; Huppert *et al*, 2006; Layard, 2005; Scottish Executive, 2003a; Scottish Government, 2009; WHO Europe, 2005).

The growing interest in the mental health of populations has highlighted the need for monitoring to assess the impact of policies and mental health improvement interventions. This has raised questions about traditional measures of mental health, which have largely focused on levels of psychiatric morbidity and associated risk and protective factors. The shift in focus has thus been accompanied by a growing interest in developing indicators (and scales) that might be used to measure different dimensions of mental health, such as mental well-being, as opposed to indicators of psychiatric morbidity, which are used to determine prevalence of mental health problems (Stewart-Brown, 2002).

The Scottish Indicators of Mental Health Programme has the central aim of establishing national mental health indicators for Scotland to enable national monitoring. These focus on both mental health problems and mental well-being. This chapter outlines the work completed and in progress. It presents the rationale and principles underpinning the Scottish Indicators of Mental Health Programme, the process involved and the main conceptual and practical challenges and constraints.

European policy context

Promoting mental health and preventing mental illness are priorities for the World Health Organization and the European Union (EU), and assessing mental health at the population level is recognised as important. At a European level for instance, the European Commission working party on mental health (established 2003) includes among its aims: 'contributing to the improvement of information; the compilation and development of a sustainable health monitoring system in the field of mental health; and participating in making mental health indicators operational' (European Commission, 2003). Both the 2005 WHO Mental Health Declaration for Europe and the 2005 EU Green paper on mental health highlighted the importance of establishing good information on mental health and the need to establish surveillance systems and indicators to assess the mental health of populations (European Commission, 2005; WHO Europe, 2005). More recently, the European Pact for Mental Health and Well-being (2008), launched at an EU mental health conference, included an agreement by participants that 'There is a need to improve the knowledge base on mental health: by collecting data on the state of mental health in the population...' (European Commission, 2008)

Other recent significant developments include:
1. A personal and social well-being module in the third wave of the European Social Survey (2006), to be repeated in the sixth wave (Huppert *et al*, 2009; 2010).

2. European Commission funded programmes concerned with establishing mental health indicators such as: MINDFUL – Mental Health Information

and Determinants for the European Level (2004–2006) – which aimed to improve the status of mental health information within the EU by building on previous work and by widening the scope of the mental health monitoring systems to cover not only mental ill-health but also positive mental health and mental health promotion and prevention (European Commission & STAKES, 2004; Korkeila, 2000; STAKES, 2001; 2005).

Scottish policy context

Similarly, improving mental health is a national public health priority for Scotland (for example, Child and Adolescent Mental Health Development Group, 2005; Scottish Executive, 2000; 2003a; 2003b; 2006a; 2006b; Scottish Government, 2009). In recognition of the lack of an overall assessment of the mental health of Scotland's population and its context, a commitment to establishing mental health indicators for Scotland was made in Improving Health in Scotland: The challenge (Scottish Executive, 2003a) and operationalised by the Scottish Government's National Programme for Improving Mental Health and Well-being (Scottish Executive, 2003c), which commissioned NHS Health Scotland to establish a core set of national, sustainable mental health indicators that could be used to create a summary mental health profile for Scotland (Scottish Indicators of Mental Health Programme, 2005). A set of 55 indicators for adults was established in December 2007 (Parkinson, 2007a). These provided a means of assessing and monitoring mental health (including mental well-being and mental health problems) and the contextual factors associated with it for Scotland's adult population (aged 16 and above) nationally over time.

Continuing the commitment to the mental health indicators, *Towards a Mentally Flourishing Scotland: Policy and Action Plan 2009–2011* (TAMFS), the Scottish Government's recent policy for mental health improvement (Scottish Government, 2009), stated clearly the need to develop 'a national picture of mental well-being and mental health problems among infants, children and young people in Scotland' to assess progress in improving mental health and to monitor future trends. NHS Health Scotland is now working to establish a similar set of mental health indicators for children and young people (aged 17 and under, including the pre-birth period, consistent with the United Nations' definition of a child (United Nations General Assembly, 1989).

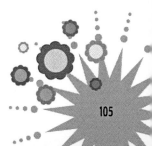

Principles, concepts and understandings behind the Scottish Indicators of Mental Health Programme

There are many definitions and terms used for mental health, which is a much debated concept, with no universally accepted definition. The way it is conceptualised, however, will affect how it is measured. Historically, assessment of population mental health has largely focused on levels of psychiatric morbidity using surveys and scales to determine prevalence of mental health problems (Stewart-Brown, 2002; WHO *et al*, 2004). Recent research suggests that mental health consists of two psychometrically distinct dimensions: mental health problems (equally referred to as mental illness, mental ill-health, mental distress, psychiatric morbidity etc.) and mental well-being (often referred to as positive mental health, well-being etc.) (Parkinson, 2007b). Good mental health is therefore more than the absence of mental health problems. The growing recognition of the importance of mental well-being has generated increased interest in developing indicators to measure mental well-being to accompany indicators of psychiatric morbidity. Accordingly, the Scottish Indicators of Mental Health Programme works with an understanding where 'mental health' is used as an overarching term covering both mental health problems and mental well-being, and is establishing mental health indicators for both these dimensions.

The Scottish Indicators Programme has taken a public mental health approach. This covers the risk and protective factors for mental health, acknowledges the importance of mental health to overall health, including physical health, and argues that how people feel is a significant public health indicator. This approach also acknowledges the complex relationship between the mental health of individuals and broader socio-economic, cultural and environmental factors. It means that the full range of contextual factors that impact on the population's mental health can be captured by the indicators.

A mixed approach, based on population health, has also been used, taking into account current policy, data, evidence base, expert opinion and theory, to obtain measurable, meaningful indicators relevant to the policy making process and for which, as far as possible, data are available at a national level (Parkinson, 2007b). The aim has been to ensure that there is a clear and robust relationship between an indicator and mental health, although for some, questions about direction of causality are an issue.

This approach means that the indicators are neither solely data- nor policy-driven. It also recognises that indicators should not be restricted to data that are currently available. With this in mind, the work has sought to influence national data collection systems and accepted that some indicators will be aspirational and not supported by available data. These aspirational indicators act as a prompt for future development, providing scope for going beyond the data that are currently collected, and a means of moving the mental health improvement agenda forwards.

The indicator sets (adults and children and young people's) are designed for national population level assessment of current experience of mental health and the associated contextual factors. They are not designed to:

1. assess the availability, appropriateness, efficiency or effectiveness of service provision

2. monitor performance

3. assess individual legislation, policies, strategies or initiatives

4. create a summary score or index.

Establishing indicators for children and young people has involved additional considerations, notably the need to follow the United Nations' Convention on the Rights of the Child principle of respect for the views of the child (article 12), acknowledging children's right to be heard and to have their views taken into account in matters that affect them (United Nations General Assembly, 1989). Ensuring that this is more than tokenistic is important. To this end, children and young people's views on what they think is important to their mental health have been determined through a literature review and through consultation (Elsley & McMellon, forthcoming 2010; Shucksmith et al, 2009).

The indicators and their assessment also need to be appropriate to the life stage of the child or young person. This is particularly challenging where the evidence underpinning a particular indicator is general in nature and not specific to children and young people. As such, it is likely that few if any indicators will be appropriate for the full age range of zero to 17, rather they will be appropriate to discrete developmental stages. Additionally, due to the significant impact that adults can have on the mental health of children and young people, indicators that relate to the behaviour of adults (those aged 18 and above) that has an impact on the mental health of children and young people, such as parental substance misuse and maternal behaviour during the pre-birth period, are also necessary.

Purpose, use and audience

The mental health indicators are designed to support and promote consistent and sustainable national monitoring of the state of mental health and associated contextual factors for Scotland's population. This will allow for the creation of mental health profiles for Scotland, which can be updated as data become available to assess trends. The indicators enable the Scottish Government and its partners to determine progress in improving population mental health, highlight key trends and inequalities between population groups and geographical areas of Scotland, data permitting, and point to where focus for future action and resource allocation should lie. They can therefore help shape and inform future policy decisions across government, and by others at national and local levels.

A profile providing the first ever systematic assessment of, and a unique insight into, the mental health and its context for Scotland's adult population was produced in 2009 and will be updated in 2011 (Taulbut *et al*, 2009). It provides a benchmark for mental health improvement for adults in Scotland.

The indicators are therefore primarily aimed at policy-makers, planners and others with responsibility at a national or local population level for the mental health of people in Scotland. The context of mental health, however, is extremely broad. The indicator set is therefore, similarly broad, which means that it will be of interest to a wide range of policy areas in addition to health and mental health.

While the focus has been on the development of national indicators, local needs for indicators are understood. Where possible, data are used from national sources with large sample sizes to allow as much disaggregation to sub-national/ population sub-group level as possible with available data. Where national data for an indicator cannot be disaggregated as required, practitioners/planners are advised to collect the appropriate data in local surveys.

Developing the indicators: process

The Indicators of Mental Health Programme has involved several key overlapping stages.

1. Determining a suitable, robust framework of constructs and a desirable set of defined mental health indicators.

2. Reviewing relevant administrative and survey data currently collected nationally in Scotland, including an assessment of other national indicators.

3. Identifying and establishing a consensus on a set of indicators, which can currently be monitored using existing data.

4. Identifying additional data needs for the desirable indicator set and recommending priorities for new data collection to fill the gaps between the data that are already available and that are required for the desirable indicator set.

5. Exploring opportunities to collect the recommended new data, and working to influence existing data collection systems to fill these additional data needs.

6. Ensuring the sustainability of data for the indicator set by liaising with the national survey teams and other data collectors to facilitate their continued collection.

Each potential indicator is evaluated against the following criteria:

1. correlation to mental health

2. relevance for the population and policy

3. assessment of the quality, strength and amount of evidence

4. whether amenable to change by intervention

5. feasibility, both in terms of current data availability and if the data are not collected whether there are questions or scales which could be used to collect the data or whether these need to be developed

6. robustness of available data.

Key expert input has helped to shape the work of the programme and has been provided by advisory groups. Due to the wide reaching nature of the programme these groups have necessarily included individuals from government, key voluntary groups and national organisations and with specific skills (eg. research and data skills.)

Consultation, electronically and via events, has also helped shape the work of the programme, allowing for a wider range of views to be obtained.

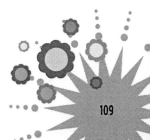

This has also helped:

1. keep expectations in line with what the indicator programme can achieve

2. gauge acceptance of the work

3. ensure the work is better aligned to the needs of wider stakeholders

4. foster greater 'buy-in', essential for seeking to gain better mental health data collection.

The indicator frameworks and indicator sets

The indicators are structured within frameworks, separate for the adult and the children and young people's sets. These recognise the complex relationships between the mental health of individuals and broader socio-economic, cultural and environmental factors (Department of Health, 2001; Friedli, 2004). They consist of constructs of two types where a construct refers to a categorising conceptual element (see table 1 on p111) (Parkinson, 2007b):

1. high level constructs of mental health status – outcome measures

2. contextual constructs – covering the factors associated with mental health; the direction of causality is often unknown so these may be determinants (the risk and protective factors) or consequences of mental health.

The contextual constructs for the adult framework are structured into three broad interconnected domains of the individual, community and structural. These are the levels at which mental health improvement works, namely:

1. strengthening individuals

2. strengthening communities

3. reducing structural barriers to mental health.

To ensure continuity with the adult mental health indicator set, the children and young people's work has made appropriate modifications to the adult framework, mainly by the inclusion of family and formal learning environment domains for the contextual constructs. The decision to include these additional domains was decided after consultation at an initiation event in April 2008 (Parkinson, 2008).

Table 1: High-level constructs				
Mental well-being			Mental health problems	
Contextual constructs				
Individual	Family (children's only)	Formal learning environment (children's only)	Community	Structural
Learning and development	Family relations	Involvement	Participation	Equality
Healthy living	Family structure	Peer and friend relationships	Social networks	Social inclusion
General health	Parental healthy living	Educational environment	Social support	Discrimination
Spirituality	Family members' health	Pressures and expectations	Trust	Financial security/debt
Emotional intelligence			Safety	Physical environment
Significant life events (children's only)				Working life (adults only)
				Violence
				Culture (children's only)

There is inevitably a degree of overlap between constructs of the frameworks and other configurations are possible. It was apparent in undertaking this work that it would be impossible to reach a unanimous agreement. What has been important overall is that the indicators essential to assess the mental health and its context are contained within the frameworks.

Building commitment: alignment with other policy developments

Mental health cuts across many policy agendas and is seen to contribute to a wide range of goals. Given this cross-cutting nature, the indicators are clearly of relevance and value to policy areas and agendas beyond health. Aligning the work with, and establishing links to, the wide range of relevant national policies, initiatives, indicators and monitoring systems is essential to ensure that, wherever possible, the indicators will be of practical benefit to a broad spectrum of users. Raising awareness of the overlap of agendas is vitally important when seeking to influence national data collections systems, to gain commitment for new data to be collected and for sustainability of existing data sources.

Since 2007, there has been a focus on outcomes planning and monitoring in Scotland. In view of this, the children and young people's indicator work is aligning as much as possible with national outcome frameworks in existence or in development for other relevant Scottish policies and programmes, in particular the Early Years Framework, Getting It Right For Every Child (GIRFEC), Curriculum for Excellence and Equally Well (Scottish Executive, 2004a, 2004b; Scottish Government, 2008a, 2008b; 2008c; 2010).

Addressing data gaps

While much relevant data, both routine administrative sources and from national Scottish surveys, are collected in Scotland, and a mixture of data from several sources is drawn on for the indicators, obvious gaps exist between currently collected data and that needed for the desirable indicators.

Ensuring that new data required are collected means influencing data collection. Essential to the success of this phase is undertaking work to highlight the relevance, importance and contribution of the proposed indicator set to areas of policy other than health. This also requires efforts to be made to consult and engage with relevant data/survey managers. By building relationships within other policy fields and with those working to develop other indicators and national data, it has been possible to come together across disciplines, to meet shared goals and overlapping data needs. Capitalising on reviews of national surveys led to the collection of new data for 21 of the adult mental health indicators. This success was partly due to the wealth of support from many policy areas, organisations and academia.

To allow possible comparisons existing validated and reliable questions were sought, where possible, as the means of collection of any new data. This involved scoping questionnaires of many national and international surveys and reviewing measurement scales to determine the most appropriate (Parkinson, 2007c).

In response to a clear need for a UK validated scale to assess overall mental well-being, researchers at Warwick and Edinburgh Universities were commissioned to develop the Warwick-Edinburgh Mental Well-being Scale (WEMWBS) (Tennant *et al*, 2006). Validated in the UK initially for those aged 16 and above, WEMWBS has since been validated for use with children aged 13 to 16 (Clarke *et al*, 2010; Stewart-Brown *et al*, 2009; Tennant *et al*, 2007). From 2008, this scale is now included annually in the Scottish Health Survey providing data for an adult mental health indicator and for a Scottish Government national performance indicator. The scale is also widely used in the UK and internationally.

Questions for two of four unoperationalised adult indicators, escape facilities and attitudes to violence, have also been developed. This work used the processes of the 2009 Scottish Social Attitudes Survey to develop and test out questions (Ormston *et al*, 2010).

Constraints and limitations

The main constraints and challenges have been data limitations and limitations of the evidence base (Parkinson, 2007b).

Several issues are evident with the identified data, which have important implications for the indicators. For survey data this relates to the following:

1. **Sustainability** – guaranteeing that the required questions for the indicators are continued in future surveys/data collection exercises and remain unaltered. Changing policy agendas are, however, a major challenge and make it difficult to guarantee that all required data will remain sustainable for the foreseeable future.

2. **Sample size** – an issue when disaggregation of data is desired to compare regions within Scotland or to compare population groups. Of the national surveys, those with larger sample are used in preference.

3. **Representativeness** – many national surveys are designed as household or school-based surveys, so certain sections of the population will not be represented in the data.

4. **Ethnicity** – questions for assessment need to be developed and phrased within ethnic group and culture in mind, to reflect that the concept of mental health is understood in different ways by different ethnic groups.

A key challenge has been the ongoing debate about what are the necessary and sufficient elements that constitute and contribute to mental health and defining the underpinning constructs. In many cases there is no consensus on mental health outcomes (especially for mental well-being), and there is no easy way of distinguishing between cause and effect. This is due to several limitations of the current evidence base, both methodological and conceptual. These include:

▶ the equivocal nature and/or scarcity of evidence for some areas of the evidence base

▶ the use of different terminologies, definitions and means of assessing mental health in studies making it hard to draw clear conclusions

▶ a lack of longitudinal studies that leads to uncertainty about the direction of causality; a lot of the evidence comes from cross-sectional studies that only indicate associations

▶ few suitable studies in some areas of the evidence base, and in some cases, gaps in evidence relating to children and young people specifically, meaning that generalisations and extrapolations have to be made from literature on adult mental health in some instances

▶ the majority of the evidence base coming from studies assessing factors that affect mental health problems rather than mental well-being; it is yet unknown what elements of these may be the same

▶ studies controlling for differing confounding variables to differing extents.

The quality and quantity of the evidence varies and there is a considerable need for further research on the social determinants of both mental health problems and mental well-being. Other research needed includes further analyses of existing datasets, to investigate in greater detail factors associated with mental health and to address the limitations in the evidence base. Longitudinal studies are also essential to examine the dynamics of associations identified in cross-sectional studies and to help establish whether these are coincidental or causal, and the direction of causality of significant relationships.

Although not all construct areas and indicators are equal in terms of importance of their impact on the mental health, limitations in the evidence base make it difficult to agree a relative weighting. In view of this, no attempt has been made in the work to rank or weight the constructs or indicators. It is also recognised that the indicators do not act in isolation although, for monitoring purposes, the indicators are assessed individually. For these reasons and to gain a fuller profile, the indicators work has not sought to create an index or indexes as other indicator sets have, for example, *Child Poverty in Perspective: An overview of child well-being in rich countries*, Innocenti Report Card 7 (UNICEF, 2007).

Conclusion

The Scottish Indicators of Mental Health Programme has been and continues to be an exciting opportunity to ensure adequate monitoring of mental health and an assessment of the impact of interventions across a range of policy domains. In addition to their value at a national policy level, the adult indicators have been put to wider use than initially envisaged, for example, to inform local NHS Board strategies and outcomes frameworks. Therefore, this programme has provided a resource for those working at many different levels across a range of disciplines and topics.

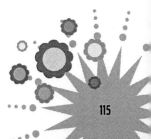

References

Child and Adolescent Mental Health Development Group (2005) *The Mental Health of Children and Young People: A framework for promotion, prevention and care* [online]. Edinburgh: Scottish Executive. Available at: www.scotland.gov.uk/Resource/Doc/77843/0018686.pdf (accessed August 2010).

Clarke A, Friede T, Putz R, Ashdown J, Adi Y, Martin S, Flynn P, Blake A, Stewart-Brown S & Platt S (2010) W*arwick-Edinburgh Mental Well-being Scale (WEMWBS). Acceptability and validation in English and Scottish secondary school students. The WAVES project* [online]. Glasgow: NHS Health Scotland. Available at: www.healthscotland.com/uploads/documents/12339-WAVES%20Final%20Report.pdf (accessed August 2010).

Department of the Environment, Food and Rural Affairs (DEFRA) (2005) *Securing the Future – UK Government sustainable development strategy* [online]. London: The Stationery Office. Available at: www.defra.gov.uk/sustainable/government/publications/uk-strategy/documents/SecFut_complete.pdf (accessed August 2010).

Department of Health (2001) *Making It Happen: A guide to delivering mental health promotion* [online]. London: DH. Available at: www.dh.gov.uk/prod_consum_dh/groups/dh_digitalassets/@dh/@en/documents/digitalasset/dh_4058958.pdf (accessed August 2010).

Department of Health (2005) *Making it Possible: Improving mental health and well-being in England* [online]. Leeds: Care Services Improvement Partnership/National Institute for Mental Health in England Available at: www.apho.org.uk/resource/view.aspx?RID=70037 (accessed August 2010).

Eckersley R (2005) *Well and Good: Morality, meaning and happines* (2nd ed). Melbourne: Text Publishing.

Elsley S & McMellon C (forthcoming 2010) *Checking it Out: A consultation with children and young people on a draft framework for children and young people's mental health indicators*. Glasgow: NHS Health Scotland.

European Commission (2003) *Mandate: Mental Health Working Party (MHWP)* [online]. Available at: http://ec.europa.eu/health/ph_information/implement/wp/mental/docs/wpmh_mandate_en.pdf (accessed August 2010).

European Commission (2005) *Green Paper – Promoting the Mental Health of the Population: Towards a strategy on mental health for the European Union* [online]. Brussels: European Commission. Available at: http://ec.europa.eu/health/ph_determinants/life_style/mental/green_paper/mental_gp_en.pdf (accessed August 2010).

European Commission (2008) *European Pact for Mental Health and Well-being. EU high-level conference together for mental health and well-being Brussels, 12–13 June 2008* [online]. Brussels: European Commission. Available at: http://ec.europa.eu/health/ph_determinants/life_style/mental/docs/pact_en.pdf (accessed August 2010).

European Commission & STAKES (2004) *Action for Mental Health Activities Co-funded from European Community Public Health Programmes 1997–2004*. Luxembourg: European Commission.

Friedli L (2004) *Mental Health Improvement 'concepts and definitions': Briefing paper for the National Advisory Group*. Edinburgh: Scottish Executive.

Huppert F, Baylis N & Keverne B (Eds) (2006) *The Science of Well-being*. Oxford: Oxford University Press.

Huppert FA, Marks N, Clark A, Siegrist J, Stutzer A, Vitters ØJ, Wahrendorf M (2009) Measuring well-being across Europe: description of the ESS well-being module and preliminary findings. *Social Indicators Research* **91** (3) 301–315.

Huppert FA, Marks N, Siegrist J, Carmelo V, Vitters ØJ (2010) *Question Module Design Team (ESS Round 6) Application Form for Repeat Modules* [online]. Available at: www.europeansocialsurvey.org/index.php?option=com_content&view=category&layout=blog&id=22&Itemid=48 (accessed August 2010).

Korkeila JJA (2000) *Measuring Aspects of Mental Health* [online]. Helsinki: National Research and Development Centre for Welfare and Health (STAKES). Available at: http://groups.stakes.fi/NR/rdonlyres/5DD0D44F-9B09-480E-A668-4E9285C10976/0/measuringaspectsofmh.pdf (accessed August 2010).

Layard R (2005) *Happiness: Lessons from a new science*. London: Allen Lane.

Ormston R, Bromley C, Curtice J, Reid S & Sharp C (2010) *Development of Survey Questions on Attitudes to Violence and Escape Facilities*. Final report, March 2010. Glasgow: NHS Health Scotland.

Parkinson J (2007a) *Establishing a Core Set of National, Sustainable Mental Health Indicators for Adults in Scotland: Final report* [online]. Glasgow: NHS Health Scotland. Available at: www.healthscotland.com/uploads/documents/5798-Adult%20mental%20health%20indicators%20-%20final%20report.pdf (accessed August 2010).

Parkinson J (2007b) *Establishing a Core Set of National, Sustainable Mental Health Indicators for Adults in Scotland: Rationale paper* [online]. Glasgow: NHS Health Scotland. Available at: www.healthscotland.com/uploads/documents/5289-Final%20rationale%20paper.pdf (accessed August 2010).

Parkinson J (Ed) (2007c) *Review of Scales of Positive Mental Health Validated for Use with Adults in the UK: Technical report* [online]. Glasgow: NHS Health Scotland. Available at: www.healthscotland.com/uploads/documents/7546-952-HSPMHScalesreport04.2.08[2].pdf (accessed August 2010).

Parkinson J (2008) *Establishing a Core Set of National, Sustainable Mental Health Indicators for Children and Young People in Scotland: Report of the launch event of 21 April 2008* [online]. Glasgow: NHS Health Scotland. Available at: www.healthscotland.com/uploads/documents/7709-C&YP%20 MH%20Indicators%20event%2021st%20April%202008%20report%20Final.pdf (accessed August 2010).

Scottish Executive (2000) *Our National Health: A plan for action, a plan for change* [online]. Edinburgh: Scottish Executive. Available at: www.scotland. gov.uk/Resource/Doc/158732/0043081.pdf (accessed August 2010).

Scottish Executive (2003a) *Improving Health in Scotland – The challenge* [online]. Edinburgh: The Stationery Office Bookshop. Available at: www. scotland.gov.uk/Resource/Doc/47034/0013854.pdf (accessed August 2010).

Scottish Executive (2003b) *Partnerships for Care: Scotland's Health White Paper* [online]. Edinburgh Scottish Executive. Available at: http://scotland.gov. uk/Resource/Doc/47032/0013897.pdf (accessed August 2010).

Scottish Executive (2003c) *National Programme for Improving Mental Health and Well-being: Action Plan 2003–2006* [online]. Edinburgh: Scottish Executive. Available at: www.scotland.gov.uk/Resource/Doc/47176/0013801. pdf (accessed August 2010).

Scottish Executive (2004a) *A Curriculum for Excellence: The curriculum review group* [online]. Edinburgh: Scottish Executive. Available at: www. scotland.gov.uk/Resource/Doc/26800/0023690.pdf (accessed August 2010).

Scottish Executive (2004b) *Getting it Right for Every Child* [online]. Edinburgh: Scottish Executive. Available at: www.scotland.gov.uk/Topics/ People/Young-People/childrensservices/girfec (accessed August 2010).

Scottish Executive (2006a) *Delivering for Health* [online]. Edinburgh: Scottish Executive. Available at: www.scotland.gov.uk/ Publications/2005/11/02102635/26356 (accessed August 2010).

Scottish Executive (2006b) *Delivering for Mental Health* [online]. Edinburgh: Scottish Executive. Available at: www.scotland.gov.uk/Resource/ Doc/157157/0042281.pdf (accessed August 2010).

Scottish Government (2008a) *Curriculum for Excellence Building the Curriculum 3: A framework for learning and teaching* [online]. Edinburgh: Scottish Government. Available at: www.scottish.parliament.uk/business/research/briefings-10/SB10-10.pdf (accessed August 2010).

Scottish Government (2008b) *Early Years Framework* [online]. Edinburgh: Scottish Government. Available at: www.scotland.gov.uk/Resource/Doc/257007/0076309.pdf (accessed August 2010).

Scottish Government (2008c) *Equally Well: Report of the ministerial task force on health inequalities* [online]. Edinburgh: Scottish Government. Available at: www.scotland.gov.uk/Resource/Doc/229649/0062206.pdf (accessed August 2010).

Scottish Government (2009) *Towards a Mentally Flourishing Scotland: Policy and action plan 2009–2011* [online]. Edinburgh: Scottish Government. Available at: www.scotland.gov.uk/Resource/Doc/271822/0081031.pdf (accessed August 2010).

Scottish Government (2010) *Curriculum for Excellence website. Learning Teaching Scotland* [online]. Available at: www.ltscotland.org.uk/curriculumforexcellence/index.asp (accessed August 2010).

Shucksmith J, Spratt J, Philip K & McNaughton R (2009) *A Critical Review of the Literature on Children and Young People's Views of the Factors that Influence their Mental Health* [online]. Glasgow: NHS Health Scotland. Available at: www.healthscotland.com/uploads/documents/10772-Views%20of%20C&YP%20on%20what%20impacts%20on%20their%20mental%20health%20-%20Final%20report.pdf (accessed August 2010).

STAKES (2001) *Minimum Data Set of European Mental Health Indicators. Proposed set of mental health indicators; definitions, description and sources*. Helsinki: National Research and Development Centre for Welfare and Health (STAKES).

STAKES (2005) *Mental Health Information and Determinants for the European Level (MINDFUL): Interim technical implementation report*. Helsinki: National Research and Development Centre for Welfare and Health (STAKES)

Stewart-Brown S (2002) Measuring the parts most measures do not reach: a necessity for evaluation in mental health promotion. *Journal of Mental Health Promotion* **1** 4–9.

Stewart-Brown S, Tennant A, Tennant A, Platt S, Parkinson J & Weich S (2009) Internal construct validity of the Warwick-Edinburgh Mental Well-being Scale (WEMWBS): a Rasch analysis using data from the Scottish Health Education Population Survey. *Health and Quality of Life Outcomes* **7** 15.

Taulbut M, Parkinson J, Catto S & Gordon D (2009) *Scotland's Mental Health and its Context: Adults 2009* [online]. Glasgow: NHS Health Scotland. Available at: www.healthscotland.com/uploads/documents/9179-AdultMHfullreportwebPDF.pdf (accessed August 2010).

Tennant R, Fishwick R, Platt S, Joseph S, & Stewart-Brown S (2006) *Monitoring Positive Mental Health in Scotland: Validating the Affectometer 2 scale and developing the Warwick-Edinburgh Mental Well-Being Scale for the UK* [online]. Glasgow: NHS Health Scotland. Available at: www.healthscotland.com/uploads/documents/5758-Affectomter%20WEMWBS%20Final%20Report.pdf (accessed August 2010).

Tennant R, Hiller L, Fishwick R, Platt S, Joseph S, Weich S, Parkinson J, Secker J & Stewart-Brown S (2007) The Warwick-Edinburgh Mental Well-being Scale (WEMWBS): development and UK validation. *Health and Quality of Life Outcomes* **5** 63.

UNICEF (2007) *Child Poverty in Perspective: An overview of child well-being in rich countries, Innocenti Report Card 7* [online]. Florence: UNICEF Innocenti Research Centre. Available at: www.unicef-irc.org/publications/pdf/rc7_eng.pdf (accessed August 2010).

United Nations General Assembly (1989) *Convention on the Rights of the Child. UN General Assembly Document A/RES/44/25* [online]. Available at: www.un.org/documents/ga/res/44/a44r025.htm (accessed August 2010).

World Health Organization Europe (2005) *Mental Health Declaration for Europe Facing the Challenges, Building Solutions*. Helsinki: WHO Europe.

World Health Organization, Victorian Health Promotion Foundation & University of Melbourne (2004) *Promoting Mental Health: Concepts, emerging evidence, practice* [online]. Geneva: WHO. Available at: www.who.int/mental_health/evidence/MH_Promotion_Book.pdf (accessed August 2010).

Chapter 7

Early years and public health: a case study from the Glasgow experience

Linda de Caestecker and Michael Killoran-Ross

Introduction

The early years of life are a critical time for mental health and thus, for policy-makers in health care and more specifically public health. In the early years experience, the parent (caregiver)/child relationship is vital to a child's development, to his or her future psychological well-being, and to a range of long-term outcomes such as educational attainment, social networks, and employability (Shonkoff & Phillips, 2000). One of the most important opportunities for children to develop good mental health, empathy, the ability to create and learn, and to have a positive sense of self is to have a small group of adults in early life with whom the child forms an attachment and who respond appropriately and effectively to the child's needs. This chapter will consider briefly the importance of early life experiences, and will focus on parenting education as a key intervention in the promotion of good mental health in children. Additionally, this chapter will provide descriptions of, and evidence for, the Positive Parenting Programme (Triple P) as a direct result of the authors' experience of adopting this programme in the Starting Well

Health Demonstration Project in Glasgow, Scotland (Sanders, 1999; Ross & de Caestecker, 2003) and in a more recent large-scale roll-out (Prinz *et al*, 2009). The implementation of Triple P will be used as a case study to illustrate some of the challenges faced by health planners in ensuring a population-based provision of parenting support.

The early years, mental health and nurturing relationships

There is increasing evidence to suggest that the early experiences of children influence brain development (The Scottish Government, 2007). Infant brains develop rapidly in the first year of life and development is selective and purposeful. During this period, the most dramatic changes in brain structure are observed in the area involved in social behaviour, and development is dependent upon, and unfolds within, the context of nurturing relationships. The infant's instinct is to seek out relationships and the crucial role for parents/caregivers is to respond to and enhance this relationship. These relationships therefore, are among the most important influences of psychological well-being among children. The term 'parenting' is used to capture the '...focused and differentiated relationship that the young child has with the adult (or adults) who is/are most emotionally invested in and consistently available to him/her' (Shonkoff & Philips, 2000). Although this relationship is usually between the child and either a birth or adoptive parent, it may be filled by other primary caregivers.

The mother/child relationship is the primary relationship for most children, with early research focused largely on mothering (Shonkoff & Phillips, 2000). In the research literature, the contribution of men was initially limited to an analysis of the economic contributions made to family life by men, or the absence of father figures in the family. Contemporary research has demonstrated that fathers are, on one hand, more involved in family life than was the case in the past. However, there is also evidence to suggest that increasing numbers of young children are now raised in single mother households. The consequences of these differing experiences for children's development remain largely unexamined.

Parenting has been a central focus for developmental inquiry from the beginning of the field of developmental psychology. Early studies sought to consider the relationship between styles of parenting and competent behaviour in children. These studies have led to an ongoing interest in management/control functioning and the emotional quality of parental/child relationships. However, this essentially static view of parental behaviours and attributes has been challenged by evidence suggesting that parenting changes over time, that it varies between and among children, and that parenting is not only received by the child, but also shaped by the child's own behaviours (Grusec & Goodnow, 1994; Holden & Miller, 1999).

There is evidence to suggest that where early child/parent relationships have begun badly, improvements can occur. It appears that many children learn, develop, or establish problem behaviours because parents either lack or inconsistently use key parenting skills. In the research literature, there is now a wealth of evidence, including several comprehensive reviews, demonstrating that cognitive behaviourally-based parenting programmes can support parents in adopting appropriate and consistent parenting behaviours, can prevent problem behaviours in children, and can support parents and families in the prevention of future mental health problems (Scott, 2007, Scott *et al*, 2001; Barlow & Stewart-Brown, 2000). It appears that these approaches can also benefit children with other disorders including ADHD and autism. Reductions in maternal depression and stress and marital conflict, and increases in parental satisfaction in the parenting role have also been reported. A systematic review of the effectiveness of group structured parent education programmes in children aged three years to 10 years indicated that these programmes can be effective in producing positive change in both parental perceptions of children's behaviour and on behaviour when objectively measured. The review also found that these observed changes were maintained over time (Barlow & Stewart-Brown, 2000).

There is a strong imperative for society to ensure that everything is done to maximise the potential for effective child/parent relationships from the outset. Although the quality of a parent's caregiving can be strengthened, this is not necessarily an easy task. The quality of caregiving has its origins in diverse elements of family ecology, including the quality of the individual parent's past (such as their own parenting experience), marital relationships, and a variety of social contextual features (work-related pressures, community violence, welfare policies, etc.) It is our contention that in spite of a large range of potential obstacles, the policy-driven pursuit and practical implementation of measures aimed at supporting parents in their parenting responsibilities by the public sector should emerge as a crucial priority.

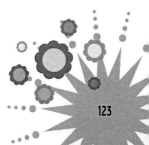

The Glasgow story begins

Parenting surveys have often demonstrated that primary care professionals are the group most frequently initially consulted by parents and caregivers of children with emotional or behavioural problems (for example Sanders *et al*, 1999). The role of primary care is to detect problems at an early stage, provide advice to parents for mild to moderate child behaviour problems, and to refer to specialist services for moderate to severe problems. Within the primary care team, health visitors have a pivotal role in engaging with issues of child behaviour and parent/child interaction but they require access to appropriate professional development, high quality training, and equally high quality educational resources if they are going to undertake this role competently.

Partly in response to these imperatives, the Starting Well Health Demonstration Project: the Scottish National Demonstration Project in child and family health, was established in Glasgow in 2000 (Ross & de Caestecker, 2003; Ross & de Caestecker, 2005). The project aimed to demonstrate that child health could be improved by a programme of activities that supported families and that provided them with access to enhanced community-based resources. The three essential components of the project were:

▶ intensive home-based support

▶ the provision of a strengthened network of community-based support services for children and their parents

▶ partnership working and the development of integrated service responses targeted to family need.

The project has been described comprehensively in the literature, where evaluation data has also been presented. The results of the independent evaluation suggested statistical trends indicating improvements in child well-being and family functioning; however, the short timescale of the evaluation (18 months) mitigated against more robust findings (Shute & Judge, 2005). For the purposes of this chapter, emphasis will be placed on the intensive home-based component of the project.

There were explicit objectives in the project aimed at both the promotion of health and well-being of young children, and at the promotion of health and well-being of families.

The objectives for child health included:

▶ the provision of a range of opportunities for the promotion of children's health

▶ a reduction in the adverse consequences of risk factors on children's health and well-being

▶ improvements in opportunities for young children to socialise with other children.

For families, objectives included:

▶ explicit attempts to improve parental self-esteem, psychological well-being, empowerment and a sense of achievement in the parenting role

▶ enhancements in parental knowledge and understanding of key issues of child development and parenting

▶ increases in parental abilities to effectively cope with fundamental issues in parenting.

Project teams were led by health visitors and included lay workers (health support workers), community nursery nurses, community support facilitators (who provided an interface between the project and local family/child initiatives), a bilingual worker and administrative staff. Health visitors, led by a health visitor co-ordinator (senior health visitor), provided individual care and also acted as team leaders. The advantage to basing the project within health visitor practice was that these health professionals are well accepted within communities across Great Britain and as they are routinely in contact with every family, they are believed to offer stigma-free service provision.

The provision of parenting support was a key component of the project with the Positive Parenting Programme (Triple P) selected by the project team as the mechanism for providing this. It was perceived that a comprehensive model of parenting education would be of benefit to the local population. Therefore although training was initially offered to all members of the project team this was extended to multidisciplinary and multi-agency partners throughout the Glasgow area.

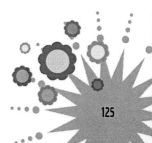

The Positive Parenting Programme (Triple P)

The Positive Parenting Programme (Triple P) is a multi-level parenting and family support strategy developed by Professor Matt Sanders and colleagues at the University of Queensland in Brisbane, Australia (Sanders, 1999). The programme aims to prevent severe behavioural, emotional and developmental problems in children by enhancing the knowledge, skills and confidence of parents. It incorporates universal, selective and targeted interventions organised across five levels on a tiered continuum of increasing strength.

There have been a number of trials examining the impact of Triple P interventions in primary care settings. Two population trials supporting a public health delivery model of Triple P are of particular interest. The Every Family trial demonstrated the effectiveness of the system of Triple P interventions in an Australian context (Sanders *et al*, 2005). In less than three years, the trial demonstrated a reduction of 22% in the mental health problems of children (defined as behavioural and emotional concerns). Furthermore, there was a reduction of 22% in the number of parents reporting emotional distress, and community parenting practices were improved by reducing the use of coercive parenting methods by 32%. Another population based trial of Triple P was implemented in South Carolina (USA) (Prinz *et al*, 2009). This trial involved 18 counties that were randomly assigned to either Triple P or a 'service-as-usual' condition. The Triple P condition involved over 600 service providers, who were trained in various levels of Triple P, and a universal media and communication strategy. The aim of the project was to examine the extent to which implementation of the Triple P system could reduce the prevalence of child maltreatment at a population level. Preventative effects (with large effect sizes) for three independent population indicators (substantiated cases of child maltreatment, child out-of-home placements and child maltreatment injuries) differentiated the Triple P system condition from the service-as-usual condition, taking into consideration baseline levels of these indicators. The study was the first of its kind to randomise communities to implement an evidence-based parenting intervention as a prevention strategy, and to demonstrate a positive impact on population indicators of child maltreatment. These findings do, however, need to be considered in light of the limitations observed by the authors, including the 'gross' nature of the measures, which served to underestimate the prevalence of harmful parenting practices and the issue of maintenance of the improved parenting practices over time.

The Glasgow story continued

The Starting Well Project ended in 2006, however, as an enduring legacy, the project proved to be informative in supporting the development of models of service delivery in child health in Glasgow, and the introduction to Glasgow of Triple P was an important part of that development. In 2008, NHS Greater Glasgow and Clyde, in association with local authority partners, agreed that a population-based parenting programme was required. This decision was based on a recognition of the challenges in health inequalities faced by the people of Glasgow, and the well-documented record of poor health, low income and poverty observed in the local area. In an attempt to promote population-level improvements in health, it was agreed that a clear focus on early years was essential, and from this perspective, parenting education emerged as a crucial strategy. As had been established by experience in Starting Well, it was observed that the success of any parenting education programme would depend on the implementation of universal and targeted approaches involving the media, and the co-ordinated efforts of primary care (health) professionals, social work services, and education services working collaboratively as part of a comprehensive parenting support system to improve the health status and well-being of children. Triple P was selected as the parenting education programme of choice for Glasgow, owing to the practical experience gained in working with the programme within Starting Well, the significant number of multi-agency staff already trained in its delivery, and the credibility of the programme, which has an international evidence base.

The rationale for the implementation of a universal parenting prevention strategy targeted on an entire population was to ensure a population based change in parenting practices and a normalisation of the behaviours associated with accessing parenting support. Importantly, it was also felt that a universal strategy would prove vital in engaging families considered to be 'hard to reach' or better expressed as 'seldom heard'. One of the unique components of the Triple P is the extensive use of media and other forms of information provision (websites, advertisements, and newspapers) serving to promote family knowledge of key parenting messages and mechanisms for accessing parenting education.

In planning the comprehensive implementation of Triple P in Glasgow, a broad range of challenges were apparent, including:

▶ promoting parental access to parenting education
▶ staff training and development

▶ access to appropriate financial resources

▶ agreement across agencies in the selection of a suitable programme.

The first two of these challenges will be considered here in detail: parental access to parenting education programmes, and the closely related issue of staff training and development. There was an awareness, for example, that despite the fact that family based interventions are effective in the treatment of many common childhood behavioural problems, these interventions are not traditionally widely available in the community and therefore do not make as significant an impact on the prevalence of children's behavioural difficulties as they could. There are few examples of successful dissemination of psychological interventions, and although there is growing research evidence from randomised controlled trials about treatment/prevention of behavioural or emotional problems through parenting interventions, this evidence has had limited impact on the prevalence rates of childhood behaviour or emotional problems because so few people access these services. This difficulty can be due to lack of effective engagement with parents but it also reflects a lack of training and management support for frontline staff to deliver the programmes.

In Glasgow, there has been a reluctance from some professional groups to adopt a single comprehensive parenting education programme. This reluctance was observed in the early implementation of the Starting Well Project in 2000, and has persisted. In discussion with practitioners, it appears that some would prefer to use a variety of different standardised programmes, adopting a 'pick and mix' strategy in parenting education. It also appears that many services would prefer the continued use of locally developed, non-empirically supported interventions with, which they have become comfortable. Changing the practice of professionals is a complex interaction between the quality of the intervention, the quality of the training for practitioners, the post-training environment, and the practitioners' feelings of self-efficacy in implementing the programme. Common barriers to implementation of evidence-based programmes include misperceptions that it would be impossible to use the programme within usual caseload responsibilities, a lack of access to supervision, and a lack of dedicated time for programme implementation. Interestingly, the literature confirmed our experience: where the mode of delivery or content of a programme varies markedly from a professional's 'comfort zone', there may be a greater need for support in the workplace through the provision of training, supervision and peer support.

Meeting the challenges 1: improving access to parents

In developing the programme there was an awareness that the success of a large-scale implementation of Triple P would depend upon a number of factors:

▶ effective promotional and recruitment strategies to engage parents

▶ appropriate local venues for group interventions that are close to public transport

▶ delivery of interventions at appropriate times including weekends and evenings

▶ adequate workplace supervisory support for the programme providers.

Triple P was promoted to parents using a strategic package which included an explanatory letter, promotional posters, brochures, a registration form, a business card, and a resource order form to order books. In each of the administrative areas of NHS Greater Glasgow and Clyde, parenting co-ordinators contacted agencies and services dealing with families and young people (eg. child care centres, after school care initiatives, crèches, kindergartens, preschools, primary schools, play groups, community and child health centres, GP practices, etc.) The promotion campaign involved informing all health education and welfare professionals in the area by letter about the programme and the promotional package associated with it. As demonstrated in other roll-out examples of Triple P, greater community education through mass media regarding parenting issues can directly influence parenting practices and may increase early help seeking (Sanders et al, 2005, Prinz et al, 2009). Press releases were therefore organised and a process of extensive engagement with local newspapers and radio partners began, alongside direct community engagement activities such as displaying of posters and dissemination of leaflets within local areas.

Although the use of media was important in promoting awareness of the programme, and in advertising access points, simple 'user-friendly' material presented across the popular media was also seen as an important intervention in its own right. Strategies such as positive parenting 'tips' presented on radio stations, in weekly newspaper columns, and in editorial and feature articles, have been used successfully in the implementation of Triple P in other settings. This level of intervention may be particularly useful for parents who have sufficient personal resources, such as motivation, literacy, commitment and support to implement suggested strategies with only brief parenting advice. However, a media strategy is less likely to be an effective single strategy for parents who have a child with severe behavioural difficulties, or where the parent has few personal resources. Although a media strategy may help normalise the concept of accessing services. The effective use of the media provides its own challenges and depends on a host of contributing factors, including the development of good working relationships with media personnel, a good communications team with dedicated time to implement and work with the media, and capacity for the opportunistic 'placing' of parenting messages relating to other news items.

Meeting the challenges 2: working with providers

Triple P has a well-established training programme with developed accreditation processes. However, based on experience in Starting Well, it was recognised that the direct training was only the beginning of the change process that the team hoped to initiate. In providing professional development to staff within services, research has highlighted the importance of supporting the supervisors/ managers of staff providing the programme. Effective strategies adopted to ensure managerial support included orientation briefings, procedure guidelines, and regular updates. After initial training, practitioners benefited from appropriate 'back-up' mechanisms such as email trouble-shooting, follow-up training, question and answer forums, regular monitoring, and review sessions exploring progress within implementation and towards performance indicators. The establishment of supervision networks, and dedicated parenting co-ordinators has been of significant importance in developing and implementing the programme. Implementation has also been enhanced by efforts aimed at offering support to overcome administrative obstacles and a myriad process issues associated with the organisation of training (venues, equipment, etc).

With regard to specific professional groups, the introduction of a comprehensive parenting education programme represents a significant change in the role of many health visitors. Research conducted in the State of Queensland (Australia), where there was a commitment to provide Triple P to parents from 30 child health centres across the State, demonstrated that as well as requiring political support, the success of the programme depended on a number of support mechanisms being put in place for health care staff. Examples of these support mechanisms include briefing and orientation days, a comprehensive training programme, data collection systems, analysis and evaluation processes, establishment of co-ordinator roles, 'trouble-shooting' as required and logistical support. Additionally, the need to clarify programme expectations, to correct misinformation, and to 'debunk' myths about the programme's applicability and philosophy was recognised and acted upon.

Conclusion

There is overwhelming evidence to suggest that the relationship between a parent (caregiver) and a young child in the early years is critical to a child's development, and to his or her future psychological well-being. In an attempt to promote this crucial relationship, and to promote population-level health benefits, NHS Greater Glasgow and Clyde and local authority partners have adopted the Triple P Programme, as the parenting education programme of choice. Triple P was selected on the basis of both earlier experience in The Starting Well Project (2000–2005) in Glasgow, and on its crediblity as an internationally recognised evidence-based programme. The roll-out of Triple P is being staged over a three-year period from 2010 to 2013 and has an extensive evaluation in place, which will provide further evidence on the effectiveness of Triple P as a programme for improving the health and well-being of children and families.

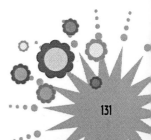

References

Barlow J & Stewart-Brown S (2000) Review article: behaviour problems and parent training programmes. *Journal of Development Behavioural Paediatrics* **21** 356–370.

Grusec JE & Goodnow JJ (1994) The impact of parental discipline methods on the child's internalisation of values: a reconceptualisaion of current points of view. *Developmental Psychology* **30** (1) 4–19.

Holden GW & Miller P (1999) Enduring and different: a meta-analysis of similarity in parent's child rearing. *Psychological Bulletin* **125** 223–254.

Prinz RJ, Sanders MR, Shapiro CJ, Whitaker DJ & Lutzker JR (2009) Population-based prevention of child maltreatment: the US Triple P system population trial. *Prevention Science* **10** 1–12.

Ross MK & de Caestecker L (2003) The Starting Well Health Demonstration Project: the best possible start in life? *International Journal of Mental Health Promotion* **5** 5–12.

Ross MK & de Caestecker L (2005) Guest editorial – Introduction to the special issue early years interventions: learning through a UK/US dialogue. *Journal of Primary Prevention* **26** (3).

Sanders MR, Tully LA, Baade PD, Lynch ME, Heywood AH, Pollard GE & Youlden DR (1999) A survey of parenting practices in Queensland: implications for mental health promotion. *Health Promotion Journal of Australia* **9** 112–121.

Sanders MR (1999) Triple P–Postive Parenting Programme: towards an empirically validated multilevel parenting and family support strategy for the prevention of behavior and emotional problems in children. *Clinical Child and Family Psychology Review* **2** 71–90.

Sanders M, Ralph A, Thompson R, Sofronoff K, Gardiner P, Bidwell K & Dwyer S (2005) *Every Family: A public health approach to promoting children's wellbeing*. Brief Report. Brisbane, Australia: The University of Queensland.

Scott S (2007) Conduct disorders in children. *British Medical Journal* **334** 646.

Scott S, Spender Q, Doulan M, Jacobs B & Aspland H (2001) Multi-centre control trial of parenting groups for childhood antisocial behaviour in clinical practice. *British Medical Journal* **323** 194–203.

Shonkoff J & Phillips DA (Eds) (2000) *From Neurons to Neighborhoods: The science of early childhood development*. Washington DC: National Academy Press.

Shute J & Judge K (2005) Evaluating 'Starting Well', the Scottish National Demonstration Project for Child Health: outcomes at six months. *Journal of Primary Prevention* **26** (3) 221–240.

The Scottish Government (2007) In: *Health in Scotland 2006: Annual Report of the Chief Medical Officer*. Edinburgh: The Scottish Government.

Further reading

Attride-Stirling I, Davies H, Day C & Sclare I (2000) Someone to talk to who will listen: addressing the psychosocial needs of children and families. *Journal of Community Applied Social Psychology* **11** 179–191.

Braidy LM, Nagin DS, Trembley RE, Bates JE, Brame B & Dodge KA (2003) Developmental trajectories of childhood disruptive behaviours and adolescent delinquency: a six site cross national study. *Developmental Psychology* **39** 222–245.

Coid J (2003) Formulating strategies for the primary prevention of adult antisocial behaviour: 'high risk' or 'population strategies'? In: DB Farrington & J Coid (Eds) *Early Prevention of Adult Anti-social Behaviour*. Cambridge: Cambridge University Press.

Edwards RT, Ceilleachair A, Bywater T, Hughes D & Hutchings J (2007) Parenting programme for parents of children at risk of developing conduct disorder: cost effectiveness analysis. *British Medical Journal* **334** 682–685.

Hutchings J, Gardner F, Bywater T, Daley D, Witiker C & Jones K (2007) Parenting intervention in SureStart services for children at risk of developing conduct disorder: pragmatic randomised control trial. *British Medical Journal* **334** 678–682.

Melzer H, Gatward R, Goodwin R & Ford T (1999) *The Mental Health of Children and Adolescents in Great Britain. Report of a survey carried out by the Social Survey Division of the Office for National Statistics*. London: Office of National Statistics.

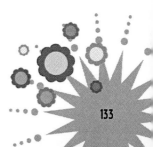

Chapter 8

Promoting mental health and preventing mental health problems through school settings

Katherine Weare

Introduction

Approaches

Mental health work operates under many different headings, with schools, social services and health services using a variety of terms. 'Mental health' is a term commonly used by the health and social care sectors, where it is usually a synonym for mental illness, difficulties and problems. There is a great deal of useful work carried out within this approach, and concerns about mental health problems of children and young people are well founded – it is indeed a growing epidemic. Exact estimates vary, but it would appear that about one-fifth of teenagers under the age of 18 years suffer from developmental, emotional or behavioural problems, one in eight have a mental disorder, most commonly depression, and many young people have problems with alcohol and drugs (Harden *et al*, 2001). Childhood mental illness affects

adult life too with one-third of people who are clinically depressed as adults experiencing their first episode before the age of 21 (Harden *et al*, 2001). So it is unsurprising that concerns about mental health problems of the young are growing as is an interest in what it takes to break into the recurrent cycle, thus helping to reduce all the vast personal misery, and social and economic burden mental health problems bring.

There are also models of mental health, which are aimed at the promotion of positive mental health for everyone, including those without major problems: the so-called 'universal approach'. These models start with an overall focus on positive mental health and well-being, in terms of people's strengths, capacities and skills, within which a concern for mental health problems is then located. Such work operates under a range of terms, such as 'positive psychology', 'emotional intelligence', and 'emotional literacy' and within schools, 'social and emotional learning' (Weare, 2004). More precise foci on specific key mental health competences include 'persistence' and 'grit' (Dweck, 2000) which in turn build on the seminal concept of 'resilience' (Seligman, 1996; Krovetz, 1999), which is the ability to bounce back from difficulties and disappointments.

The conditions for mental health are often summarised under the heading of social and psychological 'risk and resilience' factors that can serve to create problems or to help people to overcome them (Health Education Authority, 1997; Newman & Blackburn, 2002). Risk factors are often associated with social and economic deprivation and include a family history of psychiatric disorder, violence, childhood neglect, family breakdown, and unemployment. Psychological protective factors include positive parenting, sound education, employment, housing, financial security, and belonging to a supportive family and community. These factors can create a sense of hopefulness about the future and they exert an influence on how individuals respond to stressful or traumatic life events. Schools can play a role in breaking into this cycle and promoting the factors that create resilience. Mental health has also been characterised as a set of skills or capacities, the absence or presence of which influence mental health. They include emotional management, self-awareness, optimism, resilience, a sense of coherence, social skills, and empathy (Macdonald & O'Hara, 1998; Weare, 2000).

Mental health promotion in schools

During the last 20 years calls for school to become involved in both promoting positive mental health and tackling mental health problems have been growing steadily. This ties in with a general trend for the way schools are viewed as having a broad role in preparing young people for life by providing opportunities to develop life skills such as emotional and social intelligence, relationship building skills and resilience, and in formulating identities (Greenberg *et al*, 2003). Such skills are useful throughout life and have been shown to be particularly vital during childhood and adolescence, helping young people negotiate the challenges of maturation (Newman & Blackburn, 2002), including risky behaviour.

School based interventions

There is a growing number of mental health based interventions in schools. The world leader in terms of the quantity of interventions and rigorous efforts to evaluate them is the US, where there are thousands of what are in effect mental health programmes, although under a range of names. These interventions usually take the form of major 'programmes' within particular localities that mainly focus on skills development of a cognitive behavioural kind. These programmes are developed by teams of experts, with a major contribution by psychologists. Such interventions are usually 'manualised', in other words pre-written and intended to be delivered exactly as designed, which makes them easier to both evaluate and market. Systematic reviews have shown that 20 or so such interventions are clearly successful, judged on the most rigorous of criteria (Zins *et al*, 2004; CASEL, 2003, 2009a; Shucksmith *et al*, 2007; Adi *et al*, 2007). Typical examples include Promoting Alternative Thinking Strategies (PATHS) (PATHS, 2009), Second Step for Violence Prevention (Committee for Children, 2009), and the Metropolitan Child Study (2009).

Australia also has some well-evaluated programmes (Shucksmith *et al*, 2007; Adi *et al*, 2007) such as Roots of Empathy (2009), MindMatters (2009), and Friends (2009). Australian work tends to have a broad focus on the kind of settings and environments that promote mental health and on regional or national strategies. The current national strategy, Kidsmatter (2009) is a broad enabling framework, which appears to be promoting effective work (Slee *et al*, 2009).

As with Australia, work in Europe often focuses on mental health promoting environments, on enabling frameworks and on local adaptability. Two examples are the European Network of Health Promoting Schools (now known as Schools for Health in Europe), and the German framework, The Good and Healthy School. Work in Europe tends not to be systematically evaluated. Settings based work is often seen to be difficult to evaluate as it is so complex, and there is not the appetite for funding evaluative research that there is in the US.

The UK falls somewhere between the environmental focus of Europe and Australia and the skills focus of the US, and also tends to have a strong steer from government. Since the 1980s the 'healthy school' has been a major focus of work, within which emotional well-being and anti-bullying are major themes (Department for Children, Schools and Families/NHS, 2009). The emphasis has been on the whole school, a settings approach, with some curriculum input often in the context of personal, social and health education and circle time in particular. Flowing from this work, the national government funded programme Social and Emotional Aspects of Learning (SEAL) was created in England in the 1990s (Department for Children, Schools and Families, 2009b). It focuses on teaching both pupils and staff social and emotional skills and on creating environments which promote mental health. This has provided a platform for work on mental health in schools, with the programme operating in most primary and many secondary schools.

Some schools and local authorities across England and Wales are using other universal programmes, often alongside the general framework provided by SEAL. Examples of these are PATHS (2009), Second Step (Committee for Children, 2009), the Dino Dinosaur Curriculum (Incredible Years, 2010), and Emotional Literacy in Middle Schools (Maurer & Brackett, 2004). All of these programmes are from the US. However, in addition, Zippy's Friends (Partnerships for Children, 2009) is being used, which was developed in Europe. Homegrown initiatives include those from Antidote (2003), a UK-based organisation that has attempted to help schools create and assess 'emotionally literate' school and classroom environments. This initiative has an emphasis on positive and communicative relationships.

Targeted approaches, which have a focus on children and young people with problems have long had support from the voluntary sector in the UK where a wide range of programmes exist. Examples include The Place2Be (2009), who are supporting counsellors in schools and Pyramid Clubs (Continyou, 2009), which attempt to identify children with problems and provide support and quiet, safe places for them. More recently in England, the large-scale government funded Targeted Mental Health in Schools project (TaMHS) (Department for Children, Schools and Families, 2009a) has funded 'pathfinders' (usually local authorities) to follow 'evidence-informed practice' to help children and families experiencing problems. This role includes encouraging all the relevant agencies to work together to deliver flexible, responsive and effective early intervention mental health services.

Wales and Scotland have tended to employ a more devolved approach, which focuses on local initiatives. Scotland has a history of being very active in mental health work in schools, with the role of central government being to provide leadership and policy co-ordination, while encouraging local approaches to develop and be applied. Several Scottish projects have been created in this environment and these include Being Cool in School (Better Behaviour Scotland, 2009) and Creating Confident Kids (City of Edinburgh Council, 2009). The Scottish Curriculum for Excellence (Learning and Teaching Scotland, 2009) includes a series of specific outcomes for health and well-being.

The evidence base

All this global activity on mental health in schools has been underpinned by a growing evidence base. Systematic reviews of programmes show that, although many programmes are not successful, well designed ones can be effective in some circumstances when well delivered (Shucksmith *et al*, 2007; Adi *et al*, 2007). Well designed programmes can impact on:

▶ mental health (Wells *et al*, 2003)

▶ alcohol and drug use, early sexual experience, violence and bullying (Greenberg *et al*, 2003)

▶ improved behaviour (Durlak & Wells, 1997)

▶ crime (Caplan *et al*, 1992)

▶ improved school performance (Zins *et al*, 2004).

A meta-analysis of work in the US (CASEL, 2009b) looked at 207 programmes and suggested that, taken together, they showed an overall 11% improvement in achievement tests, a 25% improvement in social and emotional skills, and a 10% decrease in classroom misbehaviour, anxiety and depression.

Evaluation in Europe has been more sporadic and less well-funded but some homegrown European work is now starting to pass systematic review, which demonstrates their effectiveness. For example, work on anti-bullying in Scandinavia and Italy (NICE, 2009), stress management in Germany, and behaviour management in the Netherlands (Adi *et al*, 2007).

The principles of effective programmes

In the knowledge that not all programmes are effective, there is now a strong interest in working out what principles drive effective interventions, and an increasing number of meta-analyses are starting to identify the characteristics of effective programmes (Catalano *et al*, 2002; Weare & Gray, 2002; Zins *et al*, 2004; Devaney *et al*, 2006; CASEL, 2003).

Effective programmes are founded on sound theories of child development, incorporating approaches that demonstrate beneficial effects on children's attitudes and behaviour through scientific research (CASEL, 2003). They are implemented consistently and run over a prolonged period of time: one-off interventions are rarely, if ever, effective (Shucksmith *et al*, 2007). Programmes need to start early and the most effective programmes are those that target the youngest children (Carr, 2002).

Effective programmes are more likely to be multi-modal, and ideally 'whole school', rather than restricted to one part of the school. Mental health work should be integrated across a whole range of school activity, including the curriculum (Lister-Sharpe *et al*, 2000; Adi *et al*, 2007; Catalano *et al*, 2002; CASEL, 2003). The more effective programmes help staff develop their own mental health, and pay attention to their own skills in order to model skills they want pupils to learn, helping to ensure that the school environment is safe, well ordered, warm and respectful (Weare, 2000; 2004; Antidote, 2003; Morris & Casey, 2006).

Effective programmes include explicit work on the development of the relevant mental health skills in students, staff and in some cases parents (Catalano *et al*, 2002; Shucksmith *et al*, 2007; Adi *et al*, 2007). Skills development helps everyone, but children with mental health problems particularly need to develop skills such as resilience to help them overcome their difficulties. Parental involvement is an essential ingredient in most successful programmes, so that students have opportunities to practise their skills in the real world and are not experiencing mixed messages (CASEL,

2003; Adi *et al*, 2007). Some of the more successful programmes also positively involve pupils by encouraging peer learning.

Any additional specialist and therapeutic help for those with more severe difficulties is best located within the context of a broad, universal approach (Stewart-Brown, 1998). This universal approach provides a supportive environment, a critical mass of people who can help those with difficulties, and reduces stigma (Weare & Gray, 2002). Against this universal backdrop, children with more specific and/or extreme difficulties need vigorous and intensive extension work (Hunter-Carsch *et al*, 2006), which needs to start early (Rutter *et al*, 1998). For children with mild levels of difficulty, small amounts of early intervention may be sufficient (Shucksmith *et al*, 2007). Some demonstrably helpful interventions include play based approaches, nurture groups, parental liaison, parenting skill development, and small group sessions to develop cognitive problem solving and social skills, such as those used by the Penn Prevention Programme (Jaycox *et al*, 1995) and in the UK by Primary SEAL (Department for Children, Schools and Families, 2009a; Shucksmith *et al*, 2007).

Children whose problems are more intense and complex need to be identified early, have their problems and needs appraised sensitively by skilled professionals and receive more intensive help. This help should be provided in one-to-one or small group sessions, delivered by specialists and tailored to their particular problem. Due regard should be given to family context and structured, intensive work with the whole family should be considered. Approaches need to be clearly therapeutic, with cognitive behaviour therapy and play based therapies shown to be particularly effective (Shucksmith *et al*, 2007). Effective targeted work involves putting the child at the centre of strong, joined up, teamwork between the various agencies involved (Shucksmith *et al*, 2007; Department for Children, Schools and Families, 2009a). Teams should work together to develop common assessment frameworks, support improved information sharing, and provide closely integrated services (eg. Department of Health, 2006).

Conclusion

Across the world there has been increasing recognition of the important role that schools can play in promoting mental health and preventing mental health problems, and some valuable evidence-based work is emerging.

However, there are threats to this progression, and in particular it remains to be seen whether the financial crisis which is having such a widespread impact on public services will result in cutbacks on what is, mistakenly, sometimes seen as peripheral to the central task of schooling. It has to be hoped not, as in such times of stress and pressure, work to promote emotional resilience and help reduce the unacceptably high levels of mental health problems already experienced by young people will be needed more than ever.

References

Adi Y, Killoran A, Janmohamed K & Stewart-Brown S (2007) *Systematic Review of the Effectiveness of Interventions to Promote Mental Wellbeing in Primary Schools: Universal approaches which do not focus on violence or bullying*. London: National Institute for Clinical Excellence

Antidote (2003) *The Emotional Literacy Handbook: Promoting whole school strategies*. London: David Fulton Publishers.

Better Behaviour Scotland (2009) *Being Cool in School* [online]. Available at: http://www.betterbehaviourscotland.gov.uk/initiatives/cool.aspx (accessed July 2010).

Caplan M, Weissberg RP, Grober JS, Sivo PJ, Grady K & Jacoby C (1992) Social competence promotion with inner-city and suburban young adolescents: effects on social adjustment and alcohol use. *Journal of Consulting and Clinical Psychology* **60** 56–63.

Carr A (Ed) (2002) *Prevention: What works with children and adolescents?* London: Taylor and Francis.

CASEL (2003) *Safe and Sound: An educational leader's guide to evidence-based social and emotional learning programmes* [online]. Available at: http://www.casel.org/downloads/Safe%20and%20Sound/1A_Safe_&_Sound.pdf (accessed August 2010).

CASEL (2009a) [online]. Available at: http://www.casel.org. (accessed August 2010).

CASEL (2009b) *Social and Emotional Learning and Student Benefits* [online]. Available at: http://www.casel.org/downloads/EDC_CASELSELResearchBrief.pdf (accessed August 2010).

Catalano RF, Berglund L, Ryan AM, Lonczak H S & Hawkins J (2002) Positive youth development in the United States: research finding on evaluations of positive youth development programmes. *Prevention and Treatment* **5** article 15.

City of Edinburgh Council (2009) *Creating Confident Kids* [online]. Edinburgh: City of Edinburgh Council Available at: http://www.edinburgh.gov.uk/internet/Learning/Learning_publications/CEC_creating_confident_kids (accessed August 2010).

Committee for Children (2009) *Second Step for Violence Prevention Program* [online]. Washington: Committee for Children. Available at: http://www.cfchildren.org/ (accessed August 2010).

Continyou (2009) *Pyramid Clubs: About Pyramid* [online] Coventry: Continyou. Available at: http://www.continyou.org.uk/what_we_do/children_and_young_people/pyramid/about_pyramid (accessed August 2010).

Department for Children, Schools and Families (2009a) *Targeted Mental Health in Schools Project: Using the evidence to inform your approach*. A practical guide for headteachers and commissioners. Nottingham: London: DCSF.

Department for Children, Schools and Families (2009b) *Social and Emotional Aspects of Learning* [online]. Available at: http://nationalstrategies.standards. dcsf.gov.uk/inclusion/behaviourattendanceandseal (accessed August 2010).

Department for Children, Schools and Families/NHS (2009) *Healthy Schools* [online]. Available at: http://www.healthyschools.gov.uk (accessed August 2010).

Department of Health (2006) *Child and Adolescent Mental Health Service Mapping* [online]. London: Department of Health and University of Durham. Available at: http://www.dur.ac.uk/camhs.mapping/ (accessed August 2010).

Devaney E, Utne O'Brien M, Resnik H, Keister S & Weissberg R (2006) *Sustainable Schoowide Social and Emotional Learning: Implementation guide*. University of Illinois and Chicago, College of Liberal Arts and Sciences: CASEL.

Durlak J & Wells A (1997) Primary prevention mental health programs for children and adolescents: a meta-analytic review. *American Journal of Community Psychology* **25** (2) 115–152.

Dweck C (2000) *Self Theories: Their role in motivation, personality and development*. New York: Psychology Press.

Friends (2009) *Friends for life: addressing learning outcomes. Using the FRIENDS for children Program in Australian Primary Schools* [online]. Available at: http://www.friendsinfo.net/downloads/FRIENDS%20SyllabusQLD. pdf (accessed August 2010).

Greenberg MT, Weissberg RP, O'Brien MU, Zins JE, Fredericks L, Resnik H & Elias MJ (2003) *American Psychologist* **58** (6/7) 466–474.

Harden A, Rees R, Shepherd J, Ginny B, Oliver S & Oakley A (2001) *Young People and Mental Health: A systematic review of research on barriers and facilitators*. London: EPPI-Centre.

Health Education Authority (1997) *Mental Health Promotion: A quality framework*. London: Heath Education Authority.

Hunter-Carsch M, Tiknaz Y, Cooper P & Sage R (2006) *The Handbook of Social, Emotional and Behavioural Difficulties*. London and New York: Continuum.

Public Mental Health Today © Pavilion Publishing (Brighton) Ltd 2010

Incredible Years (2010) *Dino Dinosaur Curriculum* [online]. Seattle: Incredible Years. Available at: http://www.incredibleyears.com/ (accessed August 2010).

Jaycox L, Gillham J, Reivich K & Seligman MEP (1995) Prevention of depressive symptoms in school children: two-year follow-up. *Psychological Science* **6** 343–351.

Kidsmatter (2009) *Australian Primary Schools Mental Health Inititiative* [online]. Available at: http://www.kidsmatter.edu.au (accessed August 2010).

Krovetz ML (1999) *Fostering Resiliency: Expecting all students to use their hearts and minds well*. Thousand Oaks, CA: Corven Press (Sage).

Learning and Teaching Scotland (2009) *Curriculum for Excellence* [online]. Available at: http://www.ltscotland.org.uk/curriculumforexcellence/ (accessed August 2010).

Lister-Sharp D, Chapman S, Stewart-Brown SL & Sowden A (2000) Health promoting schools and health promotion in schools: two systematic reviews. *Health Technology Assessment* **3** (22).

Macdonald G & O'Hara K (1998) *Ten Elements of Mental Health: Its promotion and demotion*. Glasgow: Society of Health Promotion Specialists.

Maurer M & Brackett M (2004) *Emotional Literacy in the Middle School*. New York: Dude Publishing.

Metropolitan Child Study (2009) [online]. Chicago: University of Illinois. Available at: http://www.psych.uic.edu/fcrg/macs.html (accessed August 2010).

MindMatters (2009) [online]. Available at: http://www.mindmatters.edu.au/default.asp (accessed August 2010).

Morris E & Casey J (2006) *Developing Emotionally Literate Staff*. London: Paul Chapman.

Newman T & Blackburn S (2002) *Transitions in the Lives of Young People: Resilience factors*. Edinburgh: Scottish Executive.

NICE (National Institute for Clinical Excellence) (2009) *Promoting Young People's Social and Emotional Wellbeing in Secondary Education* [online]. Available at: http://www.nice.org.uk/nicemedia/pdf/PH20Guidance.pdf (accessed August 2010).

Partnerships for Children (2009) [online]. Available at: http://www.partnershipforchildren.org.uk/zippy-s-friends (accessed August 2010).

PATHS (2009) [online]. Available at: http://www.channing-bete.com/prevention-programs/paths/ (accessed August 2010).

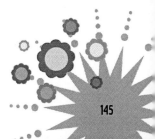

Roots of Empathy (2009) [online]. Available at: http://www.rootsofempathy.org (accessed August 2010).

Rutter M, Hagel A & Giller H (1998) *Anti-social Behaviour and Young People*. Cambridge: Cambridge University Press.

Seligman MEP (1996) *The Optimistic Child: A proven programme to safeguard children against depression and build lifelong resilience*. New York: Harper Collins.

Slee P, Lawson M, Russell A, Askell- Williams H, Dix K, Owens L, Skrzypiec G & Spears B (2009) *Kidsmatter Evaluation Summary*. Adelaide, South Australia: Centre for Analysis of Educational Futures, School of Education, Flinders University.

Shucksmith J, Summerbell C, Jones S & Whittaker V (2007) *Mental Wellbeing of Children in Primary Education (targeted/indicated activities)*. London: National Institute of Clinical Excellence.

Stewart-Brown S (1998) Public health implications of childhood behaviour problems and parenting programmes. In: A Buchanan & B Hudson (Eds) *Parenting, Schooling and Children's Behaviour*. Aldershot: Ashgate.

ThePlace2Be (2009) [online]. Available at: http://www.theplace2be.org.uk/ (accessed August 2010).

Weare K (2000) *Promoting Mental, Emotional and Social Health: A whole school approach*. London: Routledge.

Weare K (2004) *Developing the Emotionally Literate School*. London: Sage.

Weare K & Gray G (2002) *What Works in Promoting Children's Emotional and Social Competence?* Report for the Department of Education and Skills, London: Department of Education and Skills.

Wells J, Barlow J & Stewart-Brown S (2003) A systematic review of universal approaches to mental health promotion in schools. *Health Education* **103** (4) 197–220.

Zins JE, Weissberg RP, Wang MC & Walberg H (2004) *Building Academic Success on Social and Emotional Learning*. Columbia: Teachers College.

Chapter 9

The mental health of veterans

Jacquie Reilly and Jacqueline M Atkinson

Introduction

Worldwide combat related mental health has become high profile in government and media agendas. In the UK, 4,000 new cases of mental illness were diagnosed among the armed forces in 2007 alone, with those returning from Iraq and Afghanistan most likely to suffer from post-traumatic stress (Corbett *et al*, 2008). Combat Stress, the British ex-servicemen's mental health charity also reported a 53% rise in the number of veterans seeking help from 2005–2008 (Rayment, 2008). Personnel who fought in earlier campaigns are also now coming forward, looking for treatment for psychological problems that they have developed following deployment, sometimes developing many years later. In recent times the public health challenges of the psychological problems resulting from conflict were raised in relation to the first Gulf war (Atkinson, 1991a,b). With older conflicts it has been estimated that ex-personnel have had to wait an average of 14 years after leaving the military to be given a diagnosis (www.combatstress.org.uk). This has led to concerns about the services' ability to cope.

One senior Ministry of Defence (MoD) official was reported anonymously in the British press as saying:

> '...we are facing an explosion of psychiatric problems not just from serving military personnel but also from those who served in campaigns dating all the way back to the Second World War. It is a huge problem and something which requires a cross-governmental solution.' (Rayment, 2008)

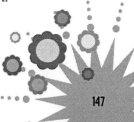

A senior member of Combat Stress echoed this stating that:

'...there is a strong possibility that we face being swamped by new veterans seeking our help. ...we need to develop more capacity for the future because we are already creaking.'
(Rayment, 2008)

These issues came to the forefront of the public agenda because of growing numbers of reports of problems being encountered by ex-military personnel, which were not viewed as being treated effectively by the health service.

In response to these concerns the UK government announced measures to give veterans priority treatment. In November 2007 the then Health Minister Alan Johnson and Veterans Minister Derek Twigg announced changes to the level of support available to armed forces veterans. This included the expansion of NHS treatment for veterans (based on clinical need), in addition to the development of community mental health services, where clinicians could be accessed who had experience of military health problems and could provide a direct pathway to the NHS.

Launching the new pilot community mental health services, Derek Twigg said:

'The new community health pilots will be staffed by qualified mental health professionals. By working with us, these professionals will be able to develop further their understanding of the military ethos and military operations, and to enhance and keep up-to-date their expertise in veterans' mental health, enabling them to give better support to our people. I also warmly welcome the announcement by the Department of Health giving greater priority for treatment to former members of the armed forces.'
(Twigg, 2007)

Once tested, the initial pilots will be developed across Scotland and England.

Types of problems associated with veterans

While a majority of veterans may cope well on leaving the military environment, a small percentage leave with psychiatric and other problems, which can affect their lives. The main types of mental health problems associated with veterans' health, according to Combat Stress, are depressive illness, anxiety disorders, phobias, panic disorders, alcohol abuse, drug abuse and suicide, and social problems such as divorce and unemployment.

A clinical audit carried out by Combat Stress found that the levels of various problems encountered vary, for example, depressive disorders are cited at between 5–75% of veterans seeking treatment, anxiety 2–40%, phobias 15–30%, panic disorders 5–37%, alcohol abuse 6–55% and drug abuse at around 25% (Combat Stress, 2008).

Reservists deployed to combat zones are more likely to develop more mental health problems than regular service personnel (Hotopf *et al*, 2006), especially post-traumatic stress disorder (PTSD) (Iversen *et al*, 2009).

Depression

Depression is common among military personnel, both current and veterans (Iversen & Greenberg, 2009). A recent study of both veterans and serving personnel indicated that of the 13.5% who had a neurotic disorder 3.7% had a major depressive disorder and 7.3% had a minor depressive disorder (Iverson *et al*, 2009).

Post-traumatic stress disorder

Although depression is one of the major mental health issues for veterans, (Iversen & Greenberg, 2009), PTSD has a much higher profile and remains one of the more contentious issues in relation to veterans' health. Although it has been highly publicised in the mass media, the exact number of those affected is unclear. The Ministry of Defence suggested that actual rates were low at around 4% of those deployed to Iraq and Afghanistan (Fear *et al*, 2010). PTSD is more common in reservists, however, who are deployed to combat zones (Iversen et al, 2009). Alongside the common symptoms of PTSD, Combat Stress state that veterans also experience a sense of futility, as well as a tendency toward isolation and a feeling of detachment from others. This is particularly felt toward civilians, whom veterans feel 'do not understand them'. The hyper-arousal and hyper-vigilance can lead to becoming violent towards themselves or others.

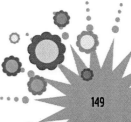

If left untreated PTSD can have negative effects on individuals' behaviour, causing problems within families, employment and on how a veteran copes in the wider non-military environment (Stevenson, 2000; Kang & Hyams, 2005). While the armed services, ex-military charities and the NHS do provide mental health care, many veterans and currently serving personnel are reluctant to seek help. They often conceal their condition for fear of stigma, embarrassment or job loss even where they may recognise that they need psychiatric help. A study in the USA looked at levels of depression, anxiety and PTSD in combat infantry units. Of the 6,201 soldiers involved, less than 50% affected would consent to some from of psychotherapy (Hoge *et al*, 2004). This reluctance must be addressed within both the military and the NHS if more effective treatment is to be offered to a growing population now being deployed to war zones.

Suicide

A recent study of suicide rates among those who left the military between the years 1996 to 2005 revealed a total of 224 suicides in this period. It was found that in comparison with the general population, the risk of suicide was higher in men aged 16–19 years and 20–24 years but lower for those between 30–59 years. The rates for women were not higher than the general population. The risk of suicide was most closely associated with gender (men), age at discharge, being unmarried, coming from a lower rank, being untrained and when service has been for fewer than four years. The conclusion drawn was that men aged under 25 years who leave the UK armed forces were at increased risk of suicide, and this was more common within two years of leaving the service (Kapur *et al*, 2009).

Alcohol misuse

Alcohol misuse is a problem for veterans and recent research has described it as a pervasive problem within the military in general. Fear *et al* (2010) estimated that 13% of the UK's service personnel were abusing alcohol to the extent that it was impacting on their health.

This culture of alcohol use within the services and its use when veterans are suffering from psychological symptoms has led to the suggestion that:

> '...this group is at increased risk of the social complications of excessive drinking such as violence and relationship breakdowns. Although having introduced some alcohol control policies, the armed forces need to reassess whether they are rigorous enough.'
> (*Lancet* editorial, 2010)

An American study showed that high rates of alcohol misuse after deployment were being reported among those returning from conflicts. It was suggested in this study that younger service members are at an increased risk of new-onset heavy and binge drinking, which could lead to alcohol related problems in the future (Jacobson *et al*, 2008). Given the number of people being deployed at this time, this may become an important public health issue for the future.

Homelessness

The homeless organisation Homeless Link carried out a survey in 2010 that showed that while levels of homelessness among veterans were not excessively high, they were widespread: half of the day centres in England reported dealing with veterans. There are a number of factors which make veterans more likely to be homeless, including PTSD, which may prevent ex-service personnel from living unsupported. It also highlighted that veterans can face falling into patterns of rough sleeping (Homeless Link, 2010).

In Scotland, while progress is being made in relation to the development of housing, specifically for ex-military personnel, there are still barriers as demand outstrips supply. A Poppy Scotland report (2006) on housing for all veterans showed that there were over 900 accommodation units (managed by nine separate organisations). In relation to the qualifying criteria for such housing a number of points were highlighted: suitable accommodation for single people and childless couples was limited, priority for allocation seemed to go to those on a war pension (an issue for those leaving services on medical grounds) and that hostel accommodation for needy or homeless veterans was only available in specific areas. Lengthy waiting lists were common and it was possible that some veterans would never be housed (Poppy Scotland, 2006).

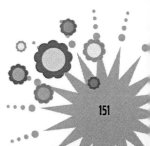

Work is in progress to develop these services further, with the Joint Service Housing Advice Office (JSHAO) providing information on housing options to veterans both while serving and when they come out of the military.

Unemployment

Although a National Audit Office report found that 94% of ex-service personnel found work within six months of leaving (National Audit Office, 2007), employment rates for people with a mental health problem are relatively low in general. A UK Labour Force Survey showed that only 18.4% of those with a mental illness were employed (Office of National Statistics, 2001). It has been argued that employers are reluctant to employ people with a mental health problem, with only 37% saying they would recruit people in this category (Department of Work and Pensions, 2002). The specific problems faced by veterans with mental health problems make it problematic to work in a civilian environment, which is reflected in historical and contemporary employment rates (Iversen & Greenberg, 2009).

Veterans in prison

In 2009, a report by the National Association of Probation Workers (NAPO) stated that the proportion of veterans in the prison population had more than doubled in six years. The report stated that approximately 12,000 veterans were on probation or parole (6% of the total), while 8,500 were in prison, that is 8.5% of the jail population. It was suggested that misuse of alcohol and drugs were key factors in veterans' offending behaviour with a high proportion of crimes linked to domestic violence. The study found that chronic misuse of alcohol and drugs were major factors in half of 90 cases where veterans had been given a community sentence. Almost half of the veterans were suffering from PTSD or depression. The most common conviction was for violence in a domestic setting, which occurred in 39 cases. In 10 cases the main offence was against a child (NAPO, 2009). Other research carried out by the Defence Analytical Services and Advice (DASA) suggests the figure may be much lower at 3%, or 2,500 veterans in prison (DASA, 2010). It is clear that there needs to be a concerted effort to find out exactly what the size of this problem is in order to effectively treat those with mental health problems in a prison setting.

In 2010 the Justice Unions Parliamentary group (JUPG) called for more action on servicemen and women returning from active combat. They made recommendations, which included:

▶ giving those returning from combat a psychological assessment before they leave the service

▶ giving special attention to alcohol or drug issues

▶ asking police to monitor arrested veterans and refer them if necessary to specialist help

▶ requiring GPs to ask if patients have served in the forces

▶ completion of a thorough justice ministry survey, using probation and prison officers, to ascertain how many veterans are currently in the criminal justice system.

(Justice Unions Parliamentary Group, 2010).

Routes to treatment for mental health problems

There is some debate about whether there need to be separate, dedicated services for veterans, or whether they can be best served through general NHS mental health services. Currently, there are a number of different routes to receiving treatment. The Department of Health and Ministry of Defence established the Medical Assessment Programme (MAP) in 1993 (based at St Thomas's Hospital in London) to look into the health issues of those who had served in the 1990/1991 Gulf conflict. This service was later opened to those who have served in Iraq and Afghanistan and who had taken part in Porton Down. Latterly, a mental health assessment has been offered to any ex-service personnel with operational service since 1982. This includes veterans of the Falklands conflict (Ministry of Defence, 2010).

An important part of treating ex-service personnel is to understand military culture and the impact of conflict. Work is being undertaken to ensure that NHS professionals have the appropriate skills and support in order to effectively treat veterans with mental health problems. A study of MAP's referrals of Gulf veterans with PTSD to specialised centres concluded that this could be beneficial (Lee *et al*, 2005). In 2007 six community mental health pilot projects were set up across the UK. In March 2010, in response to a question in the

House of Commons, it was announced that this would be rolled out across the UK by 2011–2012. In addition, Combat Stress professionals will work in the NHS as champions for the mental health of veterans (O'Brien, 2010). A positive practice guide for working with veterans has also been produced (Department of Health, 2009). Since 2006 a dedicated reserves mental health programme has been available to veterans (Ministry of Defence, 2006).

Another pathway to support is through Combat Stress, the veterans' mental health charity. Combat Stress provides treatment and support to ex-service men and women suffering from conditions such as PTSD, depression and anxiety disorders. These services include clinical therapies such as cognitive behavioural therapy (CBT) and eye movement desensitisation and reprocessing (EMDR) as well as other non-clinical interventions to veterans. The charity has three treatment centres in England and Scotland for short-stay treatments and is also developing community outreach teams nationwide.

Innovative interventions are being developed both within the NHS and voluntary services. One new approach is that of horticultural therapy, which has a well established tradition for positively affecting well-being and quality of life for certain groups (Relf, 1999; Haycock, 2001; Neuberger, 2008) introduced by the new charity, Gardening Leave.

Case study: the Gardening Leave project

Gardening Leave was founded in 2007 as a charity to provide horticultural therapy to veterans with combat related mental health problems. The pilot project is based at the Scottish Agricultural College, Ayr and takes referrals from the nearby Combat Stress centre, Hollybush House. In 2010 a second project with a wider outreach programme started in London, attached to the Royal Hospital at Chelsea (Parry, 2010).

The activities offered are in addition to clinical interventions. As well as the gardening activities, there are opportunities to work on restoring an old glasshouse, and fishing in the river running through the site. The site houses and develops the national poppy collection, which has particular resonance for service personnel. An evaluation of the Scottish based project found that veterans attending the project felt that this was therapeutic and beneficial to their well-being. It helped individuals better cope with many elements of their illness, learn new skills and feel safe in an inclusive and understanding environment (Reilly & Atkinson, in press). Specific benefits for veterans included:

▶ a renewed sense of purpose

▶ something to look forward to

▶ improvement in mood and stress levels

▶ regaining confidence

▶ feeling that they were in a safe place

▶ feeling that their problems were understood

▶ the satisfaction of growing plants.

In addition, outdoor, physical activity was important in helping sleep, remaining calm and reducing agitation. Likewise, learning new, or regaining old skills was felt to be important. These skills were then transferred to everyday life as many veterans developed their own gardens away from the site and often passed on skills and knowledge to others. Many spoke of being able to give something back.

Not to be underestimated was that the project was veterans only, employing staff with specialist understanding of the military. The knowledge that everyone was 'in the same boat' contrasted with commonly stated feelings of being adrift and misunderstood in the civilian world.

Conclusion

Overall, there have been renewed efforts to understand the issues affecting the mental health of those in the armed forces both during and following combat when trying to reintegrate into civilian life. At a policy level there has been an awareness that the high numbers of armed personnel now being deployed into active service, presents an important mental health challenge and that, as a society, we have a duty to recognise that the men and women who are carrying out these duties are often doing so in very difficult circumstances and need to be supported effectively both during combat and on their return. However, if we are to address this challenge effectively then attention also needs to be given to the stigma attached to mental health problems, which prevents many services personnel and veterans from seeking help. Attitudes to early diagnosis, help-

seeking and to contributory issues such as the use of alcohol need to change, and for this to happen more needs to be known about how this stigma operates and what would work to address this. These are key issues to tackle in preventing the escalation of mental health problems both in serving personnel and veterans.

References

Atkinson JM (1991a) Factors contributing to military casualty rates during war. *Psychiatric Bulletin* **15** 199–200.

Atkinson JM (1991b) The demand for psychiatric services as a result of the Gulf War. *Psychiatric Bulletin* **15** 201–203.

Combat Stress (2008) *Clinical Audit Data and Psychometric Analyses 2005–2008*. Leatherhead: Combat Stress.

Corbett C, White S & Blatchley N (2008) *UK Armed Forces Psychiatric morbidity: Assessment of presenting complaints at MOD DCMHs and association with deployment on recent operations in the Iraq/Afghanistan theatres of operation April–June 2007*. London: Defence Analytical Services Agency.

Defence Analytical Services and Advice (2010) *Estimating the Number of Prisoners in England and Wales Who are Ex-armed Forces* [online]. DASA: Ministry of Defence. Available at: www.dasa.mod.uk (accessed July 2010).

Department of Health (2009) *Improving Access to Psychological Therapies Programme: Veterans. Positive practice guide* [online]. Available at: www.1254742500_rrHB_veterans_positive_practice_guide (accessed July 2010).

Department of Work and Pensions (2002) *Trends in Employment for the Disabled*. London: HMSO.

Fear T, Jones M, Murphy A, Hull L, Iversen A, Coker B, Machell L, Sundin J, Woodhead C, Jones N, Greenberg N, Landau S, Dandeker C, Rona R Hotopf M & Wessely S (2010) What are the consequences of deployment to Iraq and Afghanistan on the mental health of the UK armed forces? A cohort study. *Lancet* **357** (9728) 1783–1797.

Haycock L (2001) Horticultural therapy and post traumatic stress recovery. *Journal of Therapeutic Horticulture* **12** 100.

Hoge CW, Castro CA, Messer SC, McGurk D, Cotting DI & Koffman RL (2004) Combat duty in Iraq and Afghanistan, mental health problems and barriers to care. *New England Journal of Medicine* **351** 13–22.

Homeless Link (2010) *Survey on Needs and Provision (SNAP)* [online]. Available at: Homeless Link www.homeless.org.uk/veterans (accessed July 2010).

Hotopf M, Hull L, Fear NT, Browne T, Horn O, Iversen A, Jones M, Murphy D, Bland D, Earnshaw M, Greenberg N, Hughes JH, Tate AR, Dandeker C, Rona R & Wessely S (2006) The health of UK military personnel who deployed to the 2003 Iraq war: a cohort study. *Lancet* **367** 1731–1741.

Iversen A & Greenberg N (2009) Mental health of regular and reserve military veterans. *Advances in Psychiatric Treatment* **15** 100–106.

Iversen AC, van Staden L, Hughes JH, Browne T, Hull L, Hall J, Greenberg N, Rona RJ, Hotopf M, Wessely S & Fear NT (2009) The prevalence of common mental disorders and PTSD in the UK military: using data from a clinical interview-based study. *BMC Psychiatry* **9** 68.

Jacobson I, Ryan M, Hooper T, Smith T, Amoroso P, Boyko E, Gackstetter G, Wells T & Bell N (2008) Alcohol use and alcohol-related problems before and after military combat deployment. *Journal of the American Medical Association* **300** (6) 663–675.

Justice Unions Parliamentary Group (2010) *Veterans in the Criminal Justice System: Co-ordinated National Action Plan*. Justice Unions Parliamentary Group. London: The Stationery Office.

Kang HK & Hyams K (2005) Mental health care needs among recent war veterans. *New England Journal of Medicine* **352** 1289–1289.

Kapur N, While D, Blatchley N, Bray I & Harrison K (2009) Suicide after leaving the UK armed forces – a cohort study. *Public Library of Science Medicine* **6** e26.

Lancet (2010) Editorial: The mental health of UK military personnel revisited. *Lancet* **375** (9727) 1666.

Lee HA, Gabriel R & Bale A (2005) Clinical outcomes of Gulf veterans' medical assessment programme referrals to specialised centers for Gulf veterans with post-traumatic stress disorder. *Military Medicine* **170** 400–405.

Ministry of Defence (2006) *Reserves Mental Health Programme (RMHP)* [online]. Available at: http://www.nhs.uk/NHSEngland/Militaryhealthcare/Documents/rmhp.pdf (accessed July 2010).

Ministry of Defence (2010) *Medical Assessment Programme* [online]. Available at: http://www.mod.uk/DefenceInternet/FactSheets/MedicalAssessmentProgramme.htm (accessed July 2010).

National Association of Probation Officers (2009) *Armed Forces and the Criminal Justice System* [online]. Available at: www.napo.org.uk/about/veteransincjs.cfm (accessed July 2010).

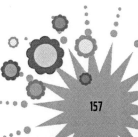

National Audit Office (2007) *Leaving the Services: Official Report*. London: National Audit Office.

Neuberger K (2008) Some therapeutic aspects of gardening in psychiatry. *Acta Horticulturae* **790** 83–90.

O'Brien M (2010) *Written Ministerial Statements, 11 January*. Health: Medical Care (veterans) Hansard. London: The Stationery Office.

Office of National Statistics (2001) *Labour Force Survey* [online]. Available at: http://www.statistics.gov.uk/statbase/Source.asp?vlnk=358 (accessed July 2010).

Parry N (2010) Planting seeds of hope. *British Journal of Wellbeing* **1** (3) 50.

Poppy Scotland (2006) *Meeting the Need: A report into addressing the needs of veterans living in Scotland*. Edinburgh: Poppy Scotland.

Rayment S (2008) Britain is facing an explosion of psychiatric disorders amongst serving and former members of the armed forces. *Daily Telegraph*, 4 October.

Reilly J & Atkinson JM (in press) Veterans views of the Gardening Leave project for ex-military personnel with PTSD. *Journal Public Mental Health*.

Relf PD (1999) Then role of horticulture in human well-being and quality of life. *Journal of Therapeutic Horticulture* **X** (79).

Stevenson VE (2000) Premature treatment termination by angry patients with combat related post-traumatic stress disorder. *Military Medicine* **165** 422–424.

Twigg D (2007) *Veterans World* [online] 9. Available at: veterans-uk.info/vets_world/issue9/news5.html (accessed July 2010).

Chapter 10

Later life: challenges and opportunities

Sandra Grant, Fiona Borrowman and Isabella Goldie

Introduction

In any discussion of the public health needs of older people the starting point is the demographic shift (or 'ticking time-bomb'), whereby not only is the proportion of older people in the population increasing, due to low birth rates and increased longevity, but there is a disproportionate increase in the 'older old' over the age of 85. The structure of society is changing rapidly. By 2020 two in five people in the UK will be over 50 years of age and one in five will be over 65. The oldest age group (85 and over) is growing the fastest with an increase in the proportion of the population from 1.9% in 2004 to an estimated 2.7% by 2020. By 2050 in Europe 30% of the population will be over 65 years of age and 11% over 80 years old (Office of National Statistics, 2009). This will have a major impact on society not only in terms of family structure and roles but also on economic issues related to wealth production and the costs of care. It is one of the most significant and challenging issues to be faced this century.

While providing support for people in later life poses a significant public health challenge, much of the emphasis is commonly placed on the negative aspects of this. The positive implications are given less attention. There is a steadily increasing number of older people, mainly retired from paid work, who remain healthy and are able to contribute actively to society – a strength not a 'burden'. Any public mental health strategy has to take account of the contributions of older people as well as their potential mental health support needs.

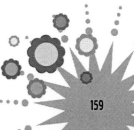

Socio-cultural factors

The age at which one becomes 'old' depends on whose definition is being used, and for what purpose. Access to certain benefits and allowances and the planning and organising of services currently require a cut-off point (usually 60–65 years). This often does not coincide with a personal identity of leaving 'middle' age behind. For the purposes of planning mental health improvement in later life it has become customary to take the age of 50 as the time to concentrate on impending issues such as retirement, bereavement and failing health. Although this makes sense in terms of working 'upstream' it is not welcomed by the 'younger, old' who are aware of how much they contribute as active members of society and reject the stigmatisation and discrimination that has become attached to ageing.

This changing demographic pattern, linked partly to changes in lifestyle, reflects the complexity of developing mental health strategy for a group of people with very different life experiences and expectations. At the present time this is exemplified by the impact of the world wars and their aftermath. Because of the time-specific factor of war there is a unique opportunity to view the ageing population in three particular cohorts: those alive around and just after the first world war, those growing up between the wars and those born during or after the second world war. This chapter will focus on the second two groups: before and after the 1939–1945 war.

For the people who were adults at the beginning of the war, now in their 80s and 90s, many recall the days when regular medical help and opportunities for further education were only available for the wealthy. Peace for many had brought a return to family life and the safety net of a welfare state that was previously unthinkable. Most of their formative years were spent at a time when the family unit was central with little time to consider personal needs. They tend to make few complaints and demand little now.

The subsequent generation, the large numbers of children born when troops returned into the security of peace time, the so-called 'baby boomers', are now themselves reaching retirement age. These children grew up in a time of relative optimism and opportunity and came of age in a period of cultural change that stressed youth, liberalism, confidence and high expectations. They experienced a growing awareness of the concept of 'self' and of an entitlement to good health including mental health. Many are now retiring financially secure. This is the group that will become increasingly assertive and challenging about the lack of opportunities for older people: a resource that can be called upon in the changing society.

Although people are now living longer this does not mean that they are living longer disability free. As Marmot (2010) discussed, levels of disability show that more than three-quarters of the population do not have disability-free life expectancy as far as the age of 68. This places additional responsibilities on families and can create intergenerational pressure, with adults of working age often balancing caring for their older relatives alongside meeting the needs of their own children. However, older relatives can also be a support by helping to look after grandchildren. This is a positive development; being needed and making a valuable contribution is an important feature for maintaining positive mental health. In reality it can also become a burden and stressor.

Some people are at the other end of the spectrum of involvement, with a very limited social network, especially after the transition of leaving work or of bereavement. One of the most important protective factors against mental illness is social relationships. The growth in one-person households of older people is substantial, especially among widows given the gender difference in life expectancy. If they are not in institutional care, 76% of men and 94% of women over the age of 65 live alone. The changing structure of families and the move towards residential care options has left many older people increasingly isolated.

> 'Isolation is partly the consequence of an emphasis on independence and the fact that more elderly people are living alone or in institutions, rather than with extended families, over the last 50 years. It also has to do with ageism, what Dr Arbore calls "the cruelest of the isms" because it "isolates people, makes them feel powerless, makes them retreat". While elders are respected in many societies, they are disregarded in cultures that exalt productivity and youth. Age-based residential segregation has increased in the last half-century with the spread of nursing homes, assisted-living facilities and other senior housing. These are critical resources for people without other sources of help, but they can leave people cut off from the rest of society.'
> (Sigrist, 2010)

This sense of older people being a burden on family and/or society is exemplified in the debate about how to finance older people's care, especially if they need residential support. How much should be self-funded and what happens when the money runs out? How does the state pay? These are difficult stressors for a person growing older. These debates and society's prevailing attitude to ageing has an impact on how people view themselves as they age. It is very difficult to be part of a society that views ageing negatively and not internalise some of these views oneself.

Mental health

Mental health is not evenly distributed across society as a whole and there exists a direct relationship between position on the social gradient and mental health (Marmot, 2010). A report by Friedli (2009) lays out the evidence that poor mental health is both a cause and a consequence of social, economic and environmental inequalities. Friedli argues that the 'poverty gap' causes mental and physical health problems owing to the chronic low level of stress attached to coping with daily deprivation and disadvantage. Deprivation can have a negative impact on mental health at all ages but the cumulative effect over a lifetime can be especially devastating in later years. A salient factor is the unequal prevalence of disability in later life, with people in the lowest socio-economic group experiencing 17 fewer disability-free years than the wealthiest in society (Marmot, 2010).

Sometimes it is erroneously believed that it is 'normal' for older people to be depressed, rather than it being the result of a complex interaction between society, life history and present circumstances. There is increasing evidence about what improves the mental well-being of older people and makes them resilient or what makes them vulnerable to developing problems. Not surprisingly it is the same things that are important at all ages, although with a somewhat different emphasis. Within a UK inquiry into mental health in later life, older people themselves identified five key features:

▶ being valued vs. being discriminated against

▶ participating in meaningful activity vs. having nothing to do or to contribute

▶ good relationships vs. isolation and social exclusion

▶ good physical health vs. illness

▶ financial security vs. poverty.

(Age Concern and Mental Health Foundation, 2006)

The Institute for Public Policy Research (Allen, 2008) identified similar results, highlighting the effect of deprivation and poverty and the vulnerability of not only living alone, but also of living in a care home. A person can be lonely in an institutional setting and within a recent report by the Mental Welfare Commission, Scotland and the Scottish Commission for the Regulation of Care (2009), it was found that around half of all people living in a care home never went out. Given this level of exclusion, it is not surprising then that the prevalence of depression is higher in care homes than in the general older population with two in five people living in care homes experiencing depression (Mental Health Foundation, 2002).

Mental health problems

Poor mental health and mental disorders are common in later life. One in four older people suffer from mild depression, bad enough to significantly impair their quality of life. One in seven have a serious depression (illness). Every week in Scotland five people over the age of 50 kill themselves and in Europe generally, older people have the highest suicide rates, with a graded increase with age and even higher rates in those above 85 (Scottish Government, 2007). Depression and anxiety result primarily from psycho-social distress, often linked to poor physical health which itself increases with age.

As we get older the risk grows of developing a form of dementia. The prevalence rises from 2% in 65–69 year olds to 22% in people aged 85–89 years. Dementia is a brain disease that is ultimately fatal. It cannot be cured (although symptoms can be alleviated) and in most cases there is relatively little that can be done for prevention except to follow general health promotion advice. This tends to lead to a degree of nihilism and despair. A person with dementia and his/her carers have the same rights to mental well-being and support as everyone else and the same principles apply. For carers in particular, many of whom are older, there is a particular need for support and guidance. They are at a high risk of developing depression.

Not every mental health problem is age-related. People with long-standing illnesses such as schizophrenia and bipolar disorder continue to have difficulties as they grow older, although they often have reduced access to services, due to age related access thresholds.

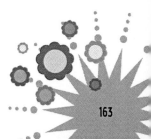

Making it happen

The question of how we address these challenges has prompted recent debate not only at a national level within the UK but also across European and international policy stages. For many years the mental health of older people has been under-represented within the policy debate, however, interest is now growing. The rationale for this may in part be due to the impact of an ageing population on productivity, but also reflects some of the current concerns around levels of disability in later life and the costs of addressing this. One example of international interest is the focus given to later life in the European Pact for Mental Health and Well-being, where a thematic conference was held to explore a way forward. The background papers to this conference 'Mental Health and Well-being in Older People – Making in Happen' (European Communities, 2009) outline seven key action areas to assist with 'making it happen':

1. policy development

2. mental health promotion

3. mental disorder prevention

4. older people in vulnerable situations

5. systems for care and treatment

6. informal carers

7. research.

This chapter will explore two of these key action areas: policy development and mental health promotion and consider the implications of implementing these.

Policy development

Policy that has an influence on the mental health of older people is far-reaching and much wider than mental health policy. The call for action in the EU background paper (European Communities, 2009) reflects the need to consider the mental health of older people across all policy and at all levels (regional, national and international). Within this paper eight cross-cutting themes were identified: empowerment of older people in society; recognition of diversity in later life; early interventions taking a life-course approach; social inclusion and social capital; inequalities and poverty; gender issues;

inter-sectoral collaboration; and research and development of the knowledge base. The need to take a broad approach to tackling these issues is clear.

> 'While there is much that can be done to improve mental health, doing so will depend less on specific interventions, valuable as these may be, and more on a policy sea change, in which policy-makers across all sectors think in terms of "mental health impact".'
> (Friedli, 2009)

Currently much of the public mental health debate takes place within the health policy arena, which limits impact on wider issues that affect people's lives. For example, within the UK inquiry (Age Concern and the Mental Health Foundation, 2006) older people identified poverty as a key issue. For many economic poverty is a life-long experience, which is exacerbated in retirement.

As called for in the EU background paper (European Communities, 2009) older people need to be involved in the design and development of all policy that has an impact on their lives, as they have an important opinion on what makes a difference. Older people should be viewed as a valuable asset with experience and knowledge that can inform policy, rather than as a 'burden' on the public purse.

The importance of reducing the impact of age discrimination is highlighted in several reports and needs to be a central policy endeavour. The UK Inquiry (Age Concern and Mental Health Foundation, 2006) found that age discrimination had a significant impact on the quality of life of older people. Age discrimination not only acts to exclude older people and reduce opportunities for participation but also results in older people internalising negative stereotypes and limiting their own lives. Discrimination can take many shapes and forms and can be direct or indirect. This form of discrimination occurs routinely but has not had the same legislative tools to support efforts to reduce it, as other forms of discriminations. Within a multicultural society, consideration needs to be given to the impact of multiple discrimination and more needs to be known about how this affects elders from within minority ethnic communities, who are living in a society where the majority view on ageing may differ in a very fundamental way from attitudes and values within the minority community. Over recent years some safeguards have been developed to protect the rights of older people and to tackle discrimination, for example in the workplace (Equality Act, 2006; ACAS, 2009). There remains a need to develop a more comprehensive legislative framework that will protect the rights of older people and make ageism illegal.

However, legislation alone will not prevent discrimination. There are indications that positive stories about growing older and living well in later life can be effective in challenging stereotypes. The media has an important role to play in representing people in a more positive way. There are examples of ways in which this has been achieved for other groups such as through concerted campaigns for people with mental health problems (Knifton & Quinn, 2008). The UK Inquiry has called for the development of media guidelines to address media reporting of later life, which should be endorsed at a policy level to ensure sufficient impact on reporting practice. Consideration should also be given to how the media can be used to place positive messages effectively in the public domain. Social marketing approaches, media advocacy and the arts can be effective in sharing real life perspectives, however, such approaches need to be developed alongside those who experience discrimination (in this case older people) and based on the evidence of what actually works to change not only attitudes but behaviour in a sustainable way (Hastings, 2008; Quinn et al, 2010).

Mental health promotion

'Health promotion is about helping people to have more control over their lives, and thereby improve their health. It occurs through processes of enabling people, advocacy, and by mediating among sectors. In essence, health promotion action involves helping people to develop personal skills, creating supportive environments, strengthening communities, influencing governments to enact healthy public policies and reorienting and improving health services.'
(Raphael et al, 1999)

Mental health promotion is a complex area that requires inter-sectoral collaboration (European Communities, 2009). Four areas for action have been highlighted in the EU background paper.

▶ The promotion of social participation and inclusion – promoting opportunities for older people to participate and contribute to community life has the potential to have a positive impact on individuals but can also enrich communities and society as a whole. Such opportunities include volunteering and paid work as well as involvement in leisure, social, educational, spiritual and cultural activities. The potential for older people to enrich community life is one which has also received international attention. Governor Quinn in the US state of Washington called for 2010 to be 'the year of the engaged older adult':

> '...a call to action for individuals, families and communities to boost learning, strengthen the workforce and enrich community life by encouraging older adults, aged 50 and older, to lend their expertise to these areas.'
> (State Journal-Register, 2010)

Within the mental health service user movement there has been a significant and influential shift from a pathology focused approach to a strengths-based 'recovery' focus. This does not mean denial of symptoms and difficulties, but rather a renewed emphasis on the strengths, supports and resilience factors within the person and in his network (McCormack, 2007). At the same time peer support mechanisms have been developed and are correlated with positive outcomes (Foot & Hopkins, 2010). Such an asset-based focus can equally be applied to older people. However, older people do not live in isolation and this approach needs to be extrapolated to communities and populations, this can apply to geographic settings or communities based on diversity such as age, gender or ethnicity. Everyone in society should have a stake in supporting the development of a mentally healthy society; one that supports a life course approach to healthy and active ageing. In the case of developing healthy communities for older people, it will mean mapping the assets and supporting active participation not just of older people, but also their communities as a whole.

Working in this way with an emphasis on the positive, requires different values and attitudes, better partnership and inter-sectoral working, and trust that the community can come up with the answers itself when given the opportunity.

▶ **Identifying supportive personal factors and lifestyle issues** – there are recognised links between physical health and the promotion of positive mental health. However, the absence of good physical health does not necessarily mean an absence of positive mental health. The EU Healthy Ageing Strategy, A challenge for Europe (Swedish National Institute of Public Health, 2006) identifies the value of encouraging good physical health as a means to promoting mental health and well-being. It calls for efforts to promote healthy lifestyles in later life such as keeping physically active, eating healthily, smoking cessation and reducing alcohol intake. These health behaviours are not only relevant for older people, as they result in health benefits at all ages (eg. Mental Health Foundation, 2006;

Arent *et al*, 2000; Swift *et al*, 2008). Efforts should be made to encourage individuals to view these behaviours as life-long and in this way supporting healthy ageing. To be effective, health promotion activity needs to present personally relevant messages showing the benefits of healthy living. Community-based initiatives should be supported where they are designed to assist in improving physical health, such as healthy cooking classes, physical activity classes and falls prevention courses. However, not everyone has equal access to leisure facilities, outdoor spaces or can afford to eat fresh fruit and vegetables on a daily basis. There are many barriers that prevent people from adopting health promoting behaviours, including poverty and living in neighbourhoods of deprivation (Marmot, 2010). Care needs to be taken to ensure that a 'health education' approach is not seen as the best and only way to promote healthy behaviour, whereby communities are given information on how they should behave regardless of local context and constraints. To be effective, a health promotion approach needs to be sensitive to context and the reality of people's lives and adopt a facilitative approach to working alongside communities. Mental health improvement staff need to see themselves as 'health facilitators' rather than 'health educators'.

▶ **Living spaces, environment and neighbourhood** – the physical environment including housing and internal living and working space; neighbourhood; and whether living in a city or a rural setting, all have an impact on mental health (Guite *et al*, 2006). The EU background paper (European Communities, 2009) identifies three areas related to living space, environment and neighbourhood that can assist in promoting the mental health of older people: providing adequate housing options; creating socially attractive neighbourhoods; and offering healthy physical and natural environments. This agenda is not one that can be taken forward by mental health policy alone. A need for effective inter-sectoral working at a policy and public service provision level is clearly called for.

WHO Global Age-friendly cities initiative (WHO, 2007) stressed the importance of involving older people in design and planning and identified issues that are useful to consider when working to create supportive environments, these include:

▶ outdoor spaces and buildings (eg. street lighting and security from crime)
▶ transportation including accessible and affordable public transport
▶ housing and the importance of supporting people's choices of residence including the development of new technologies to assist independent living

▶ social participation/social neighbourhoods; promoting opportunities for social contacts and participation in community activities.

▶ **Occupational issues and retirement policies** – the transition period of retirement or moving to a pension can have an important impact on mental health and well-being. For some older people retirement is an opportunity to relax and spend more time with family and in leisure activities. However, for other older people retirement is not a positive experience leading to isolation and loneliness. Financial situations change with retirement and moving onto a pension, for some people this greatly increases the risk of poverty. Within the current economic climate where many are experiencing reduced pension security and significant changes to the way pensions operate, poverty and financial inequity in later life will become an even greater challenge in coming years.

The EU background paper (European Communities, 2009) identifies three areas that can assist in promoting mental health in older people in relation to occupational issues and retirement policies:

1. volunteering, lifelong learning and intergenerational opportunities after working life

2. retirement planning at a local level

3. provide opportunities for flexible retirement and working.

The impact of inequalities will shape how these actions play out in reality. For example, older people who are in higher socio-economic groups may be able to take up flexible retirement options and work onto a later age but people in lower socio-economic groups, where disability rates are higher will be less able to do so. Equally, people in lower socio-economic groups experience higher levels of unemployment and employment in jobs that are manual or unsatisfying. Not all work is good for mental health and not everyone has been fortunate enough to work in employment that has had a beneficial effect. Equally, there are older people who want to retire at 65 and those who will not feel fit or well enough to continue in work. Older people need more options but they also need to have the disability free years to take these up and be able to choose whether it will improve their lives to do so.

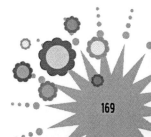

The challenges

There is no doubt that in coming years the challenge of meeting the care needs of older people will be considerable. Currently the major share of care for older people with support needs falls to informal carers. This presents an enormous resource and forms part of the solution for supporting older people in coming years. However, with the changing demographic and growing numbers of older people this may present a future challenge, as many carers feel unsupported. Sherwood *et al* (2005) identified the detrimental impact that this role has on the mental health of carers. Effective support structures need to be developed to help carers continue in this role, to do otherwise would increase the need for expensive formal care and further disrupt family relationships.

As outlined in this chapter the evidence points consistently to the importance of feeling involved, of contributing, of being a valued member of society. This is why transition points such as bereavement, retirement and moving onto a pension can be so painful. Yet society continues to exclude older people in many ways. Older people themselves need to be engaged and involved in planning and delivering any mental health improvement interventions. They need to contribute, not just feel that they are dependent. This requires a fundamental shift in the paternalistic attitudes that are so often experienced by older people when decisions are being made about their lives. An asset based approach needs to be adopted and supports put in place to facilitate meaningful involvement of older people, including those that are seldom heard, such as people living in care homes.

A potential paradox surrounds mental health promotion in later life, that by focusing on preventing negative outcomes, a sense of dependency or 'being a burden' can be reinforced. This is not to suggest that prevention strategies do not have their place. These strategies serve an important purpose in reducing the incidence of mental health problems and improving outcomes for older people that do experience problems.

Approaches to addressing these issues need to be sophisticated and targeted proportionately according to need and should build upon the evidence of what is known to work and in what context. Indeed, it can be argued that targeting interventions to where they can be most effective and efficient is a necessity in time of scarce resources. At a population level the focus should be on promoting positive mental health outcomes. This sends a clear message that getting older brings with it new possibilities and avoids a deficit model concerned only with the problems attached to ageing.

Older people have clearly identified wider issues that have a major impact on their mental health, such as poverty and discrimination. The evidence is clear that there is a correlation between mental health status and position on the social gradient. A lower position on the social gradient brings with it poorer mental health and increased prevalence of mental health problems. Marmot (2010) cautions against adopting public health strategies that do not take account of socio-economic inequalities. Whole population or 'universal' approaches can serve to further increase mental health inequalities rather than reduce them, as these initiatives will be most readily accessed by those in higher socio-economic groups with most personal resources, producing health gain rather than equity. Likewise, limited resources should not be targeted only towards those most at risk, despite the social justice imperative to do so, as this approach leaves out those at the median who also do less well than those above them on the social gradient. Instead, Marmot calls for public health interventions that are graded proportionately in accordance with need and disadvantage. He calls this approach 'proportionate universalism' (Marmot, 2010). There is a clear policy imperative to develop responses which aim to level this playing field.

The recommendations and evidence from regional, national and increasingly international work provides a body of knowledge that can be used to guide such policy development. The challenge is transferring this knowledge into practice to ensure that effective mental health improvement interventions are developed and can be sustained in the long-term. The current financial climate makes this a daunting task. It will require long-term investment and an end to a culture of short-termism. This agenda cannot be taken forward within mental health policy alone. Addressing inequalities effectively requires inter-sectoral responses and more consistent partnership approaches. The degree of this challenge cannot be overstated – there are few examples so far of governments that have managed to tackle these problems effectively. Working across the UK, Europe and beyond, the most useful way forward may be to harness a range of expertise.

Lastly, but significantly, one key theme running throughout this chapter is the level of exclusion encountered by older people. A fundamental change is required to the way in, which society views and treats older people. Everyone has a part to play in tackling this last acceptable 'ism'. Not only is the exclusion of older people unethical, the losses to society are great. Older people have a lifetime of skills and knowledge that can enrich community life and many have lived through the most challenging of times. Rather than framing the demographic shift as a negative phenomena with older people viewed as a 'burden', society needs to see older people as an asset. Perhaps a useful and positive way to reframe the 'ageing population' is as an 'experienced population'.

References

ACAS (2009) *Guidance on Age in the Workplace: A guide for employers* [online]. Available at: http://www.acas.org.uk/index.aspx?/articleid=1046 (accessed August 2010).

Age Concern & Mental Health Foundation (2006) *Promoting Mental Health and Well-being in Later Life: A first report from the UK Inquiry into Mental Health and Well-Being in Later Life*. London: Mental Health Foundation.

Allen J (2008) *Older People and Well-Being*. London: IPPR.

Arent SM, Landers DM & Etnier JL (2000) The effects of exercise on mood of older adults: a meta-analytic review. *Journal of Aging and Physical Activity* **8** 407–430.

European Communities (2009) *Background Document and Key Messages for the EU Thematic Conference: Mental health and well-being in older people – Making it happen*. EU Thematic conference on mental health of older people 19–20 April 2010, Madrid. Organised by European Commission Directorate-General for Health and Consumers and the Spanish Ministry of Health and Social Affairs with support of the Spanish Presidency of the European Union.

Equality Act 2006 (c.3) [online]. Available at: http://www.opsi.gov.uk/acts/act2006 (accessed July 2010).

Foot J & Hopkins T (2010) *A Glass Half-full: How an asset approach can improve community health and well-being* [online]. IDeA. Available at: http://www.idea.gov.uk/idk/aio/18410498 (accessed August 2010).

Friedli L (2009) *Mental Health, Resilience and Inequalities*. Copenhagen: WHO Regional Office for Europe.

Guite HF, Clark C & Ackrill G (2006) The impact of the physical and urban environmental on mental well-being. *Public Health* **120** (12) 1117–1126.

Hastings G (2008) *Social Marketing: Why should the devil have all the best tunes?* Oxford: Elsevier.

Knifton L & Quinn N (2008) Media, mental health and discrimination: a frame of reference for understanding reporting trends. *International Journal of Mental Health Promotion* **10** (1) 23–31.

Marmot M (2010) *Fair Society, Healthy Lives: The Marmot Review – Strategic review of health inequalities in England post-2010* [online]. Available at: www.ucl.ac.uk/marmotreview (accessed July 2010).

McCormack J (2007) *Recovery and Strengths Based Practice. SRN discussion paper series*. Report no. 6. Glasgow: Scottish Recovery Network.

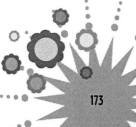

Mental Health Foundation (2002) In: *Psychiatry in the Elderly* (3rd ed). Oxford: Oxford Press.

Mental Health Foundation (2006) *Feeding Minds: The impact of food on mental health*. London: Mental Health Foundation.

Mental Welfare Commission, Scotland & Scottish Commission for the Regulation of Care (2009) *I'm Still Me*. Edinburgh: MWC.

Office of National Statistics (2009) *42nd Regional Report* [online]. Basingstoke: Palgrave Macmillan. Available at: http: www.statistics.gov.uk (accessed August 2010).

Quinn N, Shulman A, Knifton L & Byrne P (2010) The impact of a national mental health arts and film festival on stigma and discrimination. *Acta Psychiatrica Scandinavica* [online] June. Available at: http://onlinelibrary.wiley.com/doi/10.1111/j.1600-0447.2010.01573.x/abstract (accessed August 2010).

Raphael D, Steinmetz B, Renwick R, Rootman I, Brown I, Sehdev H, Phillips S & Smith T (1999) The community quality of life project: a health promotion approach to understanding communities. *Health Promotion Internations* **14** (3) 197–210.

Scottish Government (2007) *The Epidemiology of Suicide of Scotland 1989–2004: An examination of temporal trends and risk factors at national and local levels, part 4*. Edinburgh: Scottish Government.

Sherwood PR, Given CW, Given BA & von Eye A (2005) Caregiver burden and depressive symptoms: analysis of common outcomes in caregivers of elderly patients. *Journal of Aging and Health* **17** (2) 125–147.

Sigrist P (2010) *Old and Lonely: The growing specter of social isolation* [online]. Available at: http://sustainablecitiescollective.com. (accessed July 2010).

Swedish National Institute of Public Health (2006) *Healthy Ageing: a Challenge for Europe*. Östersund: Swedish National Institute of Public Health.

Swift J, Goodwin A & Clark D (2008) *Physical Activity and Mental Health: The role of physical activity in promoting mental well-being and preventing mental health problems*. Edinburgh: NHS Health Scotland.

State Journal-Register (2010) Citing: Quinn P. *Get Involved: Governor says older adults can enrich communities by volunteering* [online]. Available at: http://www.sj-r.com/seniors/x1409371056/Get-involved-Governor-says-older-adults-can-enrich-communities-by-volunteering.

WHO (2007) *Global Age-friendly Cities: A guide*. Geneva: WHO.

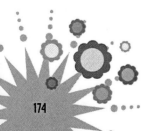

Chapter 11

Mental well-being and black and minority ethnic communities: conceptual and practical issues

Karen Newbigging and Manjit Bola

Introduction

Mental well-being is a multidimensional and complex concept and consequently there are many different and debated definitions. Mental well-being has both subjective and objective elements and it is self-evident that these will include individual, social and cultural aspects. This reflects variations in how people from different cultural backgrounds tend to think about themselves (Markus & Kitayama, 1991; Triandis, 1995), how they view their mental well-being, different views on life events and their use of strategies for maintaining positive mental health, including the value and priority accorded to seeking help or the importance placed on disclosing personal problems (Shek, 2004).

This chapter explores the concept of mental well-being from the perspective of black and minority ethnic (BME) communities, drawing on research recently

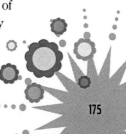

undertaken by the authors in Scotland. This leads to an exploration of the implications for practice in this area and in particular how to ensure that the mechanisms are in place to mainstream the understanding, strategies and related issues for BME communities at the beginning and throughout the process of policy and practice development. This is essential within a multicultural society, operating within a legislative framework promoting equalities.

Conceptualising mental well-being

Mental health is an ambiguous and potentially confusing term. It can be merely seen as a euphemism for mental illness as observed by Herron and Mortimer (1999), who identify two models for the relationship between positive mental health ie. mental well-being, and mental illness. The bipolar or single continuum model reflects the view that positive mental health exists at the opposing end of the same continuum from mental illness. The alternative model, the two or dual continua model, proposes that mental health consists of two dimensions; mental health problems or mental illness and mental well-being (Tudor, 1996), which has also been defined in terms of flourishing and languishing (Keyes, 2006). Separating the definition of mental well-being from mental illness means that it is possible to focus on strengths rather than deficiencies; capacity rather than loss and growth rather than remediation (Herron & Trent, 2000). The adoption of this second model of mental well-being ie. mental well-being as more than the absence of mental illness, is increasingly evident in government policies. It is encapsulated in the widely used definition from the World Health Organization, as a state 'in which the individual realises his or her own abilities, can cope with the normal stresses of life, can work productively and fruitfully, and is able to make a contribution to his or her community' (World Health Organisation, 2005, p12).

From a review of research on mental well-being, Ryan and Deci (2001) identify two broad traditions – hedonic well-being and eudaimonic well-being. Hedonic well-being is often used to refer to the subjective sense of well-being (SWB), notably happiness and life satisfaction. Eudaimonic well-being, often referred to as psychological well-being, relates to the realisation of human potential and includes meaning, self-realisation and functioning in life including personal evaluation of psychological well-being (Keyes, 2006). Although these two concepts overlap, they are derived from two distinct traditions, both arising from western philosophy – hedonism and eudaimonism. They differ fundamentally in terms of their views of what constitutes a good society and a good life, which has implications for the questions asked about how developmental and social processes relate to well-being (Ryan & Deci, 2001). Keyes *et al* (2002) suggest that both hedonic and eudaimonic traditions may reflect western, and possibly middle and upper-class definitions of what it means to live a full and satisfying life. They suggest that eastern perspectives may emphasise connection to others; meeting obligations and achieving fulfilment through carefully managed social ties.

Lay understandings of mental well-being are likely to differ from theoretical models in the way that the concept of mental well-being is expressed and will incorporate cultural beliefs and values. Similarly, the development and application of theoretical models to inform policy, practice and research endeavour will incorporate cultural assumptions about what it means to be mentally well and ideas about the self and personal identity. Ryff (1989), for example, has identified six aspects of functioning – autonomy, environmental mastery, personal growth, positive relations with others, purpose in life and self-acceptance and developed these into scales of psychological well-being. These scales have been predominantly tested on US populations. Keyes (2006) has commented on the relative lack of focus on the social dimensions within the eudaimonic tradition of research and thus proposes the concept of social well-being, with five dimensions:

▶ social coherence (whether a social life is seen as meaningful)

▶ social actualisation (whether society is seen as possessing potential for growth)

▶ social integration (a sense of belonging and acceptance by their communities)

▶ social acceptance (feel they accept other people)

▶ social contribution (sense of having something worthwhile to contribute).

(Keyes, 2006, p5)

Conceptualisations of mental well-being for Chinese and Pakistani communities

The meaning of mental well-being in different cultural contexts has been relatively unexplored (Cheng & Chan, 2005). This led NHS Scotland to commission the authors to undertake a scoping review of how Chinese and Pakistani

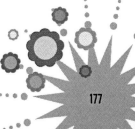

communities, which form the majority of Scotland's relatively small minority ethnic population, conceptualise mental well-being (Newbigging *et al*, 2008). The rationale was to identify the implications for strategies to promote positive mental health and well-being in these communities. The research involved:

1. reviewing the literature on mental well-being and Chinese and Pakistani communities from 1988–2008

2. interviews with 47 Chinese and South Asian community development workers working with Chinese and Pakistani communities in Scotland

3. an appraisal of the methods for undertaking research on mental well-being with Chinese and Pakistani communities.

The literature review identified a significant gap in research with little material from the UK that focused explicitly on lay conceptions of mental well-being for black and minority ethnic (BME) communities. A substantial number of studies were identified from China, reflecting the efforts of one researcher together with colleagues (eg. Shek, 1993, 1999, 2004, 2007; Shek & Chow, 2006). The studies involved cross-sectional surveys and there were few qualitative studies. Those that have used measures of mental well-being developed on Western populations are open to criticism for not taking into account the different nature of relationships, cultural values, philosophy and religion within Chinese communities. The relative absence of studies exploring lay concepts of mental well-being was notable, as was the scant literature relating to Pakistani communities. A few studies from non-UK English-speaking countries, pointed to the impact of migration, processes of acculturation and experiences within the host country on identity formation, as significant influences on how individuals and communities conceptualise mental well-being.

In addressing this research gap, our fieldwork revealed the diversity and rich cultural heritage for both communities, which have a profound influence on how mental well-being is conceptualised. It was evident that the term mental well-being was not familiar within Chinese and Pakistani communities and that the term 'mental' has negative connotations. Often it was only possible to get to a discussion of mental well-being through a discussion of mental illness or in Western terms for mental distress, notably stress or depression. Initially we thought this was because mental well-being was being framed in terms of the absence of mental illness, possibly because much of the previous engagement with these communities had been in relation to the discourse of mental illness. However, it became evident that the term did not facilitate an exploration of the concept. Particularly for some members of the Pakistani community where attempting to isolate the concept of mental well-being from other aspects of life, physical health, family, community and faith felt somewhat contrived and was not congruent with western concepts of well-being (Hussain, 2006).

> *'Mental well-being means different things to different people. The word mental is not very friendly. We never specifically think about well-being or mental health. The word isn't something which fits into [our] society.'*
> (Pakistani community worker)

For both Chinese and Pakistani communities the concept of mental well-being is embedded and integral to their lives. Often referred to as 'peace of mind', it reflects family, community, physical, material and spiritual well-being, with both communities placing a strong emphasis on family welfare and on role obligations. Relatedness, connectivity and social harmony thus emerged as central constructs.

> *'It's about balance isn't it when you talk about yin and yang and harmony. If there is harmony in the family then everyone wins. You are sharing the happiness. Conflicts are submerged. Families have to live together in harmony. In some ways I see goodness, mental health as good community well-being as a harmonious community and with that comes good health and prosperity.'*
> (Chinese community worker)

> *'So it's mindful peace. So rather than translating it into mental it would be better to say mind peace because it gives you a positive word compared to a negative one.'*
> (Pakistani community worker)

Philosophical and religious beliefs emerged as the most significant influences on conceptualisations of mental well-being from the literature review. This was particularly evident in the interviews with community workers within Pakistani communities, who indicated that Islam plays a central role in conceptualisations of mental well-being. This was found even for younger people who have received a Western education although the contribution of education to how mental well-being is understood was also recognised. Thus, mental well-being was described in terms of adherence to religious teachings with prayer as a central strategy for its maintenance. This was different for Chinese communities. While the academic literature emphasises the importance of philosophical and religious beliefs, particularly Confucianism and Taoism in Chinese conceptualisations of mental well-being, they were rarely directly referred to in the interviews

with Chinese community workers. There was an emphasis on hard work and material well-being, which may reflect the influence of Confucianism but arguably are likely to reflect the realities of life as an economic migrant. Christianity was identified as becoming increasingly important for some members of Chinese communities in Scotland. Religion and faith serve to shape beliefs about life's adversities and coping strategies that can be used. Further, they also provide access to social networks, which can serve to mobilise further support and resources for coping.

The interconnection with physical health was also a dominant theme and had a number of dimensions including: an integrated view of physical and mental well-being in contrast to western dualism; the visibility of physical health and the lack of understanding and stigma associated with emotional problems or mental illness. Age, generation, ethnic identity, cultural orientation and context were also identified as important. Conceptualisations of mental well-being may change over the life course and with the strength of ethnic identity and acculturation. Indeed there was the suggestion from both the literature review and the interviews that people may hold more than one frame of reference for conceptualising well-being ie. informed by both the majority and minority cultural beliefs.

Although there were similarities between the Chinese and Pakistani communities in terms of their conceptualisations of mental well-being, there were also important differences – for example, the framing of mental well-being within a religious discourse by workers with Pakistani communities and within a discourse of material and role obligations by workers with Chinese communities. While no direct comparisons could be drawn between Chinese and Pakistani communities and the majority community in Scotland, the literature review pointed to fundamental differences in the conceptualisations of mental well-being. In particular it was suggested that terms and concepts used in mental well-being research in the west may not be as relevant or have a profoundly different meaning in these communities.

For Chinese communities, the factors that were identified as having an impact on mental well-being included:

▶ the reasons for and experiences of migration

▶ family well-being, particularly that of children with reference to concepts of filial piety

▶ gender role expectations with a potentially negative impact for men

▶ language barriers and isolation for Chinese communities, who may find themselves part of a very small minority in Scotland's rural and dispersed communities.

The strategies mentioned by Chinese community workers to promote mental well-being included: education and mental health awareness raising; the importance of activities such as tai chi classes and opportunities to maintain ethnic identity and culture through the internet, Chinese TV and music channels.

For Pakistani communities, workers identified factors that impacted negatively on mental health as:

▶ gender role expectations in terms of family and community as having a potentially negative impact on women's mental well-being and associated with this was family living arrangements and isolation; this was particularly the case for first generation women where language serves as a barrier to integration

▶ generational issues, particularly for second and third generations and balancing community traditions and beliefs with western values was identified as impacting on well-being both for parents and children

▶ as with Chinese communities, the economic realities of meeting basic needs, socioeconomic status, and in addition, experiences of racism were identified as critical factors.

Religion, as previously discussed was identified as one of the main ways of maintaining mental well-being and helping to relieve pressure along with family and community support systems.

Strategies that community workers working within Pakistani communities had developed to strengthen mental well-being included building English language skills; raising awareness about the impact of poor mental well-being on family and children and developing methods to facilitate a dialogue around mental health issues to counter stigma and raise awareness.

Conceptual implications

The concept of mental well-being and the term mental clearly carries negative connotations for minority ethnic communities as is also evident for the majority community in Scotland (Pavis *et al*, 1996; Scott Porter, 2000). Our findings indicated the conceptualisation of mental well-being as positive well-being, happiness and peace of mind viewed by interviewees and within the literature reviews, as distinct and qualitatively different from the absence of mental illness. The study highlights the need for further primary research to explore in depth the meanings of mental well-being and the factors that influence this across different cultural groups and generations in the UK. It also points to the need to explore and find an appropriate vocabulary as the term mental well-being is too frequently interpreted in the discourse of mental illness.

Exploring the discourse about mental well-being within different communities raises the issue of not only differences in language but profound differences in relevant concepts. Kleinman (1977) used the term 'category fallacy' in relation to the application of western concepts of disease developed for a particular cultural group but applied to other cultural groups for whom they may lack coherence and where validity has not been established (Kleinman, 1987). Hussain and Cochrane (2004) argue that this concept is fundamental to understanding culturally different models of mental health/illness and that there is a problem in assuming that all concepts have relevance or are meaningful across all cultures.

There are two potential dangers in assuming conceptual equivalence across different cultural groups. First the assumption that the same term has the same meaning in different cultural contexts. The clearest example is the word happiness, used extensively as a lay concept and in research in the US, other English-speaking countries and China. However, the concept has profoundly different meanings in these different contexts. In the west, it is used to describe a state of well-being (positive affect and absence of negative affect) while it has a more profound meaning within Chinese communities (Ryan & Deci, 2001) and includes material abundance, physical health, virtuous and peaceful life and relief from death anxiety (Lu & Shih, 1997) as well as family welfare and social connections (Chan *et al*, 2007). The second danger is translating other cultural values or beliefs into western concepts and Shek (2004) warns against this in relation to the risk of translating Confucian values into western values of mastery and autonomy. Further work is clearly needed to explore meanings in different cultural contexts. It is also clear that there are multiple factors that shape individual conceptions of mental well-being and that individuals may be conversant with different models but have a preference for a particular one depending on the context. It is also important to understand that conceptualisations may change over the life course or reflect the strength of ethnic identity (British born Chinese for example).

The risks of assuming conceptual equivalence across cultures and the diversity of meaning of mental well-being both within and between different cultural groups pose a challenge to the universalist tradition. Several writers have also highlighted the differences between individualistic and collectivist cultures with Triandis (1995) describing three defining characteristics of collectivist cultures.

1. Definition of self in terms of the group as opposed to independence and autonomy.

2. A concern with the goals of the social group and enjoyment derived from doing what is right from the group perspective as opposed to the pursuit and achievement of individual goals.

3. Carrying out obligations and performing what is expected of them.

The implication of this is that narrow conceptualisations of mental well-being in terms of an individualistic self-concept, autonomy, mastery and individual achievement are problematic for a multicultural society (Lu, 2005). The collectivist self-concept and interdependent construction of mental well-being, ie. viewing the self in relation to others in family and community and the importance of social networks, has implications for promoting mental well-being and deserves further exploration. It suggests that mental well-being is maintained by having other things in place as opposed to action to be taken by the individual.

Practical implications for mental health promotion with BME communities

The conceptual issues highlighted above have a number of practical implications for policy, practice and research in relation to mental well-being within a multi-cultural society. There is current interest in developing policies that strengthen population mental well-being and it is evident that such initiatives need to be rooted in an inclusive and broad conception of mental well-being. This needs to include the dimensions of family well-being, faith and spiritual well-being, social role and standing, material well-being and the inter-dependence with physical well-being. The lack of research in this area means that there is a potential danger that western concepts and terms will be adopted uncritically, for example, in the operationalisation of concepts to derive positive measures of well-being, such as the Warwick-Edinburgh Mental Wellbeing Scale (NHS Health Scotland *et al*, 2006). The majority of the research that we identified was etic in its approach, ie. an outsider view in the positivist tradition that emphasises independence, objectivity and universalism. However, there is clearly a need for research that is emic in its approach, ie. an insider view, in the constructionist tradition that is qualitative and focuses on developing an understanding and meaning from the communities' perspective.

There has been significant progress in the last decade of developing methods for engaging with black and minority ethnic communities and other minority communities that will not only help in research but also facilitate local policy and practice development (Fountain *et al*, 2007). These methods, often referred to as 'community engagement', have the potential to develop new understandings and conversations about the issues that these communities face: the intra- and inter- group differences and how these may be incorporated within mainstream policies and practice. Community engagement methods are required that will help to build: a shared understanding; trust; and methods of co-production, and it has been suggested that this process of engagement in itself will serve to promote mental well-being within communities (Popay, 2006). Community engagement and associated participatory methods have traditionally focused on mental illness but have significant potential to enable local commissioners and providers in their work with communities, to enable them to develop strategies and interventions that truly improve the mental well-being of the whole population.

Conclusion

The approach to conceptualising mental well-being needs to be inclusive and encompass three critical dimensions – interconnection with physical health; interconnection with social and family well-being and interconnection with spiritual well-being. It is clear that similar terms lack conceptual equivalence and this must sound a warning for mental health improvement initiatives adopting and operationalising terms uncritically. This has implications for other groups where the dominant discourse may not fit, for example, lesbian, gay, bisexual and transgender people. This points to the need to ensure that there is engagement and exploration with diverse communities, in relation to the meanings that they attach to mental well-being and to the need to fully consider the implications for the development of strategies for maintaining mental well-being. Only when we are confident that this has been achieved can we make real progress in improving population mental health.

References

Chan N, Ho D, Ho W-L & Jung C (2007) *The Needs of Chinese Older People with Dementia and their Carers*. Manchester: Wai Yin Chinese Women Society.

Cheng S-T & Chan AC (2005) Measuring psychological wellbeing in the Chinese. *Personality and Individual Differences* **38** (6) 1316.

Fountain J, Patel K & Buffin J (2007) Community engagement: the Centre for Ethnicity and Health model. In: D Domenig *et al* (Eds) *Migration, Marginalisation and Access to Health and Social Services*. Amsterdam: Foundation Regenboog AMOC.

Herron S & Mortimer R (1999) Mental health: a contested concept. *International Journal of Mental Health Promotion* **1** (1) 4–8.

Herron S & Trent D (2000) Mental health: a secondary concept to mental illness. *International Journal of Mental Health Promotion* **2** (2) 29–38.

Hussain N (2006) Culturally determined care goals and the efficacy of statutory services. *International Journal of Qualitative Studies on Health and Wellbeing* **1** (3) 158.

Hussain F & Cochrane R (2004) Depression in south Asian women living in the UK: a review of the literature with implications for service provision. *Transcultural Psychiatry* **41** (2) 253–270.

Keyes C, Shmotkin D & Ryff C (2002) Optimizing wellbeing: the empirical encounter of two traditions. *Journal of Personality and Social Psychology* **82** 1007–1022.

Keyes C (2006) Subjective wellbeing in mental health and human research worldwide: an introduction. *Social Indicators Research* **77** 1–10.

Kleinman A (1977) Culture, depression and the 'new' cross-cultural psychiatry. *Social Science and Medicine* **11** (3) 11.

Kleinman A (1987) Anthropology and psychiatry: the role of culture in cross-cultural research on illness. *British Journal of Psychiatry* **151** (447) 454.

Lu L & Shih JB (1997) Sources of happiness: a qualitative approach. *Journal of Social Psychology* **137** (2) 188.

Lu L (2005) In pursuit of happiness: the cultural psychological study of SWB. *Chinese Journal of Psychology* **47** (2) 112.

Markus H & Kitayama S (1991) Culture and the self: implications for cognition, emotion and motivation. *Psychological Review* **98** 224–253.

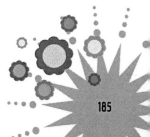

Newbigging K, Bola M & Shah A (2008) *Scoping exercise with black and minority ethnic groups on perceptions of mental wellbeing in Scotland* [online]. Scotland: NHS Scotland. Available at: http://www.healthscotland.com/uploads/documents/7977-RE026FinalReport0708.pdf (accessed August 2010).

NHS Health Scotland, University of Warwick & University of Edinburgh (2006) *The Warwick-Edinburgh Mental Well-being Scale* [online]. Available at: http://www.healthscotland.com/documents/1467.aspx. (accessed August 2010).

Pavis S, Masters H & Cunningha-Burley S (1996) *Lay Concepts of Positive Mental Health and How It Can Be Maintained*. Final report to the Health Education Board for Scotland. Edinburgh: HEBS.

Popay J (2006) *Community Engagement for Health Improvement: Questions of definition, outcomes and evaluation*. A background paper prepared for NICE by Professor Jennie Popay et al [online]. Available at: www.nice.org.uk/nicemedia/pdf/word/Community_Engagement_Scope_Final_Draft_14-3-06.doc (accessed August 2010).

Ryan RM & Deci EL (2001) On happiness and human potentials: a review of research on hedonic and eudaimonic wellbeing. *Annual Review of Psychology* **52** 141–166.

Ryff CD (1989) Happiness is everything, or is it? Explorations on the meaning of psychological wellbeing. *Journal of Personality and Social Psychology* **57** 1069–1081.

Scott Porter Research and Marketing Ltd (2000) *Pre-testing of Mental Health Week Materials: A qualitative research report*. Scotland: Health Education Board.

Shek DTL (1993) The Chinese version of the State-Trait Anxiety Inventory: its relationship to different measures of psychological well-being. *Journal of Clinical Psychology* **49** (3) 349–358.

Shek DTL (1999) Parenting characteristics and adolescent psychological well-being: a longitudinal study in a Chinese context. *Genetic, Social & General Psychology Monographs* **125** (1) 27–44.

Shek DTL (2004) Chinese cultural beliefs about adversity: its relationship to psychological well-being, school adjustment and problem behaviour in Hong Kong adolescents with and without economic disadvantage. *Childhood* **11** (1) 63–80.

Shek DTL (2007) After-school time and perceived parental control processes, parent-adolescent relational qualities, and psychological well-being in Chinese adolescents in Hong Kong. *Family Therapy* **34** (2) 126.

Shek DTL & Chow JT (2006) Development of a positive youth development program: promoting the mental health of stressful adolescents using principles of Problem Solving Therapy. *The Scientific World Journal* 6 397–405.

Triandis H (1995) *Individualism and Collectivism*. Oxford: Westview Press.

Tudor K (1996) *Mental Health Promotion: Paradigms and practice*. London: Routldege.

World Health Organization (2005) *Mental Health: Facing the challenges, building solutions*. Report from the WHO European Ministerial Conference. Copenhagen: WHO.

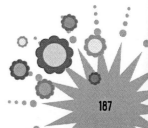

Chapter 12

Gender and mental health

Sarah Payne and Rachel Lart

Introduction

While both women and men may experience mental health problems at various points in their lives, there are important variations between them in relation to the risk of developing some conditions and in how these are treated. There are also differences in the age at which mental illness is more common. This chapter highlights the key variations between women and men in mental health and in their experiences of mental health services, and explores the implications of these for public health policy.

First, we need to clarify the meaning of 'sex' and 'gender'. The term sex is used to refer to the biological and physiological characteristics that define men and women, including not only reproductive differences but also hormonal and genetic factors. Evidence concerning the significance of biological factors for a wide range of health conditions including various mental health conditions has increased substantially in recent years (Wizeman & Pardue, 2001).

Gender refers to socially constructed differences between women and men: the roles, behaviours, activities and attributes that are seen as appropriate for men and women in a particular society. Gender impacts on health in various ways, including the expectations made of us, as men and women, the resources available to us, the health behaviours we adopt and also the ways in which health services are delivered and how well they meet our needs.

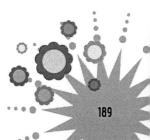

In terms of mental health, both sex and gender affect the risk of specific conditions, how well these are recognised by individuals, their family and friends and by health professionals, and how illness is treated. For example, various studies suggest that biological factors including male and female hormones play a part in depression for both men and women, although more research on this is needed (Payne, 2006; Joshi *et al*, 2010).

However, gender influences are also significant in mental health, affecting for example, exposure to risks such as poverty, discrimination, violence including gender-based violence, and stress, and also how men and women interpret symptoms of mental health problems and whether they seek help for such problems.

At both national and international levels increasing attention has been paid in recent decades to the question of gender inequalities and how to increase gender equity. Gender mainstreaming – the incorporation of a gender focus at all levels of policy making and practice – has been adopted and promoted by a number of international bodies, including the United Nations, the World Bank and the World Health Organization, as well the European Union (Payne & Doyal, 2010). Gender equality objectives have also been introduced by various countries including, for example, Australia, Canada and Sweden. In the UK the late 1990s and early part of the 21st century saw growing recognition of the importance of addressing gender in a range of policies and government departments. In 2006 the Equalities Act introduced a gender duty, which required all public sector organisations to address gender discrimination and promote gender equality in all their work. However, questions remain over whether the key differences between women and men in terms of their needs in relation to mental health services have been identified and addressed.

Overall, the prevalence of mental health problems is relatively similar for men and women. However, there are important variations in terms of both the specific condition, and also in relation to stages of the life course. While males outnumber females in figures for poor mental health in childhood, once adolescence is reached female prevalence is higher for many mental health conditions (Patel, 2005).

Depression and anxiety

Depression and anxiety are the most commonly experienced forms of mental ill-health, with around one in six people reporting such problems at any one time (McManus *et al*, 2009). Depression is around twice as common for women as men across the developed world, although the gap between women and men varies with a more marked female:male gender ratio in eastern Europe for example, compared with narrower differences in Nordic countries (Van de Velde *et al*, 2010). The degree of female over-representation and the variation in this between different countries suggests that while biology may play a part, gender is also significant. In England, figures from a community based study, the Adult Psychiatric Morbidity Survey (APMS), show that 11% of women and 7% of men were affected by mixed anxiety and depressive illnesses in 2007, with more women than men also reporting other forms of common mental disorder (McManus *et al*, 2009).

Psychoses

Psychotic illnesses including schizophrenia are less common and the figures for women and men are very similar worldwide (Bhugra, 2005). The APMS in England, for example, revealed an overall prevalence of psychotic disorder in the previous twelve months of 0.3% of men and 0.5% of women (McManus *et al*, 2009). Prevalence rates are higher for women and men in the age group 35–44, compared with other age groups and there is little difference between women and men (prevalence rate of 0.7% for men and 1.1% for women). However, among younger people, prevalence rates are greater for men, reflecting an earlier age of onset.

Alcohol use

Harmful and dependent use of alcohol is more common among men than among women, except among 16–24 year olds. Among 16–24 year olds, the figures for men and women identified as drinking in a hazardous or harmful way are not very different (Fuller *et al*, 2009a). However, among those 25 and over the gap widens. For dependent drinking, the pattern is similar, with one in eight men and one in 10 women aged 18–24 identified as having been drinking at a dependent level in the previous six months, while for older age groups the gap is larger with men outnumbering women overall by three to one. Interestingly, the prevalence of alcohol dependence has gone down slightly for men since the 2000 APMS, but has increased slightly for women in that time (Fuller *et al*, 2009a).

Drug use

Across Europe there are consistent patterns in terms of gender and illegal drug use. Men always report higher rates of illegal drug use, and within countries male to female ratios are consistently highest for more problematic drugs and patterns of use (EMCDDA, 2006). However, male to female ratios are lowest in those countries with the highest overall prevalence rates and longest history of high rates of use (EMCDDA, 2006), suggesting that as drug use becomes more widespread within a country, gender differences lessen. The UK has some of the highest prevalence rates in Europe for illegal drug use generally, and problem drug use in particular. There are just over 400,000 'problem' drug users in the UK as a whole, of whom three-quarters are men (UK Focal Point, 2008; Hay *et al*, 2008). However, data on use generally (that is, not just dependent or problem use) show a narrower gap between men and women: the Adult Psychiatric Morbidity Survey and the British Crime Survey (BCS), for example, both show that across all ages men are twice as likely to report having used an illegal drug in the last year (Hoare, 2009; Fuller *et al*, 2009b). The gap is even lower among younger groups, with around one in four men and one in five women aged 16–24 reporting use of any illegal drug in the last year (Hoare, 2009; Fuller *et al*, 2009b). Use of Class A drugs, however, remains twice as prevalent among men as women, even in that younger age group (Hoare, 2009). It is likely that this pattern reflects a higher likelihood that men who do use will go on to develop problem use. The ratio between men and women of all ages reporting any use has been fairly consistent since the BCS began in the mid-1990s, and the ratio among problem users has also remained stable over the period, suggesting that there is a genuine difference in the likelihood of young men and women users going on to develop problem or dependent use.

There has been a policy and a research focus on women drug users over the last two decades (Ettorre, 1992; Becker & Duffy, 2002; Klee *et al*, 2002; Best & Abdulrahim, 2005) but comparatively little on men's gender-specific needs. Young men in particular may be an important group to target. Some work theorising men's problem drug use suggests that issues of risk and risk taking need to be explored (Collison, 1996) to understand why men seem more likely than women to go on to develop problem drug use.

An increasingly well-recognised issue in mental health is that of co-morbidity or dual diagnosis of mental illness and substance misuse. Afuwape (2003), summarising several studies, suggests that between a quarter and a third of all users of mental health services have a current co-existing substance use problem. The National Treatment Outcome Research Study, a longitudinal study of drug users entering treatment in England, found that women were twice as likely as men to report symptoms of psychiatric disorders (Marsden *et al*, 2000), a pattern found in other studies of drug users from across Europe (Gilchrist, 2006).

Suicide and deliberate self-harm

Globally, suicide mortality is higher among men than women, although the gap between women and men varies. Male suicide mortality rates are particularly high in countries in eastern Europe – in Belarus, for example, the male rate is 63 per 100,000, while it is 54 per 100,000 in the Russian Federation and in Kazakhstan (WHO, 2010). Female suicide rates in these countries are lower, with five or six male suicides for every female suicide death.

There is only one country – China – where female suicide mortality is higher than that of men, although recent data is not available for all parts of China (WHO, 2010). Female rates are particularly marked in rural areas and some reports suggest that increasing male suicide associated with growing urbanisation will in the future narrow the gap between women and men (Yip & Liu, 2006).

In the UK, male suicide rates in 2008 were 18 per 100,000 population compared with five per 100,000 in women (Office for National Statistics, 2010). Suicide deaths have been falling for both men and women in recent years, although numbers went up slightly in 2008.

Deliberate self-harm (DSH) is more common among younger age groups, and in most countries DSH is higher among women than men (Skegg, 2005). Peak ages for DSH among men may be slightly lower than those of women (Wilkinson *et al*, 2002); and men are more likely than women to go on to completed suicide following an attempt (Skegg, 2005).

Figures for suicidal behaviour in Britain, taken from the APMS rather than data based on treatment, tend to confirm this gender difference in deliberate self-harm, with slightly more women (6%) than men (4%) reporting ever having attempted suicide (Nicholson *et al*, 2009). Women also appear to be slightly more likely to report ever having had suicidal thoughts (19% compared with 14%) (Nicholson *et al*, 2009).

Overall, then, both treatment data and figures taken from community surveys suggest differences in mental health between women and men, particularly in relation to depression and anxiety, which are reported by more women, and in relation to substance and alcohol misuse and suicide, which are more common among men. These differences have implications for mental health policy and the organisation and delivery of services, while also highlighting the question of the part played by gender stereotypes in relation to the identification of mental health problems.

Primary care services

For the majority of people experiencing symptoms of mental illness, the first point of contact with the health services is their primary physician, the general practitioner (GP). Various studies give us a picture of whether people with a common mental disorder consult their GP for this and whether there are gender differences in such consultation behaviour. Figures from the APMS suggest that most people with common mental disorders do not consult their GP (Deverill & King, 2009) while Bebbington *et al* (2000) suggest that more of those who do not consult are men.

Why might men not consult, and are there differences between the men who do, and those who do not, seek help for depression and anxiety? Increasingly, research on men, masculinity and depression suggests that male depression may be under-diagnosed for a variety of reasons. Gender stereotypes of masculinity as stoical and of depression as a female condition mean that men find it more difficult to seek help from health professionals, and more difficult to describe their distress (Emslie *et al*, 2007; Courtenay, 2000).

In addition, health professionals may fail to identify depression and anxiety among men when they do consult, partly because of gender stereotypes around candidacy for depression and anxiety, and partly because men suffering from mental health problems may 'self-medicate' with alcohol and other substances. This means that they are more likely to have their mental illness identified as substance misuse than as depression, and treated accordingly (Emslie *et al*, 2007). However, men and women also express their mental health problems in different ways: women with depression, for example, are more likely to show emotional distress and talk about sadness while men will more often act in ways that are aggressive and associated with bad temper and irritability (Kilmartin, 2005; Danielsson & Johansson, 2005) or react with overwork or risk-taking behaviour (Gadit, 2010). These differences have been described as 'acting in' depression by women, compared with 'acting out' by men (Rochlen *et al*, 2009). In addition, diagnostic criteria for depression reflect female ways of acting, including expression of emotion, fatigue, loss of pleasure in activities and depressed mood (Kilmartin, 2005) and as a result both community-based surveys based on clinical schedules and figures based on who is being treated identify female depression more readily than that experienced by men.

Research by Emslie *et al* (2007) also suggests that there are differences in what men and women seek from health care. In particular, their research suggests that men value health professionals who can help them talk about their depression and that they place more emphasis on practical results, while women are more likely to value listening skills in those they consult (Emslie *et al*, 2007).

Specialist mental health services

There are further differences between women and men in their use of specialist care, including both outpatient attendance and inpatient treatment. These differences reflect referral practices, health professionals' perceptions of need and gender stereotypes as well as severity of illness. Figures for access to all mental health services in England for 2008–09, for example, show a 19% higher use of all specialist mental health services by women than men, with the widest gap between women and men in the 75+ age group (NHS Information Centre, 2009b).

With hospital treatment, overall figures for men and women are similar, with men accounting for just over half of all inpatient episodes for mental illness (Hospital Episode Statistics, 2009). However, male admissions outnumber female admissions among those aged 18–64 while there are more female admissions among those over 65 (NHS Information Centre, 2009b).

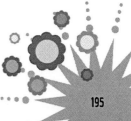

There are further differences in relation to diagnosis. More men than women are admitted to hospital for substance misuse, where men make up nearly three-quarters of those treated, and schizophrenia where men are two-thirds of those admitted to hospital (Hospital Episode Statistics, 2009). Alongside gender differences in treatment in primary care, more women than men are admitted to hospital for depression, particularly recurrent depressive disorder and anxiety and more women are also admitted for bipolar disorders. Women also make up 90% of those treated in hospital for eating disorders (Hospital Episode Statistics, 2009).

Around a third of all inpatient admissions are compulsory, and men are slightly more likely than women to be detained or sectioned as civil patients under mental health legislation. For example, in 2008–09 males made up 54% of those formally admitted to NHS facilities and 67% of those formally admitted to independent facilities (NHS Information Centre, 2009a). The gender imbalance is much larger for those admitted under the criminal justice related sections of mental health legislation; in 2008–09 men made up 90% of those admitted to psychiatric hospital as a court or prison disposal (NHS Information Centre, 2009a). However, this is broadly in line with receptions into prison, of which women make up about one in ten (Ministry of Justice, 2010). Not all patients in secure psychiatric services have been admitted through the criminal justice system, and overall, women in those services are more likely than men to have been admitted from other psychiatric services rather than through the courts or from prison (Lart *et al*,1999).

There are a number of issues in relation to inpatient treatment for men and women. For men, there are important questions over whether they are more readily admitted, due to fears on the part of health professionals over the risk they pose to themselves or others, especially when diagnosed with psychotic illnesses (Payne, 1996). The availability of inpatient beds has greatly reduced in recent years for a number of reasons, including the perceived advantages of outpatient care and the high cost of inpatient care (Priebe *et al*, 2005). The proportion of patients who are male has increased alongside the reduction of inpatient beds. In contrast, in secure services, where the number of beds has risen over the last 20 years, the proportion of men and women has remained the same (Rutherford & Duggan, 2007).

This raises various important questions about whether either men or women are being offered the treatment they need when experiencing more severe mental illness. The reduction within inpatient places has meant that those who are treated in hospital have more serious illness, but it also reflects perceptions that some forms of illness, typically those experienced more often by women and some people, present less of a threat and are more readily treated in the community (Payne, 1996; 1999). In addition, and as a consequence of these shifts in the patient population, the nature of inpatient experience has also changed, and this increases the urgency of addressing gender specific needs.

Both women and men report concerns about safety as inpatients in psychiatric treatment, and both report anxiety when psychiatric wards have more men than women. A high proportion of women with mental health difficulties have experienced gender-based violence, including physical and sexual abuse (Department of Health, 2002b), and as a result many women feel very vulnerable in mixed-sex facilities. Despite policy commitments to eradicate mixed-sex sleeping accommodation, a recent report in the UK found that three-quarters of women within inpatient psychiatric treatment were being treated on mixed-sex wards (Care Quality Commission, 2010). While some of this accommodation may include private bedrooms and bathrooms for individual patients, women still feel unsafe in such an environment where communal space is shared and there are no locks on bedroom doors.

In addition to inpatient treatment, the 2007 Mental Health Act introduced Supervised Community Treatment in England and again there are important gender patterns in how these are being used. Initial figures, for example, report that two-thirds of those on Supervised Community Treatment in March 2009 were male (NHS Information Centre, 2009a).

Specialist community mental health services also show variations between women and men in terms of who is treated, and how well it meets their needs. In 2007–08, for example, women made up 56% of those who received specialist treatment from ambulatory services, including hospital outpatient care and community care (NHS Information Centre, 2009b). Women and men each represent around half of all attendances for hospital outpatient mental health care (Hospital Episode Statistics, 2009), but there are some variations in the kinds of services they receive. For example, women receive more outpatient psychotherapy than men and men may be missing out on some forms of treatment.

Women and men can also have different needs in relation to community and outpatient services with regard to practical issues around childcare, for example, as well as concerns over safety.

Alcohol and drug misuse services and gender

Men account for over two-thirds (71%) of all inpatient episodes for mental and behavioural disorders resulting from drug and alcohol use (Hospital Episode Statistics, 2009) broadly reflecting the rates for harmful and dependent drinking and problem drug use discussed earlier. The vast majority of these episodes are emergency admissions as a consequence of alcohol use.

A survey of alcohol agencies in England suggested that only one in 20 people in need of specialist alcohol treatment uses it. However, within this, women in need of treatment were more likely to access it than men (Department of Health, 2005). Women identified as alcohol dependent in the APMS were nearly three times more likely than men to be currently receiving treatment for a mental or emotional disorder (Fuller *et al*, 2009a).

Turning to the drug treatment services, there are much better routinely collected data on use of services because of the National Drug Treatment Monitoring System (NDTMS). Overall, men account for three-quarters of all people in services in England. However, among younger (18–24) people, this falls to just under two-thirds (National Drug Evidence Centre, 2010). In Scotland, the overall ratio is slightly lower at nearly two and a half to one, falling to two to one in those under 20 (NHS Scotland ISD, 2010). The overall proportion of men to women in treatment has led to concerns that women were under-represented and that treatment services were not meeting their specific needs. The picture is probably more complex than this. What these figures suggest is that women do have proportionately equal or better access to both drug and alcohol services than men. Detailed analysis of the drug treatment figures shows that overall, women present for treatment earlier in their drug using career, engage better and are more likely to have positive results (National Treatment Agency, 2010). However, for both men and women there remain specific issues that need to be looked at through a gendered lens. For women many of these have been identified; childcare arrangements, for example, but also to do with the nature of services. Less work has been done on the gender specific needs of men in drug and alcohol treatment services.

Gender, mental health and the criminal justice system

A particularly important aspect of gender differences in mental health is the mental health of prisoners. Among the prison population, both men and women exhibit much higher levels of all mental health problems than in the general population. This pattern is found in most prison populations globally (Fazel & Danesh, 2002). The most detailed study of the mental health of the prison population of England and Wales is that undertaken by Singleton *et al* (1998), which included clinical assessment. This study found that for all psychotic and neurotic disorders and for self-harm, suicide attempts and suicidal thoughts, rates were higher for women prisoners than for men. Women prisoners also reported higher rates of drug use in the year before prison, especially of crack cocaine and opiates. The exception to this pattern was alcohol use; men were more likely to report harmful or hazardous drinking in the previous year.

There is good evidence that women offenders have particularly high levels of psychological need and that these needs are often linked to histories of physical and sexual abuse as both adults and children (HMIP, 2007; Lart *et al*, 1999; Byrne & Howells, 2002; Bartlett, 2003). However, while recognising the acute and complex needs of many, if not most, women in the prison system, it is also important to bear in mind the high levels of mental health needs among men. The number of women in prison is very small compared to that of men, under 5,000 compared to more than 80,000. If we imagine mental health needs as a pyramid, with levels of severity and complexity increasing further up the pyramid, the gender differences in mental health needs within the prison population as a whole may well be partly explained by the relative sizes of the prison populations. For men in prison, the issues relating to mental health we discussed earlier for the population as a whole are concentrated and made more acute by the prison setting.

Gender in mental health policy

Although there are important differences between women and men in terms of their risks of mental health difficulties and their experiences of treatment, these are complex. It seems likely that men's depression in particular is under-diagnosed and under-treated, and that this reflects gender differences in how depression is experienced and expressed, differences in health professionals' beliefs about 'candidacy' for depression and also differences in the degree of stigma attaching to depression for men. Male suicide rates in particular may reflect this failure to treat men for their depression.

Equally, men are more likely to experience disorders relating to drug and alcohol misuse while women are more likely to seek and access treatment for these disorders. Again this is partly explained by gender stereotypes as well as variations in behaviour. Men are slightly more likely than women to be treated in hospital, particularly in younger age groups, are more likely to be detained under mental health legislation, and more men are now being treated compulsorily in the community.

For women, there are similar problems reflecting gender stereotypes. Women's distress is more likely to be diagnosed as depression, and treated in the community, which may mean they are less able to access and benefit from inpatient treatment. Or this may mean that women's difficult lives are more likely to be pathologised. In addition, the way in which specialist mental health services are delivered – particularly the use of mixed sex accommodation and day services – means that women are likely to feel unsafe and insecure, adding to their distress.

So how well does mental health policy address these gender differences? In England and Wales a Women's Mental Health Strategy was introduced in 2002 (Department of Health, 2002b). The strategy outlined specific considerations that policy-makers and health professionals needed to consider in relation to women with mental health problems, including the need for women to be involved in service planning, delivery and evaluation, the need for single-sex facilities and for female-only crisis centres.

In spite of this, there is as yet no equivalent 'men's mental health strategy'. The National Suicide Prevention Strategy for England (Department of Health, 2002a) identified young men as a high-risk group. The strategy established a pilot project addressing mental health promotion for younger men and aimed to improve the clinical management of young men with alcohol and substance misuse, in recognition of their increased risk of suicide and deliberate self-harm. However, the Alcohol Harm Reduction Strategy does not specifically address the needs of either men or women (Prime Minister's Strategy Unit, 2004).

Following the 2006 Equalities Act all public sector organisations, including both NHS facilities and treatment and independent facilities receiving public sector funding, are required to eliminate gender discrimination and promote gender equality. The gender equality duty does not prohibit single sex services, and psychiatric institutions and other facilities are highlighted by the Department of Health as organisations where such services would be seen as appropriate and acceptable (Department of Health, 2007).

Conclusion

In recent years mental health policy in the UK has largely addressed gender specific issues in relation to women, through the Women's Mental Health Strategy. Through this strategy, efforts have been made to gender mainstream the commissioning of mental health services, although some problems still remain. However, men's specific needs have been less well recognised, despite the Equalities Act (2006), which requires the health sector to address gender inequalities. Less attention has been paid, in research terms, to how we might deliver gender sensitive and gender appropriate mental health care and support services for both men and women who experience mental health problems. However, if gender inequalities in mental health are to be addressed there needs to be investment in research that looks further 'upstream' at prevention strategies. Much is known about gender differences in relation to experiencing and reporting mental health problems, however, there remains a need to understand how best to develop prevention strategies that are gender sensitive and gender appropriate. Likewise, research is required that allows us to fully understand how we promote positive mental health for both men and for women across society. Overall, public mental health policy needs to consider how we address the gender inequalities in society that affect mental health, in addition to developing mental health improvement policies that address risk and protective factors within a gender context.

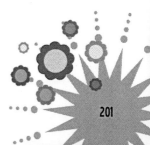

References

Afuwape S (2003) *Where Are We With Dual Diagnosis? A review of the literature*. London: Rethink.

Bartlett A (2003) *Expert Paper on Social Division and Difference: Women*. Liverpool: NHS Programme on Forensic Mental Health Research and Development.

Bebbington P, Meltzer H, Brugha TS, Farrell M, Jenkins R, Ceresa C *et al* (2000) Unequal access and unmet need: neurotic disorders and the use of primary care services. *Psychological Medicine* **30** 1359–1367.

Becker J & Duffy C (2002) *Women Drug Users and Drugs Service Provision: Service-level responses to engagement and retention*. London: Home Office.

Best D & Abdulrahim D (2005) *Women in Drug Treatment Services*. London: National Treatment Agency.

Bhugra D (2005) The global prevalence of schizophrenia. *Public Library of Science Medicine* **2** (5) 151.

Byrne MK & Howells K (2002) The psychological needs of women prisoners: implications for rehabilitation and management. *Psychiatry, Psychology and Law* **9** (1) 34–43.

Care Quality Commission (2010) *Count Me In Census 2009*. London: Care Quality Commission.

Collison M (1996) In search of the high life. Drugs, crime, masculinities and consumption. *British Journal of Criminology* **36** (3) 428–444.

Courtenay WH (2000) Constructions of masculinity and their influence on men's well-being: a theory of gender and health. *Social Science and Medicine* **50** (10) 1385–1401.

Danielsson U & Johansson EE (2005) Beyond weeping and crying: a gender analysis of expressions of depression. *Scandinavian Journal of Primary Health Care* **23** 171–177.

Department of Health (2002a) *National Suicide Prevention Strategy for England*. London: DH.

Department of Health (2002b) *Women's Mental Health: Into the mainstream. Strategic development of mental health care for women*. London: DH.

Department of Health (2005) *Alcohol Needs Assessment Project (ANARP)* London: DH.

Department of Health (2007) *Creating a Gender Equality Scheme: A practical guide for the NHS*. London: DH.

Deverill C & King M (2009) Common Mental Disorders. In: S McManus, H Meltzer, T Brugha, P Bebbington & R Jenkins (Eds) *Adult Psychiatric Morbidity in England, 2007: Results of a household survey*. London: NHS Information Centre.

EMCDDA (2006) *A Gender Perspective on Drug Use and Responding to Drug Problems: Annual Report 2006*. London: EMCDDA.

Emslie C, Ridge D, Ziebland S & Hunt K (2007) Exploring men's and women's experiences of depression and engagement with health professionals: more similarities than differences? A qualitative interview study. *BMC Family Practice* **8** 43.

Ettorre E (1992) *Women and Substance Use*. Basingstoke: Macmillan.

Fazel S & Danesh J (2002) Serious mental disorder in 23,000 prisoners: a systematic review of 62 surveys. *Lancet* **359** 545–550.

Fuller E, Jotangia D & Farrell M (2009a) Alcohol misuse and dependence. In: S McManus, H Meltzer, T Brugha, P Bebbington & R Jenkins (Eds) *Adult Psychiatric Morbidity in England, 2007: Results of a household survey*. London: NHS Information Centre.

Fuller E, Jotangia D & Farrell M (2009b) Drug misuse and dependence. In: S McManus, H Meltzer, T Brugha, P Bebbington & R Jenkins (Eds) *Adult Psychiatric Morbidity in England, 2007: Results of a household survey*. London: NHS Information Centre.

Gadit A (2010) Depression in males: is this matter more serious? *Journal of Pakistan Medical Association* **60** (6) 504–505.

Gilchrist GP (2006) Gender differences in the prevalence of psychiatric morbidity among opiate users: a European perspective. In: A Baldacchino & J Corkery (Eds) *Comorbidity: Perspectives across Europe*. London: European Collaborating Centres in Addiction Studies.

Hay G, Gannon M, MacDougall J, Millar T, Williams K, Eastwood C & McKeganey N (2008) *National and Regional Estimates of the Prevalence of Opiate Use and/or Crack Cocaine Use 2006/7: A summary of key findings. Home Office Research Report 9*. London: Home Office.

HMIP (2007) *The Mental Health of Prisoners: A thematic review of the care and support of prisoners with mental health needs*. London: HM Inspectorate of Prisons.

Hoare J (2009) *Drug Misuse Declared: Findings from the 2008/09 British Crime Survey*. London: Home Office Statistics.

Hospital Episode Statistics (2009) *Hospital Episode Statistics* [online]. Available at: http://www.hesonline.nhs.uk/Ease/servlet/ContentServer?siteID= 1937&categoryID=203 (accessed 5th July 2010).

Joshi D, van Schoor NM, De Ronder W, Schaap LA & Cornijs HC (2010) Low free testosterone levels are associated with prevalence and incidence of depressive symptoms in older men. *Clinical Endocrinology* **72** 232–240.

Kilmartin C (2005) Depression in men: communication, diagnosis and therapy. *Journal of Men's Health and Gender* **2** (1) 95–99.

Klee H, Jackson M & Lewis S (Eds) (2002) *Drug Misuse and Motherhood*. London: Routledge.

Lart R, Payne S, MacDonald G, Beaumont B & Mistry T (1999) *Women and Secure Psychiatric Services: A literature review*. York: NHS Centre for Reviews and Dissemination.

Marsden J, Gossop M, Stewart D, Rolfe A & Farrell M (2000) Psychiatric symptoms among clients seeking treatment for drug dependence. Intake data from the National Treatment Outcomes Research Study. *British Journal of Psychiatry* **177** 285–259.

McManus S, Meltzer H, Brugha T, Bebbington P & Jenkins R (2009) *Adult Psychiatric Morbidity in England, 2007: Results of a household survey*. London: NHS Information Centre.

Ministry of Justice (2010) *Statistics on Women and the Criminal Justice System*. London: Ministry of Justice.

National Drug Evidence Centre (2010) *Statistics from the National Drug Treatment Monitoring System(NDTMS)1 April 2008–31March 2009*. Manchester: National Drug Evidence Centre.

NHS Information Centre (2009a) *In-patients Formally Detained in Hospital Under the Mental health Act 1983 and Patients Subject to Supervised Community Treatment: 1998–99 to 2008–09*. London: NHS Information Centre.

NHS Information Centre (2009b) *Mental Health Bulletin: Third report from Mental Health Minimum Dataset (MHMDS) annual returns, 2004–2009*. London: NHS Information Centre.

NHS Scotland ISD (2010) *Drug Misuse Statistics Scotland 2009*. Edinburgh: Information Services Division.

Nicholson S, Jenkins R & Meltzer H (2009) Suicidal thoughts, suicide attempts and self-harm. In: S McManus, H Meltzer, T Brugha, P Bebbington & R Jenkins (Eds) *Adult Psychiatric Morbidity in England, 2007: Results of a household survey*. London: NHS Information Centre.

National Treatment Agency (2010) *Women in Drug Treatment: What the latest figures reveal*. London: NTA.

Office for National Statistics (2010) *Statistical Bulletin: Suicide rates in the United Kingdom 1991–2008*. London: ONS.

Patel V (2005) *Gender in Mental Health Research*. Geneva: WHO.

Payne S (1996) Psychiatric care in the community: does it fail young men? *Policy and Politics* **24** (2) 193–205.

Payne S (1999) Outside the walls of the asylum? Psychiatric treatment in the 1980s and 1990s. In: P Bartlett & D Wright (Eds). *Outside the Walls of the Asylum: The history of care in the community 1750–2000*. London: Athlone Press.

Payne S (2006) *The Health of Men and Women*. Cambridge: Polity.

Payne S & Doyal L (2010) Revisiting gender justice in health and social care. In: E Kuhlmann & E Annandale (Eds). *Handbook on Gender and Healthcare*. London: Palgrave Macmillan.

Priebe S, Badesconyi A, Fioritti A, Hansson L, Kilian R, Torres-Gonzales F *et al* (2005) Reinstitutionalisation in mental health care: comparison of data on service provision from six European countries. *British Medical Journal* **330** 123–126.

Prime Minister's Strategy Unit (2004) *Alcohol Harm Reduction Strategy for England*. London: Cabinet Office.

Rochlen A, Paterniti D, Epsteain R, Duberstein P, Willeford L & Kravitz R (2009) Barriers in diagnosing and treating men with depression: A focus group report. *American Journal of Men's Health,* on-line advance publication.

Rutherford M & Duggan S (2007) *Forensic Mental Health Services: Facts and figures on current provision* [online]. London: The Sainsbury Centre for Mental Health. Available at: https://www.centreformentalhealth.org.uk/publications (accessed August 2010).

Singleton N, Melzer H, Gatward R, Coid J & Deasy D (1998) *Psychiatric Morbidity among prisoners in England and Wales*. London: The Stationery Office.

Skegg K (2005) Self-harm. *Lancet* **366** 1471–1483.

UK Focal Point (2008) *2008 National Report to the EMCDDA: United Kingdom New Developments, Trends and In-depth Information on Selected Issues*. London: EMCDDA.

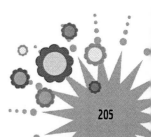

Van de Velde S, Bracke P & Levecque K (2010) Gender differences in depression in 23 European countries. Cross-national variation in the gender gap in depression. *Social Science and Medicine* **71** (313) 3–5.

Wilkinson P, Taylor G, Templeton L, Mistral W, Salter E & Bennett P (2002) Admissions to hospital for deliberate self-harm in England 1995–2000: an analysis of Hospital Episode Statistics. *Journal of Public Health Medicine* **24** (3) 179–183.

Wizeman T & Pardue M (2001) *Exploring the Biological Contributions to Human Health: Does sex matter?* Washington DC: National Academy Press.

World Health Organization (2010) *Suicide rates per 100,000 by country, year and sex* [online]. Available at: http://www.who.int/mental_health/prevention/suicide_rates/en/print.html (accessed 5th July 2010).

Yip PSF & Liu KY (2006) The ecological fallacy and the gender ratio of suicide in China. *British Journal of Psychiatry* **189** 465–466.

Chapter 13

Improving public mental health: the role of people with a psychiatric diagnosis

David Crepaz-Keay

Introduction

Public mental health and mental health promotion have moved from the most remote of margins to the centre of evidence-based approaches in a relatively short period of time. Concepts like health, well-being, mental capital and even happiness form part of the professional lexicon. But what, in this brave new world, is the place of 'mad' people, 'the mentally ill', people with a psychiatric diagnosis?

Why 'people with a psychiatric diagnosis'?

Language in the world of mental health is never straightforward and this chapter (and indeed, this book) will use a range of terms. Issues in mental health promotion are inextricably linked with discrimination and stigma, and these require a marker. A psychiatric diagnosis provides such a marker, regardless of whether it is accurate, agreed or accepted by the person diagnosed. Life is different for people with a psychiatric diagnosis.

Why do diagnosis and/or personal experience of mental ill-health matter

Public mental health is no longer focused on illness prevention and has a strong emphasis on population and community based interventions rather than concentrating on individuals. This chapter explains why, even in this context, it is important to engage, involve and indeed devolve to people with psychiatric diagnoses. This chapter will outline some of the roles in promoting mental health and preventing mental ill-health that are best done by, or with people with direct personal experience of mental ill-health. It is important to remember that a significant proportion of people have experienced mental ill-health and so any population based approach will need to consider ways to make sure they are included.

Mental and physical health and illness

We are now used to the notion that mental health is not the same thing as the absence of mental illness. This should not, however, allow us to ignore the fact that people with a psychiatric diagnosis are much less likely to be healthy, and mentally healthy (McManus *et al*, 2009). They die younger (Phelan *et al*, 2001), are more likely to be poorer, less likely to be in a relationship (Thornicroft, 2006) and more likely to be out of work (Crowther *et al*, 2001). The Marmot Review (Marmot, 2010) uses the relationship between a variety of socioeconomic factors and both life expectancy and disability free life expectancy to analyse a range of determinants of public health. This relationship is termed the social gradient in health, and the report identified that:

> 'Mental health is very closely related to many forms of inequality. The social gradient is particularly pronounced for severe mental illness. For example, in the case of psychotic disorders the prevalence among the lowest quintile of household income is nine times higher than in the highest. While the particularly high rate of psychotic disorder in the lowest quintile may, to some extent, result from downward social drift, this is unlikely to account for the social gradient. In particular, the social gradient is also evident for common mental health problems, with a two-fold variation between the highest and lowest quintiles.'
> (Marmot, 2010)

In short, the proportion of people with severe mental ill-health who account for the poorest 20% of the population is nine times the size of the proportion in the wealthiest 20% (or twice the size for mental ill-health as a whole) and this discrepancy is primarily about poorer people being more likely to have severe mental ill-health but that mental ill-health itself may lead to poverty. The relationship between mental ill-health and inequality is not limited to poverty. Opportunities to improve mental health and increase resilience may well be less accessible to people with a psychiatric diagnosis (Friedli, 2009).

Discrimination

Discrimination has a number of potential impacts on health and mental health. It affects people's home life, relationships and working life (Thornicroft, 2006). Discrimination in employment has contributed to higher levels of unemployment amongst people with a psychiatric diagnosis. Discrimination has a direct effect on people's willingness to seek help (Schomerus et al, 2009; Zartaloudi & Madianos, 2010). Though there is a significant number of countries that have national anti-discrimination or anti-stigma programmes, the majority have not been evaluated (WHO, 2008); service user involvement is one of the few approaches that is known to work (Thornicroft, 2006). It is also possible that self-management and peer support will help challenge discrimination by providing opportunities for people to use their experience of managing their own mental ill-health as a mechanism for demonstrating their capabilities rather than 'disabilities'.

Consequences of treatment

People with diagnoses such as schizophrenia and bipolar disorder tend to be on prescribed medication that, while offering some therapeutic benefit, also carries risks to physical and mental health and well-being (Hamer & Haddad, 2007). The term 'side effects' tends to marginalise the negative impacts, but they can be central to an individual's experience. Common effects include weight gain, cardiovascular problems, kidney problems, photo-sensitivity and motor dysfunction (see any psychiatric treatment data sheet, British National Formulary or similar). There is also evidence that there is a significant difference between the way we measure quality of life when evaluating initiatives that does not correlate well with how individuals perceive their experience. This suggests that we need to find new ways of measuring the negative impact of psychiatric treatment to ensure that research reflects impact as felt by the people receiving treatment (Bebbington *et al*, 2009).

Lifestyle and behaviour

People with a psychiatric diagnosis appear to be more likely to have unhealthy lifestyles, particularly with regard to diet and exercise, and alcohol, smoking and illicit substances use (Brown *et al*, 1999; McCreadie *et al*, 1998). There is also evidence that, for people living with mental ill-health, behavioural interventions offer only modest gains that diminish over time, and that to have a sustained impact, interventions need to have a longer-term component (Kemp *et al*, 2009).

Who defines illness, health and recovery?

The notion of recovery has been part of statutory mental health services in the UK and in a number of other countries for some time. Definitions vary, although one example is the Scottish Recovery Network's definition developed from their narrative research study:

> *'Recovery is being able to live a meaningful and satisfying life, as*
> *defined by each person, in the presence or absence of symptoms.*
> *It is about having control over and input into your own life. Each*
> *individual's recovery, like his or her experience of the mental health*
> *problems or illness, is a unique and deeply personal process.'*
> (Scottish Recovery Network, 2007)

For other information on recovery see Scottish Recovery Network's website. Though the concept of recovery was initially favourably received by many people with a psychiatric diagnosis as a way of shifting control from a purely medical approach to a more holistic view, there are some concerns that recovery has been professionalised and others worry that recovery has become a 'brand' and that simply relabelling services as 'recovery orientated' makes little difference.

A more important controversy in 'recovery' reduces down to who defines recovery ie. whether recovery is defined by professionals (clinicians decide when people have recovered), work/benefit status (recovery means getting back to work) or by individuals themselves (see Jenkins *et al*, 2007; Pilgrim, 2008; Lal, 2010) for a sample of the discussions. This is hardly new territory – many of the criticisms of psychiatry and mental health services over the years have been about how mental illness or 'madness' is defined, and who owns the definitions. Neither public mental health, nor mental ill-health prevention are immune from such criticisms. When the focus is on either illness (or relapse) prevention or improving the mental health of people with a psychiatric diagnosis, then there is a need to empower people to take control of their own lives.

Self-management

Self-management is about putting patients (or, in mental ill-health, people with a psychiatric diagnosis) in direct control of the management of their condition. There are a number of approaches to self-management but they tend to focus on one or more of the following: problem solving; goal setting; identifying triggers and indicators of deteriorating health; and people responding to those for themselves before relying on clinician led intervention. The common theme is a structured approach that develops over time and is informed by people's experience. This approach is built around the principle of the patient taking more control over identifying changes and in turn their initial response to these. Peer support builds on this approach by encouraging group work and mutual support that enables people to draw on each other's experiences.

Self-management has been developed as an approach for a range of long-term medical conditions. The Stanford Patient Education Research Center has developed a wide range of evidence-based interventions for a spectrum of long-term health conditions (see http://med.stanford.edu/patienteducation/). These programmes have been widely adopted and include work in Spain and the UK, however, these are focused on physical ill-health rather than mental ill-health. Self-management as an approach has been much less widely used in mental ill-health, although there are some examples. The development of psychoeducation for bipolar disorder (formerly manic depression) has been developed by Bipolar Disorders Program, IDIBAPS, Hospital Clinic, Barcelona (Colom & Vieta, 2004) and is designed to help people understand and manage their own mental ill-heath more effectively. This programme has been designed by and is delivered by clinicians. MDF the BiPolar Organisation has been running self-management training for people with bipolar disorder since 1998. The MDF course differs in that it was developed by and is delivered by people with a diagnosis of bipolar disorder and although it is well regarded by people who have experienced the training it has not to date been formally evaluated.

In 2009, the Mental Health Foundation launched a self-management training intervention in Wales. This training was developed and is being delivered by people with a range of psychiatric diagnoses (typically schizophrenia, personality disorders, bipolar disorder or severe long-term depression) but the training is more life skills than condition management orientated; this programme will be subject to long-term evaluation as the programme proceeds. Goal setting and problem solving lie at the heart of the approach we have chosen and by the end of the project (circa 2012) the Mental Health Foundation (in partnership with MDF, the BiPolar Organisation) will have developed around 60 peer support groups across Wales supporting more than 700 people. These people will have defined their own goals and will be supporting each other in trying to achieve them. An early analysis of goals set shows increasing exercise, weight loss and smoking cessation as among the most important. These are all consistent with health and mental health promotion goals and help to support the idea that involving people with psychiatric diagnoses supports, rather than disrupts promotion.

Conclusion

A clear divide was once made between the worlds of mental illness and mental health promotion. In the former, after years of campaigning and hard graft, service user involvement is now firmly established as an essential element; in the latter, service user involvement was seen as unnecessary as everyone is a member of the public. Neither the simple distinction, nor the clumsy conclusion stands up to today's scrutiny. Mental health promotion professionals and indeed, all those interested in effective health promotion, should understand that people with a psychiatric diagnosis face some of the most significant public health risks and are often last to have their mental health needs recognised and met. Community involvement is now accepted as an essential part of any health promotion agenda; practice will improve significantly when involving people with a psychiatric diagnosis attains the same status. Those who are interested in increasing involvement will find many willing and able service user groups who would be delighted to put talk of illness, diagnosis and treatment to one side and put promoting health and mental health centre stage.

References

Bebbington PE, Angermeyer M, Azorin JM, Marwaha S, Marteau F & Toumi M (2009) Side-effects of antipsychotic medication and health-related quality of life in schizophrenia. *Acta Psychiatrica Scandinavica* **119** (438) 22–28.

Brown S, Birtwistle J, Roe L & Thompson C (1999) The unhealthy lifestyle of people with schizophrenia. *Psychological Medicine* **29** (3) 697–701.

Colom F & Vieta E (2004) Improving the outcome of bipolar disorder through non-pharmacological strategies: the role of psychoeducation. *Revista Brasileira Psiquiatria* **26** (Supl III) 47–50.

Crowther RE, Marshall M, Bond GR & Huxley P (2001) Helping people with severe mental illness to obtain work: a systematic review. *British Medical Journal* **322** 204–208.

Davidson L, Chinman M, Sells D & Rowe M (2006) Peer support among adults with serious mental illness: a report from the field. *Schizophrenia Bulletin* **32** (3) 443–450.

Friedli L (2009) *Mental Health, Resilience and Inequalities*. Copenhagen: WHO.

Hamer S & Haddad PM (2007) Adverse effects of antipsychotics as outcome measures. *British Journal of Psychiatry* **50** 64–70.

Jenkins R, Lancashire S, McDaid D, Samyshkin Y, Green S, Watkins J, *et al* (2007) Mental health reform in the Russian Federation: an integrated approach to achieve social inclusion and recovery. *Bulletin of the World Health Organization* **85** (11) 858–866.

Kemp V, Bates A & Isaac M (2009) Behavioural interventions to reduce the risk of physical illness in persons living with mental illness. *Current Opinion in Psychiatry* **22** (2) 194–199.

Lal S (2010) Prescribing recovery as the new mantra for mental health: does one prescription serve all? *Canadian Journal of Occupational Therapy* **77** (2) 82–89.

Marmot M (2010) *Fair Society, Healthy Lives – Strategic review of health inequalities in England post-2010*. London: The Marmot Review.

McCreadie R, MacDonald E, Blacklock C, Tilak-Singh D, Wiles D, Halliday J *et al* (1998) Dietary intake of schizophrenic patients in Nithsdale, Scotland: case controlled study. *British Medical Journal* **317** 784–785.

McManus S, Meltzer H, Brugha T, Bebbington P & Jenkins R (2009) *Adult Psychiatric Morbidity in England, 2007 – Results of a household survey*. London: The Health & Social Care Information Centre.

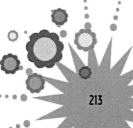

Phelan M, Stradins L & Morrison S (2001) Physical health of people with severe mental illness: can be improved if primary care and mental health professionals pay attention to it. *British Medical Journal* **322** 443–444.

Pilgrim D (2008) 'Recovery' and current mental health policy. *Chronic Illness* **4** (4) 309–310.

Schomerus G, Matschinger H & Angermeyer M C (2009) The stigma of psychiatric treatment and help-seeking intentions for depression. *European Archives of Psychiatry And Clinical Neuroscience* **259** (5) 298–306.

Scottish Recovery Network (2007) *Recovering Mental Health in Scotland* [online]. Available at: http://www.scottishrecovery.net/What-is-Recovery/what-is-recovery.html (accessed August 2010).

Thornicroft G (2006). *Actions Speak Louder… Tackling discrimination against people with mental illness*. London: Mental Health Foundation.

World Health Organization (2008) *Policies and Practices for Mental Health in Europe – Meeting the challenges*. Copenhagen: WHO.

Zartaloudi A & Madianos M (2010) Stigma related to help-seeking from a mental health professional. *Health Science Journal* **4** (2) 77–83.

Chapter 14

Stigma and discrimination

Elizabeth Corker and Graham Thornicroft

Introduction

Stigma and discrimination faced by people with a mental illness is widespread (Thornicroft *et al*, 2009) and offers a key public health challenge. Stigma (plural stigmata) was originally used to refer to an indelible dot left on the skin after stinging with a sharp instrument, sometimes used to identify vagabonds or slaves (Cannan, 1895; Gilman, 1982; Gilman, 1985). More recently, stigma has come to mean 'any attribute, trait or disorder that marks an individual as being unacceptably different from "normal" people with whom he or she routinely interacts, and that elicits some form of community sanction' (Goffman, 1963; Hinshaw & Cicchetti, 2000; Scambler, 1998).

In relation to the stigma of mental illness, this is usually considered to be an undesirable attribute in terms of social normality (Goffman, 1963). This has been an area of research for many decades and has been reported since the times of ancient Greece (Simon, 1992).

Understanding stigma and discrimination

There is now a voluminous literature on stigma (Corrigan, 2005; Link & Phelan, 2001). The most complete model of the component processes of stigmatisation has four key elements (Link & Phelan, 2001).

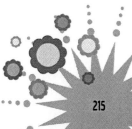

1. Labelling, in which personal characteristics are signalled or noticed as conveying an important difference.

2. Stereotyping: the linkage of these differences to undesirable characteristics.

3. Separating: the categorical distinction between the mainstream or normal group and the labelled group as in some respects fundamentally different.

4. Status loss and discrimination: devaluing, rejecting and excluding the labelled group. Interestingly, more recently, the authors of this model have added a revision to include the emotional reactions that may accompany each of these stages.

(Link *et al*, 2004)

Research has established that mental illness is more stigmatising than physical illnesses (Corrigan *et al*, 2000; Scambler, 1998) and that more stigmatising attitudes are directed towards people diagnosed with schizophrenia compared with depression (Mann & Himelein, 2004) and eating disorders (Corrigan *et al*, 2000), demonstrating not only that mental illness is more stigmatising than physical illness, but also the existence of a hierarchy of stigma within psychiatric diagnoses.

Shortcomings of work on stigma and discrimination

Five key features have limited the usefulness of stigma theories. First, while these processes are undoubtedly complex, academic writings on stigma (which in the field of mental health have almost entirely focused on schizophrenia) have made relatively few connections with legislation concerning disability rights policy (Sayce, 2000) or clinical practice. For example, legislation such as the Americans with Disabilities Act in the USA and the Disability Discrimination Act (DDA) in the UK are now being applied to cases involving mental illness (23% of all DDA cases in the UK). Second, most work on mental illness and stigma has been descriptive, overwhelmingly describing attitude surveys or the portrayal of mental illness by the media. Very little is known about effective interventions to reduce stigma. Third, there have been notably few direct contributions to this literature by service users (Chamberlin, 2005). However, ongoing work involving the authors at the Institute of Psychiatry, Kings' College London is seeking to address the previous two issues by measuring and recording the direct experiences of stigma and discrimination experienced by mental health service users. Fourth, there has been an underlying pessimism that stigma is deeply historically rooted and difficult to change. This has been one of the reasons for the reluctance to use the results of research in designing and implementing action plans. Fifth, stigma theories have de-emphasised cultural factors and paid little attention to the issues related to human rights and social structures.

Recently there have been early signs of a developing focus upon discrimination. This can be seen as the behavioural consequences of stigma, which act to the disadvantage of people who are stigmatised (Sayce, 2000). The importance of discriminatory behaviour has been clear for many years in relation to the personal experiences of service users, in terms of the devastating effects upon personal relationships, parenting and childcare, education, training, work and housing (Thornicroft, 2006). Indeed, these voices have said that the rejecting behaviour of others may bring greater disadvantage than the primary condition itself (Hinshaw & Stier, 2008).

Stigma can therefore be seen as an overarching term that contains three important elements:

1. problems of knowledge – ignorance

2. problems of attitudes – prejudice

3. problems of behaviour – discrimination.

Ignorance: the problem of knowledge

At a time when there is an unprecedented volume of information in the public domain, the level of accurate knowledge about mental illnesses (sometimes called 'mental health literacy') is meagre (Crisp et al, 2005). In a population survey in England, for example, most people (57%) believe that the statement 'someone who has a split personality' describes a person who is mentally ill (Department of Health, 2010). Most (64%) thought that 10% of the population or less would experience a mental illness at some time in their lives.

There is evidence that deliberate interventions to improve public knowledge about depression can be successful, and can reduce the effects of stigmatisation. In a campaign in Australia to increase knowledge about depression and its treatment, some states and territories received an intensive, co-ordinated programme, while others did not. In the former, people more often recognised the features of depression, were more likely to support help seeking for depression, or to accept treatment with counselling and medication for their own mental health problems (Jorm *et al*, 2005).

A series of government surveys in England has been carried out from 1993 to 2009 and gives a mixed picture. On one hand, there are some clear improvements, for example, the proportion thinking that people with mental illness can be easily distinguished from 'normal people' fell from 29% to 19% (Department of Health, 2010). On the other hand, views became significantly less favourable over this time for several items, eg. we need to adopt a more tolerant attitude to people with mental illness (decreased from 92% to 87%). An increase in knowledge about mental illness thus does not necessarily improve either attitudes or behaviour towards people with mental illness.

Prejudice: the problem of negative attitudes

Although the term prejudice is used to refer to many social groups which experience disadvantage, for example minority ethnic groups, it is employed rarely in relation to people with mental illness. The reactions of a host majority to act with prejudice in rejecting a minority group usually involves not just negative thoughts but also emotions such as anxiety, anger, resentment, hostility, distaste, or disgust. In fact, prejudice may more strongly predict discrimination than do stereotypes.

Interestingly, there is almost nothing published about emotional reactions to people with mental illness apart from that which describes a fear of violence. A fascinating exception to this is work carried out in the south eastern region of the USA, in which students were asked to imagine meeting people who either did or did not have a diagnosis of schizophrenia. All three physiological measures of stress (brow muscle tension, palm skin conductance, and heart rate) were raised during imaginary meetings with 'labelled' compared with 'non-labelled' individuals. Such tension was also associated with self-reported negative attitudes of stigma towards people with schizophrenia. The authors concluded that one reason why individuals avoid those with mental illness is physiological arousal, which is experienced as unpleasant feelings (Graves *et al*, 2005). Additionally, a recent paper has compared the emotional reactions towards people with mental illness in Germany between 1990 and 2001. It was found that in regards to schizophrenia, there was more anger and fear in 2001 than in 1990 and in regards to depression there was also an increase in these negative feelings, as well as more positive emotions such as compassion and friendliness (Angermeyer *et al*, 2010). Clearly, more research is needed in the area of emotional responses to mental illness as this could be a definitive factor in the social distancing that people with mental illnesses often feel.

Discrimination: the problem of rejecting and avoidant behaviour

Attitude and social distance surveys usually ask either students or members of the general public what they would do in imaginary situations or what they think 'most people' who do, for example, when faced with a neighbour or work colleague with mental illness. Although important lessons have flowed from these findings, this work has emphasised what 'normal' people say without exploring the actual experiences of people with mental illness themselves about the behaviour of 'normal' people toward them. Further, it has been assumed that such statements (usually on knowledge, attitudes or behavioural intentions) are congruent with actual behaviour, without assessing such behaviour directly. Such research has usually focused on hypothetical rather than real situations, neglecting emotions and the social context, thus producing very little guidance about interventions that could reduce social rejection.

Stigma as a barrier to help seeking

Despite the high numbers of the general population who could be diagnosed with a mental illness, only a proportion of these actually seek professional help for these problems (Lepine *et al*, 1997). According to health behaviour theory, a person will seek help for a problem if they believe that the problem is severe enough to interfere with their daily lives; that treatment will reduce symptoms and that there are no major barriers to help seeking (Henshaw & Freedman-Doan, 2009). A major barrier for not seeking help is seen to be the stigma associated with being diagnosed with a mental illness (Corrigan, 2004; Link & Phelan, 2006; Sherwood *et al*, 2007) along with the associated embarrassment of consulting relevant professionals (Barney *et al*, 2006) and the consequences individuals envisage regarding, for example, employment and relationships. Individuals believe that seeking help is akin to admitting that they cannot cope; the likelihood of seeking help for a physical problem is higher than for a mental health problem, suggesting that seeking help for mental health problems is seen as particularly stigmatising. The consequences of failure to seek help include a continuation and perhaps worsening of symptoms and the continuation of stigma (Thornicroft, 2008).

Diagnostic overshadowing

Research has shown that those with mental illness have high rates of comorbid medical diseases and that these diseases often go untreated or even undiagnosed (Felker *et al*, 1996). Ultimately, risk of premature death both from natural and unnatural causes has been found to be higher in people with mental illness (Harris & Barraclough, 1998). The term 'diagnostic overshadowing' refers to when a clinician attributes physical symptoms to a patient's mental illness (Jones *et al*, 2008). Research commissioned by the Disability Rights Commission found that in England and Wales, people with mental illness were more likely than other people to have heart disease, high blood pressure and diabetes. Additionally, it was found that people with serious mental illness were more likely to have coronary heart disease or stroke by age 55 and those diagnosed with schizophrenia were almost twice as likely to have bowel cancer (Disability Rights Commission, 2006). Although more research is needed to ascertain exactly why diagnostic overshadowing occurs, it is clear that people with mental illness are at a higher risk of developing serious medical illnesses and that these illnesses will not be treated.

Cultural understanding of mental illness and stigma in the UK

Within the UK, the stigma and discrimination of mental illness can take on different forms, depending on the community that the individual belongs to. Research in Glasgow within Muslim, Sikh, Hindu and African/Caribbean communities has found that shame is associated with mental illness and that having a diagnosis is thought to damage the family reputation, leading to secrecy and lack of treatment. Additionally, families may see having a mental health problem as damaging for marriage prospects, as a high importance is placed on marriage. Again this is an incentive to keep mental health problems within the family a secret. The perceived causes of mental illness, such as black magic, or, within African communities specifically, drug abuse, can also exacerbate stigmatising beliefs. Finally, members of black and minority ethnic communities can face dual stigma with mental health problems and racism combining to exaggerate issues with social exclusion, misdiagnosis and under treatment (Glasgow Anti Stigma Partnership, 2007).

Global patterns of stigma and discrimination

Do we know if discrimination varies between countries and cultures? The evidence here is stronger, but still frustratingly patchy (Littlewood, 2004). Although studies on stigma and mental illness have been carried out in many countries, few have compared two or more places, and few have included non-western nations (Fabrega, 1991).

Most of the published work on stigma is by authors in the USA and Canada (Corrigan *et al*, 2003; Corrigan, 2005; Estroff *et al*, 2004; Link & Phelan, 2001), but there are also a few reports from elsewhere in the Americas and in the Caribbean (Villares & Sartorius, 2003). In a review of studies from Argentina, Brazil, Dominica, Mexico, and Nicaragua, mainly from urban sites, a number of common themes emerged.

▶ The conditions most often rated as 'mental illnesses' were psychotic disorders, especially schizophrenia.

▶ People with higher levels of education tended to have more favourable attitudes to people with mental illness.

▶ Alcoholism was considered to be the most common type of mental disorder.

▶ Most people thought that a health professional needs to be consulted by people with mental illnesses.

(de Toledo Piza & Blay, 2004)

What different countries do often share is a high level of ignorance and misinformation about mental illnesses. A survey of teachers' opinions in Japan and Taiwan showed that relatively few could describe the main features of schizophrenia with any accuracy. The general profile of knowledge, beliefs and attitudes was similar to that found in most western countries, although the degree of social rejection was somewhat greater in Japan (Kurumatani *et al*, 2004).

A recent study used the Discrimination and Stigma Scale (DISC) in a cross-sectional survey in 27 countries using language-equivalent versions

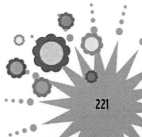

of the instrument in face-to-face interviews between research staff and 732 participants with a clinical diagnosis of schizophrenia (Thornicroft *et al*, 2009). The most frequently occurring areas of negative experienced discrimination were: making or keeping friends (47%); discrimination by family members (43%); keeping a job (29%); finding a job (29%); and intimate or sexual relationships (29%). Positive experienced discrimination was rare. Anticipated discrimination was common for: applying for work or training or education (64%); looking for a close relationship (55%), and 72% felt the need to conceal the diagnosis. Anticipated discrimination occurred more often than experienced discrimination. This study suggests that rates of experienced discrimination are relatively high and consistent across countries. For two of the most important domains (work and personal relationships) anticipated discrimination occurs in the absence of experienced discrimination in over a third of participants. This has important implications: disability discrimination laws may not be effective without also developing interventions to reduce anticipated discrimination, for example, by enhancing the self-esteem of people with mental illness, so that they will be more likely to apply for jobs.

Conclusions

If we move our point of reference from stigma to discrimination, there are a number of distinct advantages. First, attention moves from attitudes to actual behaviour, not if an employer would hire a person with mental illness, but if he or she does. Second, interventions can be tried and tested to see if they change behaviour towards people with mental illness, without necessarily changing knowledge or feelings. The key candidates as active ingredients to reduce stigma are as follows.

1. At the local level, direct social contact with people with mental illness (Link & Cullen, 1986; Pinfold *et al*, 2003a; Pinfold *et al*, 2003b).

2. Social marketing techniques at the national level.

3. People who have a diagnosis of mental illness can expect to benefit from all the relevant antidiscrimination policies and laws in their country or jurisdiction, on a basis of parity with people with physical disabilities.

4. A discrimination perspective requires us to focus not upon the 'stigmatised' but upon the 'stigmatiser'.

In summary, this means sharpening our sights upon human rights, injustice and on discrimination as actually experienced by people with mental illness (Chamberlin, 2005; Hinshaw & Cicchetti, 2000; Kingdon *et al*, 2004; Rose, 2001).

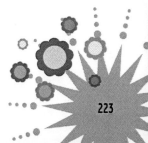

References

Angermeyer MC, Holzinger A & Matschinger H (2010) Emotional reactions to people with mental illness. *Epidemiologia e Psichiatria Sociale–An International Journal for Epidemiology and Psychiatric Sciences* **19** (1) 26–32.

Barney LJ, Griffiths KM, Jorm AF & Christensen H (2006) Stigma about depression and its impact on help-seeking intentions. *Australian and New Zealand Journal of Psychiatry* **40** (1) 51–54.

Cannan E (1895) The stigma of pauperism. *Economic Review* 380–381.

Chamberlin J (2005) User/consumer involvement in mental health service delivery. *Epidemiologica Psichiatria Sociale* **14** (1) 10–14.

Corrigan P (2004) How stigma interferes with mental health care. *American Psychologist* **59** (7) 614–625.

Corrigan P (2005) *On the Stigma of Mental Illness*. Washington DC: American Psychological Association.

Corrigan P, Thompson V, Lambert D, Sangster Y, Noel JG & Campbell J (2003) Perceptions of discrimination among persons with serious mental illness. *Psychiatric Services* **54** (8) 1105–1110.

Corrigan PW, River LP, Lundin RK, Wasowski KU, Campion J, Mathisen J, Goldstein H, Bergman M & Gagnon C (2000) Stigmatizing attributions about mental illness. *Journal of Community Psychology* **28** (1) 91–102.

Crisp A, Gelder MG, Goddard E & Meltzer H (2005) Stigmatization of people with mental illnesses: a follow-up study within the Changing Minds campaign of the Royal College of Psychiatrists. *World Psychiatry* **4** 106–113.

de Toledo Piza PE & Blay SL (2004) Community perception of mental disorders – a systematic review of Latin American and Caribbean studies. *Social Psychiatry and Psychiatric Epidemiology* **39** (12) 955–961.

Department of Health (2010) *Attitudes to Mental Illness 2010 Research Report*. London: DH.

Disability Rights Commission (2006) *Equal Treatment: Closing the gap*. London: Disability Rights Commission.

Estroff SE, Penn DL & Toporek JR (2004) From stigma to discrimination: an analysis of community efforts to reduce the negative consequences of having a psychiatric disorder and label. *Schizophria Bulletin* **30** (3) 493–509.

Fabrega H Jr (1991) The culture and history of psychiatric stigma in early modern and modern western societies: a review of recent literature. *Comprehensive Psychiatry* **32** (2) 97–119.

Felker B, Yazel JJ & Short D (1996) Mortality and medical comorbidity among psychiatric patients: a review. *Psychiatric Services* **47** (12) 1356–1363.

Gilman SL (1982) *Seeing the Insane*. New York: Wiley.

Gilman SL (1985) *Difference and Pathology: Stereotypes of sexuality, race and madness*. Ithaca: Cornell University Press.

Glasgow Anti-Stigma Partnership (2007) *Mosaics of Meaning: Full Report*. Glasgow: NHS GG&C.

Goffman E (1963) *Stigma: Notes on the management of spoiled identity*. New Jersey: Prentice Hall.

Graves RE, Cassisi JE & Penn DL (2005) Psychophysiological evaluation of stigma towards schizophrenia. *Schizophrenia Research* **76** (2–3) 317–327.

Harris EC & Barraclough B (1998) Excess mortality of mental disorder. *British Journal of Psychiatry* **173** 11–53.

Henshaw EJ & Freedman-Doan CR (2009) Conceptualizing mental health care utilization using the health belief model. *Clinical Psychology-Science and Practice* **16** (4) 420–439.

Hinshaw SP & Cicchetti D (2000) Stigma and mental disorder: conceptions of illness, public attitudes, personal disclosure, and social policy. *Development and Psychopathology* **12** (4) 555–598.

Hinshaw SP & Stier A (2008) Stigma as related to mental disorders. *Annual Review of Clinical Psychology* **4** 367–393.

Jones S, Howard L & Thornicroft G (2008) Diagnostic overshadowing: worse physical health care for people with mental illness. *Acta Psychiatrica Scandinavica* **118** (3) 169–171.

Jorm AF, Christensen H & Griffiths KM (2005) The impact of beyondblue: the national depression initiative on the Australian public's recognition of depression and beliefs about treatment. *Australian and New Zealand Journal of Psychiatry* **39** (4) 248–254.

Kingdon D, Jones R & Lonnqvist J (2004) Protecting the human rights of people with mental disorder: new recommendations emerging from the Council of Europe. *British Journal of Psychiatry* **185** 277–279.

Kurumatani T, Ukawa K, Kawaguchi Y, Miyata S, Suzuki M, Ide H, Seki W, Chikamori E, Hwu HG, Liao SC, Edwards GD, Shinfuku N & Uemoto M (2004) Teachers' knowledge, beliefs and attitudes concerning schizophrenia – a cross-cultural approach in Japan and Taiwan. *Social Psychiatry and Psychiatric Epidemiology* **39** (5) 402–409.

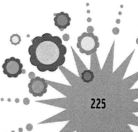

Lepine JP, Gastpar M, Mendlewicz J & Tylee A (1997) Depression in the community: the first pan-European study DEPRES (Depression Research in European Society). *International Clinical Psychopharmacology* **12** (1) 19–29.

Link BG & Cullen FT (1986) Contact with the mentally ill and perceptions of how dangerous they are. *Journal of Health Social Behaviour* **27** (4) 289–302.

Link BG & Phelan JC (2001) Conceptualizing stigma. *Annual Review of Sociology* **27** 363–385.

Link BG & Phelan JC (2006) Stigma and its public health implications. *Lancet* **365** (9509) 528–529.

Link BG, Yang LH, Phelan JC & Collins PY (2004) Measuring mental illness stigma. *Schizophrenia Bulletin* **30** (3) 511–541.

Littlewood R (2004) Cultural and national apsects to stigmatisation. In: *Every Family in the Land*. AH Crisp (Ed) (pp14–17). London: Royal Society of Medicine.

Mann CE & Himelein MJ (2004) Factors associated with stigmatization of persons with mental illness. *Psychiatric Services* **55** (2) 185–187.

Pinfold V, Huxley P, Thornicroft G, Farmer P, Toulmin H & Graham T (2003a) Reducing psychiatric stigma and discrimination – evaluating an educational intervention with the police force in England. *Social Psychiatry and Psychiatric Epidemiology* **38** (6) 337–344.

Pinfold V, Toulmin H, Thornicroft G, Huxley P, Farmer P & Graham T (2003b) Reducing psychiatric stigma and discrimination: evaluation of educational interventions in UK secondary schools. *British Journal of Psychiatry* **182** 342–346.

Rose D (2001) *Users' Voices: The perspectives of mental health service users on community and hospital care*. London: The Sainsbury Centre.

Sayce L (2000) *From Psychiatric Patient to Citizen. Overcoming discrimination and social exclusion*. Basingstoke: Palgrave.

Scambler G (1998) Stigma and disease: changing paradigms. *Lancet* **352** (9133) 1054–1055.

Sherwood C, Salkovskis PM & Rimes KA (2007) Help-seeking for depression: the role of beliefs, attitudes and mood. *Behavioural and Cognitive Psychotherapy* **35** (5) 541–554.

Simon B (1992) Shame, stigma and mental illness in Ancient Greece. In: *Stigma and Mental Illness*. PJ Fink & A Tasman (Eds)(pp 29–39). Washington, DC: American Psychiatric Press.

Thornicroft G (2006) *Shunned: Discrimination against people with mental illness*. Oxford: Oxford University Press.

Thornicroft G (2008) Stigma and discrimination limit access to mental health care. *Epidemiologa e Psichiatria Sociale* **17** (1) 14–19.

Thornicroft G, Brohan E, Rose D, Sartorius N, Leese M & Indigo SG (2009) Global pattern of experienced and anticipated discrimination against people with schizophrenia: a cross-sectional survey. *Lancet* **373** (9661) 408–415.

Villares C & Sartorius N (2003) Challenging the stigma of schizophrenia. *Revista Brasiliera de Psiquiatria* **25** 1–2.

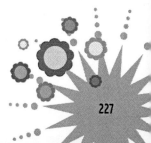

Chapter 15

Reflections upon practice and partnership working for mental health improvement

Trevor Lakey

Introduction

The complex challenge of promoting the mental health and well-being of communities requires so many different factors to be addressed that no one agency could hope to make substantial progress on their own. Partnerships can link and co-ordinate multiple skills and resources and provide a creative spark that allows a new way of seeing problems and designing solutions, to emerge. They can also foster a new balance in the relationships between different agencies and with communities – allowing new understandings and shared perspectives. There are many definitions of partnerships but this one captures the essence:

> 'Relationships involving the sharing of power, work and/or support with others for the achievement of mutual and/or compatible objectives.'
> (Ontario Ministry of Natural Resources, 1992)

Another reason why partnerships are important for mental health improvement is that they can offer a high degree of responsiveness to

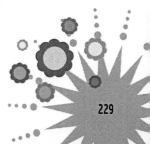

emerging or poorly defined needs, such as those affecting minority groups. The needs of such groups can often be poorly understood and addressed by mainstream services. Novel partnerships are able to bring a different 'voice' to the table and unlock new thinking and approaches.

The spectrum of partnership approaches

Partnerships to promote mental health exist for a very wide variety of purposes, with some fulfilling multiple functions. They can be national or international in scope, or operating with a regional or local focus. They can feature large numbers of partners in highly formalised structures, or be based around the collaborations of two or three groups creating a shared approach. Timescale-wise, they can be long-standing, designed to bring a sustained focus to an intractable problem. Conversely they may be designed as a quick, flexible response to an emerging need or situation, or as a means of piloting a new approach, with a view to testing its prospects for wider adoption.

The goals of partnerships can be similarly diverse. They can range from the creation of high-level interagency strategy, augmenting the provision of mainstream services through to campaigning, advocacy and awareness raising activities, collaborative research, peer support, and community led initiatives.

Tremendous examples of innovative partnership working in this field can be found all over the world. While by no means a new approach, recent years have seen a growing body of documented examples and evaluation material on emerging benefits (Jané-Llopis & Anderson, 2006). In this chapter the author draws on personal and practical examples of partnerships for mental health improvement, principally from west central Scotland, as the area the author is most familiar with and active within.

Like many things in life, simple is often the best model. For example, healthy reading schemes that utilise evidence-based book lists for mental health self-help and support, combine the expertise of primary care mental health services with the resources and accessible community spaces offered by public lending libraries (Hicks et al, 2010).

Making partnerships work: inspiration and perspiration

A few months ago the author was running a teaching session within a public health Masters course, focused on 'partnership approaches to tackle inequalities'. During the group discussion on factors that enable partnerships, one of the students described how exchanging insurance details following a car park 'shunt' triggered a discussion on health that developed into an innovative rural health partnership programme in West Africa. His contribution illustrated a fairly common feature of partnership formation: chance encounters leading to new partnerships. A good number of the mental health improvement partnership examples alluded to in this chapter came about over a cup of coffee and an exploration of ideas between colleagues.

While no one would advocate relying on 'bumping into people' as the main means of partnership formation, an openness to new ideas, partners and ways of thinking and working is a crucial first step. This is the 'inspiration' side. An inquisitiveness coupled with being prepared to informally explore complex challenges and to think differently about solutions.

The implication is that grassroots and bottom-up partnership developments can be very powerful. This in turn places a responsibility on organisations to adopt an approach that facilitates innovation. For example, do statutory agencies have policies and a culture that actively support practitioners and their managers to link with users of services and other interested parties? Do staff feel sufficiently empowered to identify valuable partnership opportunities? Or instead do staff feel stifled by impenetrable bureaucracy that blocks innovative joint working?

No partnership, however groundbreaking in concept, could flourish without the 'perspiration' as well. This is the painstaking and often unseen preparatory, developmental and infrastructural work that turns a great partnership idea into a viable, working entity capable of withstanding the stresses and strains that all joint working encounters.

Authors such as Thompson and Stachenko (1994) have identified the kinds of factors involved in facilitating effective health partnerships. These include:

1. partnership building processes
2. networks to stimulate and support change

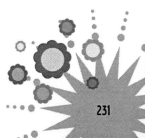

3. material resources to support the process

4. a dedicated central co-ordinating body or person

5. a communications plan.

To this list the author would add shared values and mutual respect for differences, a clearly articulated common objective, identified senior or corporate support, overt connection to wider policies and strategies, and a preparedness to take calculated risks, to push the boundaries.

More than any other factor, a partnership approach is most likely to flourish if the partners have collaborated in preparing a proper partnership agreement, backed up by a robust, pragmatic plan. Such agreements and plans clearly need to be tailored in their level of formality and comprehensiveness, in proportion to the scale of the partnership development that is being undertaken.

Having agreed the plan, partners must then continue jointly to invest in its delivery, monitoring, ongoing problem resolution and refinement. Also, of course, in the celebration of its progress and successes.

Coping with challenges, inhibitors and pitfalls

More than 15 years ago at an event launching an evaluation tool for health partnerships, the author heard a phrase about partnerships that really struck a chord: 'They are more wrestling than dancing!' In other words, there are tensions inherent in most partnerships, given the different levels of power, resource, values, and goals that will exist between partners. The implication is that successful, productive partnerships need constant care and attention. Tensions need to be managed and differences resolved throughout the process.

There are some well-recognised inhibiting factors or barriers to effective health partnerships. Examples include lack of commitment at a senior level, poor leadership, differences in outlook or core values, professional rivalries, differences in status, and deficiency in key skills. Issues such as differencing levels of resource contribution, need not of itself lead to an unstable or ineffective partnership, more important is a sense of mutual respect for the different contributions, whether these be in the form of cash or 'in kind'.

For mental health-based partnerships, there are very specific potential pitfalls relating to language, concepts and meanings. With so many interpretations and connotations around the phrase 'mental health' among individuals and within the culture of different agencies, partners would be wise to spend time in their formative stages clarifying such meanings. Positive mental health is still a relatively novel concept to many, and phrases such as well-being can also have multiple meanings. This is a particularly important consideration when working with minority ethnic communities, where western conceptualisation of mental health may not be meaningful (Newbigging *et al*, 2008).

Most partnerships will go through periods of challenge and strain. Indeed, it could be argued that the process of coping with and resolving differences between partners is what allows practice to advance, being compelled to challenge assumptions and do things differently rather than simply doing things together. As far back as 1965, Tuckman identified the stages of group development and the importance of the 'storming' stage in allowing groups to confront different perspectives and priorities and to work together to resolve these. Tuckman argued that a 'storming' stage was a pivotal point in the growth of any group, albeit not always a comfortable process. Within partnerships this is where the developmental spadework will pay off: investment in joint plans; shared induction and training; agreed review mechanisms and reporting arrangements; all supported by a clear communication plan. Above all, the partnership needs to have sufficiently confident and mature leadership to make changes to the original approach, when this is required.

Examples of partnerships for mental health improvement

In order to illustrate the range of approaches to partnership working being adopted, the author has sought the perspectives of a number of colleagues involved in a variety of partnerships for mental health improvement. These examples illustrate the principles that have been outlined by Thompson and Stachenko (1994), and give a feel for the kinds of achievements that can flow from effective joint working.

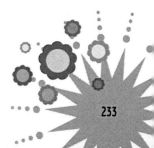

Inverclyde Alliance: a community planning partnership approach to mental health improvement

Inverclyde Alliance is a high level formal multisectoral civic partnership charged with working together to improve the quality of life for the people of Inverclyde. Encouragingly, the Alliance has chosen to give a significant focus to mental health and well-being in its community plan.

Examples of early steps taken to progress strategic action on mental health improvement include a formal signing of the 'see me' pledge. See me is the Scottish campaign to challenge the stigma of mental ill health (see me, 2010). A major interagency event aimed at exploring mental health and well-being was held in 2009, 'Towards a Mentally Flourishing Inverclyde'. This event helped to clarify the national, regional and local policy context, share learning and demonstrate the roles that partners can play in improving mental health. Good practice, gaps and future actions were also mapped.

The partnership board has recognised the cross-cutting nature of mental health and well-being and its importance in the delivery of a broad range of local outcomes with the learning from this event provided an opportunity for further reflection. Following on from this the board decided to appoint a champion who has an overview of the delivery of mental health improvement (and related) priorities.

Challenges identified by Inverclyde Alliance include the need to engage a very wide spectrum of organisations, with further work required to 'sell' the message that everyone has a role to play in improving mental health and well-being. Capacity and financial resource constraints were also identified as challenges; demanding new ways of working.

> 'Partners will need to focus on doing things better and smarter, looking to realign what we do to get the same outcomes with fewer resources.'
> (Miriam McKenna, Inverclyde Strategic Partnership Manager)

Referring back to the factors highlighted by Thompson and Stachenko (1994) on what facilitates effective partnerships, the Inverclyde Alliance approach illustrates the value of having a 'central co-ordinating body or person' on board and the 'networks to stimulate and support change'.

Lanarkshire Mental Health Improvement Partnership Group

Another partnership that illustrates a number of the facilitating elements featured by Thompson and Stachenko (1994), is Lanarkshire Mental Health Improvement Partnership Group. This partnership group has put in place a number of 'partnership building processes' and 'communications plans'.

The Lanarkshire Mental Health Improvement Partnership Group was established in May 2008 to provide co-ordination and support a collective input from key partners to the mental health improvement agenda. It also has responsibility for developing an action plan that supports the local implementation of the national objectives set in Towards a Mentally Flourishing Scotland Action Plan (Scottish Government, 2009).

The group membership includes lead colleagues from NHS Lanarkshire, North and South Lanarkshire councils, the voluntary sector, and service user and carer organisations. This group has been designed to bring together the skills and expertise to progress a mental health improvement agenda across the life span and a range of settings and for high-risk groups. The group has formal terms of reference incorporating remit, objectives, membership, budget, communication and reporting mechanisms.

The action plan development process is informed by a review of the evidence, a number of consultation events and discussions with partners and communities. The recommendations will also reflect the other high level priorities, which partners are and will be progressing (eg. early years, inequalities). Every opportunity has been taken to engage with existing groups and planning structures and to integrate with local government targets such as the Single Outcome Agreements (Scottish Government, 2007). An outcome focus is supported by an emerging mental health improvement outcomes framework being developed by NHS Health Scotland (Scottish Government, 2009), the national agency for health improvement. High level corporate 'buy in' to the agenda is supporting a comprehensive, consistent and wider reaching approach to the mental health improvement effort across Lanarkshire.

'As a result of the work of the last 18 months, we now have a clear vision for a mentally flourishing Lanarkshire, we are better connected, we are better integrated and we have a clear plan setting out our collective responsibilities.'

(Kevin O'Neill, Public Mental Health and Well-being Development Manager, NHS Lanarkshire)

Employability support

Improving the employment prospects of people who have experienced mental health problems is a crucial priority area. In 2009 the Department of Work and Pensions (DWP) appointed mental health co-ordinators across the UK to facilitate and build practical links between health and social care and Jobcentre Plus at a local level to address this priority (Perkins *et al*, 2009). The following example outlines the joint work that has taken place led by the mental health co-ordinators based in Glasgow. This work has been effective due to the 'material resources' that have been brought to the partnership by the DWP and this work benefits again from having 'a dedicated central co-ordinationg person', through the co-ordinator's role (Thompson & Stachenko, 1994).

Partners in this programme of work include Jobcentre Plus, NHS Greater Glasgow and Clyde Mental Health Partnership, Glasgow Works City Strategy, representation from the Mental Health Employability Service and service users. The group aims to improve awareness of mental health issues within Jobcentre Plus and develop better links between mental health services and Jobcentre Plus. Significant progress was achieved quite early in the process, including a joint mental health awareness session held for Jobcentre Plus staff and an awareness session on the role of Jobcentre Plus services for mental health and employability staff. These opportunities to share perspectives have increased the mutual understanding of roles and enhanced the service options for service users.

In addition, an event was held and attended by 40 local Jobcentre Plus staff and organisations who deliver contracted services. Service users provided a vital input by sharing their experiences about their journey and progression into employment.

'The role of the local DWP mental health co-ordinator has been instrumental in forging stronger links and relationships with Jobcentre Plus staff. We are tremendously encouraged that this has all been achieved within a six-month period due to the commitment of the partnership members.'
(Sylvia Collumb, Employment Programme Manager, NHS GG&C)

Food for Recovery Festival

This final example raises an important point about partnerships for mental health improvement: although they are intended to bring about improved mental health outcomes, this does not mean that they can't be fun. Glasgow Association for Mental Health has worked across the year to bring together a broad range of partners to create a Food for Recovery Festival (Scottish Recovery Network, 2010). This festival created opportunities for service users and carers to participate in food-related activities that support well-being and promote recovery, with an emphasis on the social aspects of food and the pleasure of eating. With a fantastic launch event that included cookery demonstrations, the Recipes of Hope cookery book, great food, a market hall, plus future events such as cookery courses, a community allotment open day and food growing projects, there has been real enthusiasm and engagement in the festival.

Key to its success has been a collaborative approach. The festival was planned by a steering group of service users, carers and staff, and drew on the resources and expertise of many partner agencies, including Community Food and Health (Scotland), local healthy living projects, NHS Greater Glasgow and Clyde, Glasgow City Council's culture and sports department, the local disability alliance and local colleges.

> '*Because we use a steering group approach, we know that the events and services we're offering are the ones that people want. And we're lucky to have so many highly motivated service users who have been key in making the festival such a success.*'
> (Jacqueline Croft, Operations Manager, Glasgow Association for Mental Health)

Summing up – recipes for success

Drawing together the themes highlighted in this chapter, I have shown how well-designed and supported partnerships can play a vital role in promoting the mental well-being of communities. In the current climate of public finance constraint, it becomes even more important that agencies, groups and communities work closely in partnerships to share the resources, knowledge and expertise that are available.

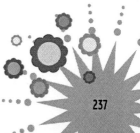

Like baking a cake, there is both art and science in successful partnerships; ingredients include being open to creativity and innovation, yet underpinning this with a rigorous approach to development, planning, infrastructures and to managing partner relations. Blend in effective leadership, the flexibility to adapt to changing circumstances, a preparedness to resolve differences, to challenge outmoded power relationships and incorporate the learning that all parties can offer. The result will be a healthy effective partnership. Partnerships bear fruit when they are resourced and sustained for sufficient time for partners to learn to work together and effectively share their respective assets.

And the proof of the pudding is in the eating: as the examples cited in this chapter demonstrate, partnerships for mental health improvement can deliver innovative, dynamic programmes that build solutions to the mental health challenges our communities face.

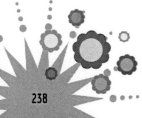

References

Hicks D, Creaser C, Greenwood H, Spezi V, White S & Frude N (2010) *Public Library Activity in the Areas of Health and Well-being: Final report.* Birmingham: Museums, Libraries & Archives Council.

Jané-Llopis E & Anderson P (Eds) (2006) *Mental Health Promotion and Mental Disorder Prevention Across European Member States: A collection of country stories.* Luxembourg: European Communities.

Newbigging K, Bola M & Shah A (2008) *Scoping Exercise with Black and Minority Ethnic Groups on Perceptions of Mental Wellbeing in Scotland* [online]. Scotland: NHS Scotland. Available at: http://www.healthscotland.com/uploads/documents/7977-RE026FinalReport0708.pdf (accessed August 2010).

Ontario Ministry of Natural Resources (1992) In: P Thompson (2000) *Planning and Implementing Collaborative International/Cross-cultural Projects: Challenges and lessons learnt.* Ontario: International Association of Facilitators.

Perkins R, Farmer P & Litchfield P (2009) *Realising Ambitions: Better employment support for people with a mental health condition.* London: Disability and Works Division, Department for Works and Pensions.

Scottish Government (2007) *Concordat Between the Scottish Government and Local Government: Scottish Budget Spending Review* [online]. Available at: http://www.scotland.gov.uk/publications/2007/11/13092240/concordat (accessed August 2010).

Scottish Government (2009) *Towards a Mentally Flourishing Scotland: Policy and action plan 2009–2011.* Edinburgh: SGHD.

Scottish Recovery Network (2010) *Food for Recovery* [online]. Available at: http://www.scottishrecovery.net/Latest-News/an-edible-take-on-recovery.html. (accessed July 2010).

See Me (2010) *Campaign and pledge information* [online]. Available at: www.seemescotland.org.uk (accessed August 2010).

Thompson P & Stachenko S (1994) Building and mobilizing partnerships for health: a national strategy. *Health Promotion International* 9 (3) 211–215.

Tuckman B (1965) Developmental sequence in small groups. *Psychological Bulletin* **63** (6) 384–99.

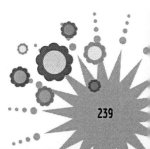

Chapter 16

Meeting the mental health needs of young people: a GP's perspective

Maryanne Freer, David Shiers, Dick Churchill, and reviewed by Joanna Friel

Introduction

Case study 1

Cathy is 15 years old and struggling. She has been distraught since her boyfriend of 10 months left her two months ago. She reacted by going out a lot with her friends, and often comes home having been drinking. She has taken up smoking though she says this is 'social'. School reports that Cathy is having problems concentrating and has become disruptive in class. She now has multiple detentions with her grades slipping and her school attendance falling. Cathy won't talk to her parents. There are continual arguments at home with Cathy refusing to eat with the family. She is often heard weeping at night. A box of laxatives has been found in her room. Since meeting a new boyfriend she has started to have urinary tract infections which she can no longer hide as she is in such pain. Alarmed that Cathy may be having 'underage sex', her mother is at her wit's end having watched her daughter spiral rapidly down from being a bright young woman with such a promising future only months ago.

Case study 2

Mike is 17 years old, and a keen sportsman who loves football and a knee injury has stopped him playing for the last few months. Previously he was always someone who would try his best to help anyone out. Recently he has been looking increasingly bad. He seems exhausted and 'distracted' at school where his grades have dropped and his participation in events diminished. Always popular before, he now has neither friends nor social life. Home life has always been difficult. His parents are separated and money is in short supply. Yet despite needing the money Mike has just dropped his weekend job. His father visits the family home regularly and then there are many fights. His father also drinks a lot. Previous allegations of domestic violence from his mother towards his father have been explored a couple of times before with no outcome. It is a very hard situation for Mike. He spends a lot of time in his room where he has started to smoke cannabis as a way to get away from it all. He feels very low.

Maybe these stories sound familiar? A young person struggling: getting into trouble, turning to drink or other substances, relationships and school performance spiralling downwards with the problems getting bigger and families not knowing what to do. Easy to get into, very difficult to get out of, what may be called the 'lobster pot syndrome'.

Stories like Cathy's and Mike's epitomise the public mental health challenge for young people. We need to consider how can we proactively deal with their issues early before breaking point? With one in five young people having a diagnosable mental health disorder, and within a context of increasingly limited economic resources, the need to provide services which deliver on primary prevention and are able to detect problems within young people at the earliest stage, have never been more needed. Not only are wider, mental well-being approaches required, but there is a growing need to develop specific targeted interventions for those more likely to develop significant problems.

General practitioners (GPs) see 75% of young people at least once a year and one in three of these young people will be experiencing a mental health problem. Arguably then the only targeted way we can address the mental health of young people across the UK is through the primary health care team. GPs have a pivotal public mental health role and can act as confidantes for young people and brokers of support for their mental health. In this chapter we will explore these issues further.

The public mental health challenge

A study by UNICEF showed that the well-being of young people in the UK was poorer than in 20 other industrialised countries (UNICEF, 2007). This is further highlighted by a survey of 16–25 year olds carried out by the Prince's Trust (2009), which showed that one in 10 youths felt 'life was not really worth living' and more than a quarter (27%) stated they were always or often depressed. Almost half (47%) said they were regularly stressed. Those not in work or education were less likely to be happy (Prince's Trust Youth Index, 2009).

The public health implications of these worrying findings are considerable. Kessler *et al*'s meta-analysis (2007) shows that we could be storing up future mental ill-health for large numbers of young people who may go on to have more significant problems and far reduced opportunities further on in their life course.

> *'Roughly half of all lifetime mental disorders in most studies start*
> *by the mid-teens and three quarters by the mid-20s. Later onsets are*
> *mostly secondary conditions. Severe disorders are typically preceded*
> *by less severe disorders that are seldom brought to clinical attention.'*
> (Kessler *et al*, 2007)

Of 4.7 million young people aged between 14 and 19 living in the UK, one in 10 is thought to have a definable mental health disorder at any one time (Office of National Statistics, 2008). To put this into the perspective of a young person, this is the equivalent of saying it could be your friend, it could be you, and it certainly will be three out of your 30 classmates (Green et al, 2005). So what do we know about the risk behaviours that can have an impact on mental health among young people in the UK?

▶ Alcohol use among children and young people is growing faster than the use of any other drug in the UK and it causes the most widespread problems (NICE, 2010).

▶ In 2006, 21% of those aged 11–15 who had drunk alcohol in the previous week consumed an average 11.4 units–up from 5.3 units in 1990 (NHS Information Centre, 2009).

▶ Children and young people aged 11–15 who regularly smoke tobacco or drink are much more likely than non-smokers and non-drinkers to use other drugs (Advisory Council on the Misuse of Drugs, 2003).

▶ Young people using cannabis by the age of 15 are three times more likely to develop illnesses such as schizophrenia. The cannabis being smoked by today's teenagers is also of much greater potency and may have even greater adverse effects than in the past (Arseneault *et al*, 2002).

▶ 11–15 year olds who smoke tobacco regularly are three times more likely to drink regularly and six times more likely to have serious psychological distress (Department of Health, 2003).

▶ Self-harm is relatively uncommon in early childhood, but increases rapidly with the onset of adolescence (Hawton *et al*, 2003). In a school survey, 13% of young people aged 15 or 16 reported having self-harmed at some time in their lives and 7% as having done so in the previous year (Hawton *et al*, 2001).

▶ Self-harm in young people may be an indicator of other problems that affect health outcomes, such as substance misuse, poor school attendance, low academic achievement and unprotected sex (Kerfoot, 1988).

▶ Young people with mental health problems are more likely to become sexually active earlier, less likely to use contraception, and consequently have teenage pregnancy rates more than twice that of their peers (Kessler *et al*, 1997).

Adolescence is associated with a marked rise in the incidence of depressive symptoms and disorders with 20% of adolescence experiencing a diagnosable depressive episode by the age of 18 years (Lewinsohn *et al*, 1993). That is one in five of our young people.

Morbidity associated with depression in children and young people continues into adulthood in about 30% of cases. This often leads to significant reduced opportunities in life, long-term social problems, and a higher risk of suicide, with 37.5% continuing to experience social dysfunction into adulthood, coupled with a high risk of criminality, and 32.3% attempting suicide between childhood and adulthood (Fombonne *et al*, 2001).

More than 95% of major depressive episodes in young people arise in children and young people with long-standing psychosocial difficulties, such as family problems, domestic violence, physical and sexual abuse, school difficulties such as bullying and exam failure, and social isolation. The most important non-familial factors are breakdown in friendships and substance misuse (Rueter *et al*, 1999).

Depression in children and young people may potentially cost the UK health services up to £3.5 million per annum for Fluoxetine treatment, £113 million for CBT treatment, and £149 million for combined CBT and fluoxetine treatments (Thomas & Morris, 2003). And of course, many young people with depression receive neither diagnosis nor treatment.

At the more severe end of the spectrum conditions like schizophrenia may first appear in adolescence. Indeed for 20% of adults with schizophrenia the illness starts under the age of 20, and for 5% under the age of 16. If you are young at the onset of schizophrenia then you can expect a poorer outlook than those for whom it starts older, typically experiencing recurrent illness and markedly impaired social functioning (Hollis, 2003). Moreover, for severe disorders like schizophrenia, the suicide risk is 150 times greater for females and 300 times greater for males compared with age-matched peers from the general population (Gould *et al*, 2003; Mortensen, 1995). Mental health admissions escalate during adolescence with admissions minimal in children under the age of 11 years but increasing 14-fold by the age of 15 years (Royal College of Psychiatrists, 2001).

It is suggested that behaviours that negatively impact on mental health may be developed as a young person but maintained into adulthood and influence life-long health ie. the exploration of drinking, drug use, violence and sexual intimacy. In addition, many of the protective and risk factors associated with the development of mental health problems are particularly evident in teenage years. Protective factors include:

▶ problem-solving skills

▶ school achievement

▶ a supportive caring parent

▶ a pro-social peer group

▶ positive involvement with significant others

▶ good physical health

▶ economic security

▶ attachment to the community

▶ access to support services.

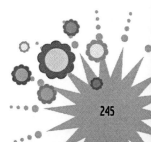

Risk factors include:

▶ family violence

▶ low parental involvement

▶ long-term parental unemployment

▶ criminality in parents

▶ social isolation

▶ neighbourhood violence

▶ poor housing conditions.

(Commonwealth Department of Health and Aged Care, 2000)

These protective and risk factors are reflected in higher rates of young people with mental health problems in families on low income or disability benefits, with parents who are unemployed, not working or who had no educational qualifications, or who are living in rented accommodation (Green *et al*, 2005).

Help-seeking from the GP

To illustrate how young people seek help from GPs let's go back to the case studies of our two young people.

Case study 1: the GP consultation

Cathy is reluctant to open up. She won't talk to her mother and avoids her teachers. Her mother recognises her urinary symptoms and insists they go to the GP. Previously, Cathy has been taken by her mother to see the GP about once a year with an occasional cold or skin rash. During the 10-minute consultation the GP is uncertain about a number of things. After an initial consultation with the mother present, she sees Cathy alone. She deals with the urinary symptoms while concentrating on building rapport. Cathy denies being sexually active although admits that her new boyfriend is pressurising her. The GP asks an open question about how life is treating her and the consultation draws to a close with Cathy disclosing how she hates school, her parents, and is very stressed. The GP books Cathy for another appointment without her mother in a week at the completion of the course of antibiotics so that she can get to know more about the 'stress'. Cathy feels a great relief.

Case study 2: the GP consultation

Mike is just not managing. His parents argue terribly and he typically deals with this by withdrawing to his bedroom and having a smoke. His mood is getting increasingly lower. He used to dream of becoming an engineer but now doesn't think he is good enough. Mike sees his GP regularly to review the knee injury. He has known his GP since he was a child, attending occasionally with asthma and respiratory infections. The GP has got to know the whole family over the years, having seen his mother frequently for backache and 'stress'. Mike feels at ease with his GP. The two of them always chat about football. Mike doesn't think his GP can help with his difficult life at home, but at one consultation the GP notices Mike appears a bit pre-occupied and asks him how things are going in general. Mike finds himself mentioning the family problems and how low he feels.

In Cathy and Mike's stories we are beginning to see how young people with mental health problems seek help, and the importance of the GP within this.

Let's explore this further. We know that young people will only seek help that is responsive and sophisticated, yet easy to access (Viner & Barker, 2005). However, what often goes unnoticed is that about three-quarters of young people attend their general practitioner at least once each year (Royal College of Paediatrics & Child Health, 2003). Some consult more frequently still: in one sample, while 28% of young people had no consultations, 20% had more than four and some as many as 18 (Churchill *et al*, 2000). These figures demonstrate that, across the UK, GPs and primary care services are in regular contact with the majority of young people, a group traditionally seen as difficult to reach (Tylee *et al*, 2007). Indeed, the GP is the health professional most consulted by young people (Kramer & Garralda, 2000) and most are satisfied with the care they receive (Jacobson *et al*, 2002).

We know young people expect the GP to treat physical health problems and indeed most young people present with physical health problems. For instance, in one study three-quarters of young people thought and expected the GP to deal with physical complaints such as sore throats, asthma and injuries (Biddle *et al*, 2006). In another, the commonest reasons for a young person consulting a GP were asthma, respiratory infections, skin conditions, trauma, musculoskeletal problems, menstrual disorders, urinary disorders and contraception (Churchill *et al*, 2000).

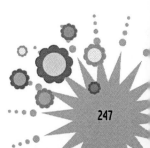

Given this expectation it is not surprising that young people may focus on some physical disorder when they see their GP, omitting to mention any underlying psychological distress unless prompted. Some present with somatisation of their emotional distress (Macdonald & Bower, 2000).

Despite this physical health presentation, the prevalence of mental health disorders for young people attending primary care is much higher than the baseline prevalence in the community. In one sample 38% of GP attendees aged 13 to 16 have evidence of a current or recent psychiatric disorder (Kramer & Garralda, 1998). That means that one in three of all the young people seeing a GP have a diagnosable mental health problem. Critically, we also find prior to suicide, the rate of consultation with a GP by a young person increases significantly in the month and week preceding death (Appleby et al, 1996). Consequently, general practice offers the ideal setting for opportunistic screening of young people for high-risk behaviours and for a mental health problem.

Interestingly, only 20–30% of young people with a diagnosable mental health problem are identified by GPs (Gledhill et al, 2003). This is not necessarily a GP recognition issue. Studies show GP recognition has a sensitivity of 61% and a specificity of 85% reflecting that GPs were able to identify the young people with more severe difficulties though a discussion of psychological issues did not always take place (Martinez et al, 2006).

Let's consider further how this may actually be reflected in practice.

The (mental) health promoting GP consultation with young people

Case study 1: turning the corner

Cathy returns to her next booked appointment. Within this second brief consultation, it remains unclear whether Cathy has an underlying mental health problem. Having established that the urinary tract symptoms have cleared up and continuing to build rapport, the GP encourages Cathy to talk about the stress she is under. Cathy needs little prompting and discloses how troubled she has been since losing her original boyfriend. She admits to crying regularly at night and going out partying with her friends to try to take her mind off it all. She blames the stress on her new boyfriend. The GP, although avoiding a stigmatising diagnosis, carefully checks out for key symptoms of risk or a major mental disorder. She then provides health information on 'stress' and problem solving approaches.

Cathy decides for herself she needs her mum's backing to leave the new boyfriend. As a family practitioner the GP is happy. Using a mental health promotion checklist, the GP discovers that Cathy loves dance, having practised ballet as a child. She suggests Cathy might restart dancing, and also recommends a website for young people packed with mental health self-help information.

The GP books Cathy for another appointment in a month's time to check on the urinary tract symptoms as well as the stress. On Cathy's return she has had no further urinary infections. Her mood is noticeably improving and she no longer cries herself to sleep. She plucked up the courage to disclose how she was feeling to her mother who supported her to leave the new boyfriend. Her mother also smoothed things over with school and Cathy has quietly slipped back into classes with no more detentions. Things are much calmer at home. The best thing has been the new dance class. Working towards an advanced award, she has stopped drinking as it affects her fitness. She has gained a new group of friends. She feels she has turned the corner. The GP doesn't book her another appointment but suggests she could return promptly if she felt she needed to.

Case study 2: getting back on track

Mike sees the GP again with his knee injury. The GP, now alerted to family problems, encourages Mike to say more. He recalls that when he referred Mike to mental health services once before, he failed to reach the service acceptance criteria. The GP knows it is important to support Mike within his generalist role by helping him build up skills that will help protect his mental health over the next couple of years and help him to achieve his aspiration to go to college to become an engineer. It seems unlikely Mike will get any family support. The GP explains the dangers of cannabis smoking. He also gives Mike the telephone number of Samaritans and a web address offering young people emotional support. The GP works through the mental health promotion check list. All the protective factors he identifies orientate around football. With the GP's encouragement Mike approaches his coach to see if there is a way to get him back on the team despite the knee injury. The coach is sympathetic. He has coached Mike for many years and has had concerns for him and decides to put him on the pitch for five minutes a match. Mike starts to get out again and picks up with his friends in the team. He gets a break from home by going away to an intensive coaching week (though his knee still restricts his playing). Even though his mood remains low, he finds himself coping better. Within the course of a conversation he mentions to his coach his dream to become an engineer. The coach has a friend who is an engineer and asks him to give Mike work experience. Mike comes back enthused. He is back on track.

These case studies illustrate how effective mental health promoting approaches can be in improving mental health and helping the young person to develop skills that will protect their mental health in the future. At no point did the potential barrier of stigma around mental health issues arise. The GPs involved, assessed whether there was any evidence of a major mental health disorder present and when they found that this was not the case, they worked to support the young people to 'get back on track' by taking a generalist approach within a small number of consultations. These were concluded satisfactorily in an non-stigmatising way, without recourse to diagnosis and treatment of mental disorder (in the conventional sense) or referral to specialist mental health services.

The GP's role

The GP consultation represents an important interface between young people, families and the world of health care professionals. As James Willis (1995) acknowledges, GPs are 'specialists in generalism' taking an interest in whatever is of interest to their clients.

At the heart of the consultation lies a positive doctor–patient relationship and its value cannot be emphasised too strongly (Jones *et al*, 1997). A key issue for young people is that they are able to consult with a trusted adult who has a role, which is very distinct from that of their parent or teacher. In developing this level of rapport we know that GP interview style is influential and can help interpret and identify hidden and often important issues, symptoms and distress and detect potentially serious risk such as suicide.

Continuity

A frequent misconception about the GP consultation is that it is a single 10-minute event. Our case histories are typical of how an evolving narrative builds up, of brief interventions over a lifetime. GPs work with their patients from the cradle to the grave and establish a continuity of relationship that no other health professional can provide.

One study found that young people who are familiar to the practice could expect more accurate identification of their levels of distress, suggesting GPs are more likely to identify mental ill-health in patients that they know. At least 50% of young participants who were correctly identified by GPs, were attending their usual practice and had several consultations (Haller *et al*, 2009). In another study young people were more likely to confide in the GP if they had higher consultation rates, possibly as a result of enhanced rapport (Churchill *et al*, 2000). Some argue if continuous care is provided only a minority of cases will be unidentified over time (Bushnell *et al*, 2005).

Working with uncertainty

GPs are used to working with clinical uncertainty where they deal with many complex social/medical problems (Dew *et al*, 2005). Indeed GPs' core competencies include: tolerating uncertainty; exploring patients' own health beliefs; exploring probability; and marginalising danger (Royal College of General Practitioners, 2010). When dealing with young people, the GP may need to work with a degree of uncertainty and offer watchful waiting, using the passage of time to test if psychological difficulties are transient (Dowrick *et al*, 2000) while avoiding a stigmatising psychiatric diagnosis where possible. The issue of avoiding diagnosis and being wary of stigma may influence not only doctors, but also parents and young people themselves. Up to 50% of young people who perceived themselves to have more serious difficulties did not raise these issues in a consultation (Martinez *et al*, 2006).

Moreover, serious disorders such as psychosis often initially present in a similar way to milder, more common ones, and rarely present with clear-cut psychotic symptoms. Alongside a tolerance of uncertainty the GP needs a high index of suspicion to avoid dismissing difficulties as just 'teenage angst'. The GP plays a crucial role as they are in a prime position to identify and mediate early intervention (Addington, 2007) thereby avoiding a crisis and improving long-term outcomes for the young person.

Existing (mental) health promotion role

Core competencies for GPs include health promotion.

'GPs should aim at a holistic approach to the patient and his or her family, where the main focus would be in promoting their health

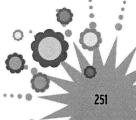

and general well-being. GPs are seen to have a responsibility for the individual patient, his or her family and the wider community and need to understand the characteristics of the community including socio-economic, ethnicity and health features.'
(Royal College of General Practitioners, 2010)

This mental health promoting role includes supporting self-care to enable a young person to make choices and decisions and take actions needed for themselves (Dew *et al*, 2005). Brief cognitive behavioural methods are already used by GPs and can be applied effectively within the 10-minute primary care consultation (David, 2006). Promoting good physical health also promotes good mental health. Our case studies illustrate the value of GPs being able to offer alternatives to prescribing such as referral to community organisations (eg. support for exercise, education, employment, housing and creative activity) (Department of Health, 2008).

Availability of wider treatment options are preferred by both young people and GPs. In one study, young people were concerned that if they admitted emotional distress to the GP they would be prescribed antidepressants, which they believed could lead to addiction and dependency (Biddle *et al*, 2006). Equally, GPs have expressed concern about the lack of alternatives to prescribing medicines (Jacobson *et al*, 2002). This is a salient point as both GPs and young people may hesitate about addressing issues at the earliest stage, where they mutually lack confidence in the treatments available (Dowrick *et al*, 2000).

What next?

GPs are already doing this work. Ways to help and support this work include the following.

1. Undertaking further audit to establish the impact of GP general care on the mental health of young people. This should aim to measure patient outcomes, clinical risk and clinical demand and should find improvements in all these areas.

2. Developing public health indicators for young people's mental health and exploring their integration into the general GP care aspects of the nGMS contract.

3. Providing effective, brief, pragmatic, case-based training as part of the GP's continued professional development, as well as through GP commissioned

CAMHS (Child and Adolescent Mental Health Service) and EIP (Early Intervention in Psychosis) train-the-trainer approaches (Sanci *et al*, 2000).

Brief training should consider:

a. effective communication skills – essential for consultations with young people for both physical and mental health problems (Donovan & Suckling, 2004)

b. mental health consultation frameworks and problem solving tools for brief consultations (Gledhill *et al*, 2003)

c. mental health self-care resources and family and community management options.

4. Ensuring GP services are accessible to young people by providing a youth friendly environment, clearly publicising the service; and maintaining principles of confidentiality, which concern young people greatly (Churchill & McPherson, 2005).

5. Supporting and linking with other well used options such as internet based information, school nurses and youth workers (Rickwood *et al*, 2007).

Conclusion

We need to acknowledge the role of the GP and recognise what they bring as a generalist and provider of holistic care. It is important to understand further the GP's current and existing work promoting the mental health of young people. The GP is able to provide targeted primary prevention in a non-stigmatising manner, that enables young people to build skills that will protect their mental health and build resilience. This role needs to be valued and we do not need to ask the GP to do 'more' by stepping out of their generalist role. Instead we need to establish that by offering appropriate, structured, brief and time-limited contact GPs are able to increase outcomes for patients, reduce clinical risk and demand. Finally, acting as confidantes for young people and brokers of their mental health, is a pivotal health promoting role that can help turn a young person's life around. This can bring with it a strong sense of professional purpose and self-worth for GPs themselves.

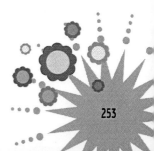

References

Addington J (2007) The promise of early intervention. *Early Intervention in Psychiatry* **1** (4) 294–307.

Appleby L, Amos T, Doyle U, Tomenson B & Woodman M (1996) General practitioners and young suicides: a preventive role for primary care. *British Journal of Psychiatry* **168** (3) 330–333.

Advisory Council on the Misuse of Drugs (2003) *Hidden Harm – Responding to the needs of children of problem drug users.* London: The Home Office.

Arseneault L, Cannon M, Poulton R, Murray R, Caspi A & Moffitt TE (2002) Cannabis use in adolescence and risk for adult psychosis: longitudinal prospective study. *British Medical Journal* **325** (7374) 1212–1213.

Biddle L, Donovan JL, Gunnell D & Sharp D (2006) Young adults' perceptions of GPs as a help source for mental distress: a qualitative study. *British Journal of General Practice* **56** (533) 924–931.

Bushnell J *et al* (2005) The effectiveness of case finding for mental health problems in primary care. *British Journal of General Practice* **55** (518) 665–669.

Churchill R, Allen J, Denman S, Williams D, Fielding K & von Fragstein M (2000) Do the attitudes and beliefs of young teenagers towards general practice influence actual consultation behaviour? *British Journal of General Practice* **50** (461) 953–957.

Churchill D & McPherson A (2005) *Getting it right in primary care: creating a child and young person friendly environment.* In: R Chambers & K Licence (Eds) Looked After Children in Primary Care. Oxford: Radcliffe.

Commonwealth Department of Health and Aged Care (2000) *Promotion, Prevention and Early Intervention for Mental Health – A monograph.* Canberra: Mental Health and Special Programmes Branch, Commonwealth Department of Health.

David L (2006) *Using CBT in General Practice – A 10-minute consultation.* London: Scion Publishing Ltd.

Department of Health (2003) *Health Survey for England 2002.* London: The Stationery Office.

Department of Health (2008) *Children and young people: promoting emotional health and well-being.* In: Information Series. London: DH.

Dew K, Dowell A, McLeod D, Collings S & Bushnell J (2005) 'This glorious twilight zone of uncertainty': mental health consultations in general practice in New Zealand. *Social Science & Medicine* **61** (6) 1189–1200.

Donovan C & Suckling H (2004) *Difficult Consultations with Adolescents.* Oxford: Radcliffe Medical Press.

Dowrick C, Gask L, Perry R, Dixon C & Usherwood T (2000) Do general practitioners' attitudes towards depression predict their clinical behaviour? *Psychological Medicine* **30** (2) 413–419.

Fombonne E, Wostear G, Cooper V, Harrington R & Rutter M (2001) The Maudsley long-term follow-up of child and adolescent depression 2. Suicidality, criminality and social dysfunction in adulthood. *British Journal of Psychiatry* **179** 218–223.

Gledhill J, Kramer T, Iliffe S & Garralda EM (2003) Training general practitioners in the identification and management of adolescent depression within the consultation: a feasibility study. *Journal of Adolescence* **26** (2) 245–250.

Gould MS, Greenberg T, Velting DM & Shaffer D (2003) Youth suicide risk and preventive interventions: a review of the past 10 years. *Journal of the American Academy of Child and Adolescent Psychiatry* **42** (4) 386–405.

Green H, McGinnity A, Meltzer H, Ford T & Goodman R (2005) *Mental Health of Children and Young People in Great Britain, 2004: Summary report.* London: Office of National Statistics.

Haller DM, Sanci LA, Sawyer SM & Patton GC (2009) The identification of young people's emotional distress: a study in primary care. *British Journal of General Practice* **59** (560) 159–165.

Hawton K, Harriss L, Hodder K, Simkin S & Gunnell D (2001) The influence of the economic and social environment on deliberate self-harm and suicide: an ecological and person-based study. *Psychological Medicine* **31** (5) 827–836.

Hawton K, Hall S, Simkin S, Bale L, Bond A, Codd S & Stewart A (2003) Deliberate self-harm in adolescents: a study of characteristics and trends in Oxford, 1990–2000. *Journal of Child Psychology & Psychiatry & Allied Disciplines* **44** (8) 1191–1198.

Hollis C (2003) Developmental precursors of child- and adolescent-onset schizophrenia and affective psychoses: diagnostic specificity and continuity with symptom dimensions. *British Journal of Psychiatry* **182** 37–44.

Jacobson L, Churchill R, Donovan C, Garralda E & Fay J (2002) Tackling teenage turmoil: primary care recognition and management of mental ill health during adolescence. *Family Practice* **19** (4) 401–409.

Jones R, Finlay F, Simpson S & Kreitman T (1997) How can adolescents' health needs and concerns best be met? *British Journal of General Practice* **47** (423) 631–634.

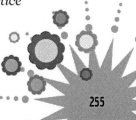

Kerfoot M (1988) Deliberate self-poisoning in childhood and early adolescence. *Journal of Child Psychology and Psychiatry and Allied Disciplines* **29** (3) 335–343.

Kessler RC, Amminger GP, Aguilar-Gaxiola S, Alonso J, Lee S & Ustün TB (2007) Age of onset of mental disorders: a review of recent literature. *Current Opinion in Psychiatry* **20** (4) 359–364.

Kessler RC, Berglund PA, Foster CL, Saunders WB, Stang PE & Walters EE (1997) Social consequences of psychiatric disorders: 2. Teenage parenthood. *American Journal of Psychiatry* **154** (10) 1405–1411.

Kramer T & Garralda M (1998) Psychiatric disorders in adolescents in primary care. *British Journal of Psychiatry* **173** 508–513.

Kramer T & Garralda M (2000) Child and adolescent mental health problems in primary care. *Advances in Psychiatric Treatment* **6** 287–294.

Lewinsohn PM, Hops H, Roberts RE, Seeley JR & Andrews JA (1993) Adolescent Psychopathology: 1. Prevalence and incidence of depression and other DSM-III-R disorders in high-school students. *Journal of Abnormal Psychology* **102** (1) 133–144.

Macdonald W & Bower P (2000) Child and adolescent mental health and primary health care: current status and future directions. *Current Opinion in Psychiatry* **13** (4) 369–373.

Martinez R, Reynolds S & Howe A (2006) Factors that influence the detection of psychological problems in adolescents attending general practices. *British Journal of General Practice* **56** (529) 594–599.

Mortensen PB (1995) Suicide among schizophrenic patients: occurrence and risk factors. *Clinical Neuropharmacology* **18** S1–S8.

National Institute for Health & Clinical Excellence (2010) *Alcohol-use Disorders: Preventing the development of hazardous and harmful drinking*. London: NICE.

NHS Information Centre (2009) *Statistics on Alcohol*. Leeds: The Health and Social Care Information Centre.

Office of National Statistics (2008) *General Household Survey 2005*. London: Office of National Statistics.

Princes Trust Youth Index (2009) [online]. Available from: http://www.princes-trust.org.uk/news_2009/wellbeing_campaign.aspxn (accessed August 2010).

Rickwood DJ, Deane FP & Wilson CJ (2007) When and how do young people seek professional help for mental health problems? *Medical Journal of Australia* **187** S35–S39.

Royal College of General Practitioners (2010) *GP Curriculum Statements* [online]. Available from: http://www.rcgp-curriculum.org.uk/rcgp_-_gp_ curriculum_documents/gp_curriculum_statements.aspx (accessed August 2010).

Royal College of Paediatrics & Child Health (2003) *Bridging the Gaps: Health care for adolescents*. London: RCPCH.

Royal College of Psychiatrists Research Unit (2001) *National In-patient Child and Adolescent Psychiatry Study (NICAPS)*. London: RCPsych.

Rueter MA, Scaramella L, Wallace LE & Conger RD (1999) First onset of depressive or anxiety disorders predicted by the longitudinal course of internalizing symptoms and parent-adolescent disagreements. *Archives of General Psychiatry* **56** (8) 726–732.

Sanci LA, Coffey CMM, Veit FCM, Carr-Gregg M, Patton GC, Day N & Bowes G (2000) Evaluation of the effectiveness of an educational intervention for general practitioners in adolescent health care: randomised controlled trial. *British Medical Journal* **320** (7229) 224–230.

Thomas CM & Morris S (2003) Cost of depression among adults in England in 2000. *British Journal of Psychiatry* **183** 514–519.

Tylee A *et al* (2007) Adolescent health 6 – youth-friendly primary-care services: how are we doing and what more needs to be done? *Lancet* **369** (9572) 1565–1573.

Viner RM & Barker M (2005) Young people's health: the need for action. *British Medical Journal* **330** (7496) 901–903.

Willis J (1995) *The Paradox of Progress*. Abingdon: Radcliffe Medical Press.

UNICEF (2007) *Child Poverty in Perspective: An overview of child well-being in rich countries. A comprehensive assessment of the lives and well-being of children and adolescents in the economically advanced nations*. Florence, Italy: UNICEF Innocenti Research Centre.

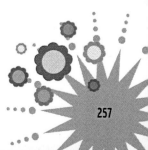

Chapter 17

Place and space

Aideen Silke

Introduction

The physical environment, by which we mean the external, tangible surroundings in which we live, exerts both positive and negative influences on mental well-being. These influences operate at both the individual and community level. Key to understanding 'place' is recognition of the significance of where we live, levels of belonging, satisfaction and trust in our local area (Deacon *et al*, 2010). Deacon *et al* found that having a poor sense of belonging and a low perception of ability to influence what goes on in an area were both strongly associated with lower mental well-being. Conversely, satisfaction with the local area was higher for those with higher levels of mental well-being, as measured by the Warwick-Edinburgh Mental Wellbeing Scale (WEMWBS) (Tennant *et al*, 2007). Recent research by CABE (2010a) has demonstrated that the impact of poorer quality urban space is more acutely felt by people living in deprived areas on low incomes, particularly black and minority ethnic groups. CABE further found that while people living in deprived areas valued local green spaces, in practice many sites that were the most convenient (eg. within local housing estates), were more often underused due to being of poor quality or actual or perceived lack of safety (CABE, 2010a). To add to this, the Office of the Deputy Prime Minister (ODPM) (2004) have found that the highest prevalence of common mental health disorders are within deprived neighbourhoods and Morris (2003) has identified a correlation between health inequalities and inequalities in the quality of the physical environment.

A recent review of health inequalities by Marmot states that:

> *'Communities are important for physical and mental health and well-being. The physical and social characteristics of communities, and the degree to which they enable and promote healthy behaviours, all make a contribution to social inequalities in health.'*
> (Marmot, 2010)

Further to this, the review found that a higher proportion of the population living in deprived areas were living in communities with the least favourable environmental conditions (Marmot, 2010). Curtin (2003) has stated that in seeking to develop healthy communities, it is social rather than medical interventions that will have the greatest impact.

Chu *et al* (2004) identified five key domains, through which the residential environment impacts on mental well-being:

▶ presence of escape facilities

▶ control over the internal housing environment

▶ quality of house design

▶ maintenance, safety, crime and fear of crime

▶ social participation.

These were later confirmed by Guite *et al* (2006), with the addition of a 6th domain: noise. At the time of publication, the nature of the relationships between factors in the physical and social residential environment and mental well-being were being tested in the case-control study 'Feeling Good About Where You Live' in Greenwich. Within this chapter these five key domains identified by Chu *et al* (2004) will be further explored.

Presence of escape facilities

Presence of local escape facilities, such as cafés, open spaces, parks and community centres, have been found to be associated with higher levels of mental well-being. The relationship between green and open space and mental well-being has been the most comprehensively established within the literature. Morris identified five elements where the evidence suggests exposure to the natural environment has a positive impact on health:

▶ enhanced personal and social communication skills

▶ increased physical health

▶ enhanced mental and spiritual health

▶ enhanced spiritual, sensory and aesthetic awareness

▶ the ability to assert personal control and increased sensitivity to one's own well-being.
(Morris, 2003)

This positive correlation between greener environments and health has been tested empirically in the Netherlands (de Vries *et al*, 2003; Groenewegen *et al*, 2006; Maas *et al*, 2006).

Open air recreation and access to outdoor spaces are an important part of many people's daily lives, and research has shown that outdoor activity provides scope for relaxation, refreshment, escape from the everyday stresses and provides opportunities to form social relationships (Macnaghten & Urry, 2000; Chiesura, 2004). Exercise is also associated with improvements in psychological and spiritual health (Hickmann *et al* 1999; Oxford Brookes University, 2001). Walking is the most common form of physical activity in adults (Owen *et al*, 2004) and increasingly schemes that promote walking in green spaces have been developed (Bird, 2004; Dawson *et al*, 2006; Lamb *et al*, 2002). Allotments are also identified as escape facilities with positive effect on physical and mental well-being and where there are opportunities for therapeutic benefits to people with physical and mental health problems (Groenewegen *et al*, 2006; Fieldhouse, 2003). Ulrich (1984) has suggested that surgical patients who had a view through their window of a natural setting recovered more quickly from their surgery and took fewer potent analgesics than matched patients in rooms with a view of a brick wall.

Faber Taylor *et al*'s (2001) study of children with Attention Deficit Disorder (ADD) found that the children functioned better after undertaking activities in green settings and that symptoms were milder for those children with greener play settings. After consideration of potential confounding factors, they suggest a causal link between experience of nature and symptoms of ADD, although they caution that confirmation of the causal link requires experimental testing (Faber Taylor *et al*, 2001).

However, within society, escape facilities are not uniformly available and CABE (2010b) found that persons living in deprived inner city areas were five times less likely to have access to good quality general green space and public parks than people in more affluent areas. Equally, persons living in deprived areas are more likely to have poorer quality mental and physical health (Marmot, 2010).

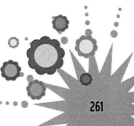

However, Chu *et al* (2004) caution that escape facilities need to be places where people actively want to go. Their simple existence is not sufficient. Furthermore, they need to be of sufficient size, quality and accessibility if they are to be used to buffer against high-density living (Rodin *et al*, 1978).

Control over the internal housing environment

Humans spend a large proportion of their time within the internal environment. Where this environment is not comfortable it can negatively impact on mental health, particularly where residents feel that they have no control and can do nothing to change their environment. However, the degree of stress caused by environmental stressors will vary by individual. The degree of control or perceived control that people have over their internal housing environment acts as an important mediator of its impact. Damp, noise, light, and temperature are the key factors; with the evidence around noise and damp being strongest.

Living in cold, damp conditions has a number of effects on physical health and on mental well-being. Guite *et al* (2006) found that residents living in damp conditions or residents concerned that they were living in cold, damp conditions were 1.88 times (95% CI, 1.20–2.42) more likely to be in the lowest quartile for mental health. Many existing conditions are exacerbated by living in a cold, damp home including reduced resistance to respiratory diseases, raised blood pressure leading to increased incidence of strokes and prevalence of heart problems, increased recovery time from common illnesses such as colds and worsening of arthritic pain.

Apart from the mental anguish and physical discomfort of living in damp conditions, social exclusion is also associated with such conditions. Damp conditions have been linked to increased absence from work and limited job opportunities due to ill health. Children and young people are also affected by damp conditions through days missed from school due to cold-related illness and educational achievement also suffers because children's attention span and physical comfort to complete homework is affected. People may be less likely to invite others into their homes if they are damp, therefore increasing the likelihood of limited social interaction. Raw *et al* (2001) describes the stigma of feeling unclean, which is felt by individuals experiencing mould and which in itself is related to depression and stress.

Recent research by Howden-Chapman *et al* (2007) investigated the impact on health inequalities of insulating existing homes, using a cluster randomised trial. Within this study, households in the intervention arm were given a series of measures to improve thermal insulation in their property. Results showed that improved insulation led to warmer bedroom temperatures, reduced odds of feeling cold or reporting damp/mould and reduced energy consumption. Significant improvements in self-reported health measures were shown, however, the reduced numbers of respiratory admissions was not significant. Households in the control arm received interventions following completion of follow-up.

The negative effects of noise on psychological, social and economic well-being have been well researched. Noise can affect quality of sleep and those repeatedly disturbed during sleep can suffer both physical and psychological stress, including paranoia, delusions, hallucinations, suicidal and homicidal impulses. Noise also impacts on people's ability to concentrate and perform mental tasks. The World Health Organization outlines how noise disturbance can accelerate and intensify the development of latent mental disorders and can contribute to the following: anxiety, stress, nervousness, nausea, headaches, emotional instability, argumentativeness, sexual impotence, changes in mood and an increase in social conflicts. Children, older people, as well as those with underlying depression may be particularly vulnerable to these effects because they may lack adequate coping mechanisms (WHO, 1999).

Lack of peace and quiet can also lead to negative social behaviour and 'annoyance reactions'. Annoyance to noise increases significantly when noise is accompanied by vibration. Social and behavioural effects of noise exposure are complex, subtle, and indirect. These effects include changes in everyday behaviour (eg. closing windows and doors to eliminate outside noises, avoiding the use of balconies, patios and yards and turning up the volume of radios and television sets). Noise can also lead to changes in social behaviour (eg. aggressiveness, unfriendliness, non-participation, or disengagement) and in social indicators (eg. residential mobility, hospital admissions, drug consumption, and accident rates). Importantly, noise can also lead to changes in mood with increased reports of depression.

The degree of annoyance produced by noise may vary with the time of day, the unpleasant characteristics of the noise, the duration and intensity of the noise, the meaning associated with it and the nature of the activity that the noise interrupted.

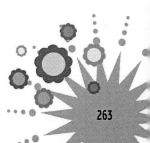

Annoyance may be influenced by a variety of non-acoustical factors such as:

▶ individual sensitivity to noise

▶ fear of the source of the noise

▶ conviction that noise could be reduced by third parties

▶ the degree to which an individual feels able to control the noise

▶ whether or not the noise originated from an important economic activity.

Other less direct effects of annoyance are disruption of one's peace of mind, the enjoyment of one's property, and the enjoyment of solitude.

Quality of house design and maintenance

Maintenance of housing is an important issue in understanding mental well-being. Evans (2003) found a relationship between physical housing quality and psychological well-being, and that symptoms of distress could be lessened by increasing the quality of housing.

High quality housing design accompanied by a maintenance regime has the ability to tackle many of the issues previously mentioned that have a negative impact on mental health, such as damp and noise. However, with relatively few new houses being built, addressing these issues primarily requires upgrading and more effective maintenance of the existing housing stock, which presents a considerable challenge.

Safety, crime and fear of crime

Crime and the fear of crime affect health both directly and indirectly. Higher levels of fear of crime are associated with poorer levels of both physical and mental health. The perception gap between actual levels of crime and levels of fear of crime is important, as perceived levels of crime are persistently higher than actual levels of crime.

Increased fear of crime is related to increased isolation (Acheson, 1998) and isolation is associated with negative mental health. Ross (1993) argues that experience of fear in the local neighbourhood and fear of being a victim of crime can lead people to limit their outdoor activities. The evidence on the link between the fear of crime and health is compelling. Green *et al*'s (2002) study of residential tower blocks in Liverpool found fear of crime was significantly associated with health status, and that feelings of safety when out alone at night were a consistent predictor of health status. Interestingly, contrary to their hypothesis, Green *et al* did not find that living in a tower block decreased feelings of safety and that feeling safe in the local environment was the key determinant of health status. This was supported by Guite *et al* (2006) in their survey of 1,012 residents in the London Borough of Greenwich, who found that not feeling safe during the day and at night were strongly correlated with lower levels of mental health and that building height was not significant.

Socially isolated environments present a public health challenge as they are a risk factor for premature morbidity and mortality. Cacioppo and Hawkley (2003) found that socially isolated young adults were more likely to find everyday stressors more stressful, to have poorer sleep efficiency, to adopt more passive coping mechanisms, to have poorer physical health, poorer maintenance of physiological function and slower wound healing.

Social participation

The World Health Organization recognises that:

'...a crucial direction for policy to promote health equity concerns the participation of civil society and the empowerment of affected communities to become active protagonists in shaping their own health.' (WHO, 2010)

This directive suggests that social participation involving vulnerable and excluded groups should seek to empower them to increase their control over decisions that influence their health and life quality. While social participation cannot be created, spaces that enable and encourage active participation can.

Participation raises self-esteem and helps people to be more open to change, which is often an important initial step in improving their health and lifestyle. Evidence suggests that engagement in local community activities builds social capital, improves health and tackles health inequalities. Furthermore, an active neighbourhood where residents feel free to participate and engage with each other is generally perceived as a safer and more desirable place to be. Finnish research found that there were three aspects of social capital, which were significantly associated with good self-rated health: membership of voluntary associations, friendship networks and religious involvement (Hyyppä & Mäki, 2003).

A review of the literature around neighbourhood accessibility, social networks and mental well-being by Parry-Jones (2006) found that informal networks and connections were important to mental well-being and that residents valued informal contact with others within a safe environment (eg. places to stop and chat on the street.) She concludes:

> '...that neither a physical nor a social determinism alone can provide a satisfactory model for the complex way in which people feel or behave in their neighbourhoods.'
> (Parry-Jones, 2006)

This is a key point and it is important that it is recognised when considering the relationship between place and space and public mental health.

Environmental stressors

In considering the relationship between place and space and mental health, it is valuable to also consider the impact of the changing environment where this is creating additional environmental stressors, particularly given the expected impact of climate change. Flooding is the most common natural disaster in Europe, and the most costly in economic terms (WHO, 2002). Flooding presents a number of risks to health including drowning or serious injury from fast-flowing water. Anxiety and depression both increase following flooding (Reacher et al, 2004; Tunstall et al, 2006). Following the 2007 floods in the UK over 70% of residents affected felt that this had an impact on their physical or emotional health (Pitt, 2008). However, the size of the impact of flooding on mental health is difficult to evaluate and onset or diagnosis is often delayed. In addition, it is difficult to measure direct association between mental health disorder and the experience of flooding.

Conclusion

As described in this chapter, the relationship between place and space and mental health is complex and multifaceted. The effect that the environment has on mental health can be both positive and negative with the impact of factors in the local environment felt at both community and individual levels. Furthermore, when considering the impact of the environment it is important to understand that this is mediated by a range of other factors that impact on mental well-being. However, as discussed, there is strong evidence which supports the argument that if there are to be significant strides made in addressing public mental health challenges, then mental health will need to be considered across a broad range of policy areas, including those that have an impact on the physical environment.

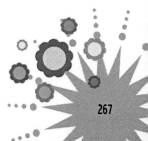

References

Acheson D (1998) *Independent Inquiry into Inequalities in Health*. London: The Stationery Office.

Bird W (2004) *Natural Fit – Can green space and biodiversity increase levels of physical activity?* Sandy, Bedforshire: Royal Society for the Protection of Birds.

CABE (2010a) *Community Green: Using local spaces to tackle inequality and improve health*. London: CABE.

CABE (2010b) *Urban Green Nation: Building the evidence base*. London: CABE.

Cacioppo JT & Hawkley LC (2003) Social isolation and health, with an emphasis on underlying mechanisms. *Perspectives in Biology and Medicine* **46** (3) S39–S52.

Chiesura (2004) The role of urban parks for the sustainable city. *Landscape and Urban Planning* **68** (1).

Chu A, Thorne A & Guite H (2004) The impact on mental well-being of the urban and physical environment: an assessment of the evidence. *Journal of Mental Health Promotion* **3** (2) 17–32.

Curtin L (2003) It takes a whole nation … to create a health system. *Nursing Administration* **27** (2) 120–127.

Dawson J, Boller I, Foster C & Hillsdon M (2006) *Evaluation of Changes to Physical Activity amongst People who attend the Walking the Way to Health Initiative*. London: The Countryside Agency.

de Vries S, Verheij RA, Groenewegen PP & Spreeuwenberg P (2003) Natural environments – healthy environments? An exploratory analysis of the relationship between green space and health. *Environment and Planning* **35** (10) 1717–1731.

Deacon L, Carlin H, Spalding J, Giles S, Stansfield J, Hughes S, Perkins C & Bellis MA (2010) *North West Mental Wellbeing Survey 2009*. Liverpool: North West Public Health Observatory.

Evans GW (2003) The built environment and mental health. *Journal of Urban Health* **80** (4) 536–555.

Faber Taylor A, Kuo F & Sullivan W (2001) Coping with ADD – the surprising connection to green play settings. *Environment and Behavior* **33** (1) 54–77.

Fieldhouse J (2003) The impact of an allotment group on mental health clients: health, wellbeing and social networking. *British Journal of Occupational Therapy* **66** (7) 286–296.

Green G, Gilbertson G & Grimsley MFJ (2002) Fear of crime and health in residential tower blocks: a case study in Liverpool, UK. *European Journal of Public Health* **12** 10–15.

Groenewegen PP, van den Berg AE, de Vries S & Verheij RA (2006) Vitamin G: effects of green space on health, well-being, and social safety. *BMC Public Health* **6** 149.

Guite HF, Clark C & Ackrill G (2006) The impact of the physical and urban environmental on mental wellbeing. *Public Health* **120** (12) 1117–1126.

Hickman SA, Lee RE, Sallis JF, Castro CM & Chen AH (1999) The association of physical activity change with self-esteem in ethnic minority women: a prospective analysis. *Journal of Gender, Culture and Health* **4** (94) 281–292.

Howden-Chapman P, Matheson A, Crane J, Viggers H, Cunningham M, Blakely T, Cunningham C, Woodward A, Saville-Smith K, O'Dea D, Kennedy M, Baker M, Waipara N, Chapman R & Davie G (2007) Effect of insulating existing houses on health inequality: cluster randomised study in the community. *British Medical Journal* **334** 460–464.

Hyyppä MT & Mäki J (2003) Social participation and health in a community rich in stock of social capital. *Health Education Research* **18** (6) 770–779.

Joseph Rowntree Foundation (2008) *The Influence of Neighbourhood Deprivation on People's Attachment to Places*. York: Joseph Rowntree Foundation.

Lamb SE, Bartlett HP, Ashley A & Bird W (2002) Can lay-led walking programmes increase physical activity in middle-aged adults? A randomised controlled trial. *Journal of Epidemiology and Community Health* **56** 246–252.

Maas J, Verheij RA, Groenewegen PP, de Vries S & Spreeuwenberg P (2006) Green space, urbanity, and health: how strong is the relation? *Journal of Epidemiological Community Health* **60** (7) 587–592.

Macnaghten P & Urry J (Eds) (2000) Bodies of nature. *Body and Society* **6** 1–202.

Marmot M (2010) *Fair Society, Healthy Lives: The strategic review of health inequalities in England 2010*. London: The Marmot Review.

Morris N (2003) *Health, Well-Being and Open Space: Literature review*. Edinburgh: Edinburgh College of Art and Heriot-Watt University.

Office of the Deputy Prime Minister (2004) *Mental Health and Social Exclusion: Social Exclusion Unit report*. London: ODPM.

Owen N, Humpel N, Leslie E, Bauman A & Sallis JF (2004) Understanding environmental influences on walking: review and research agend. *American Journal of Preventative Medicine* **27** (1) 67–76.

Oxford Brookes University (2001) *Outdoor Conservation Work Beats Depression*. Oxford: Oxford Brookes.

Parry-Jones S (2006) *Neighbourhood Accessibility, Social Networks and Mental Well-being: A literature review*. Unpublished.

Pitt M (2008) *The Pitt Review: Lessons learnt from the 2007 floods*. London: Cabinet Office.

Raw GJ, Aizlewood CE & Hamilton R (2001) *Building Regulations, Health and Safety*. London: Building Research Establishment.

Reacher M, McKenzie K, Lane C, Nichols T, Iversen A, Hepple P, Walter T, Laxton C & Simpson J (2004) Health impacts of flooding in Lewes: a comparison of reported gastrointestinal and other illness and mental health in flooded and non-flooded households. *Communicable Disease and Public Health* **7** (1) 1–8.

Rodin J, Solomon S & Metcalf J (1978) Role of control in mediating perception of density. *Journal of Personality and Social Psychology* **36** 989–999.

Ross C (1993) Fear of victimization and health. *Journal of Quantitative Criminology* **9** (2) 159–175.

Tennant R, Hiller L, Fishwick R, Platt S, Joseph S, Weich S, Parkinson J, Secker J & Stewart-Brown S (2007) The Warwick-Edinburgh Mental Well-being Scale (WEMWBS). Development and UK validation. *Health and Quality of Life Outcomes* **5** 63.

Tunstall SM, Tapsell SM, Green CH, Floyd P & George C (2006) The health effects of flooding: social research results from England and Wales. *Water and Health* **4** (3) 365–380.

Ulrich RS (1984) View through a window may influence recovery from surgery. *Science* **224** (4647) 420–421.

World Health Organization (1999) *Guidelines for Community Noise*. Geneva: WHO.

World Health Organization (2010) *Social Participation* [online]: Geneva: WHO. Available at: http://www.who.int/social_determinants/thecommission/countrywork/within/socialparticipation/en/index.html (accessed July 2010).

World Health Organization Europe (2002) *Floods: Climate change and adaption strategies for human health*. Geneva: WHO.

Public Mental Health Today © Pavilion Publishing (Brighton) Ltd 2010

Chapter 18

Strengthening mental health within communities

Carol Tannahill, Ade Kearns and Lyndal Bond

Introduction

Consideration of the community dimension to mental health is important for a number of reasons. Most of us live in communities, work in communities, belong to communities of interest by dint of our beliefs, values and activities, use services and amenities located in our communities, and socialise with others from the same communities. In short, most aspects of life happen in communities, and our identity is affected by their image and reputation. Our lives are profoundly affected by the quality of those communities and by the behaviours of others within them.

Although we may be members of more than one community, there is usually a dominant community identity with which we are most strongly aligned. Often this dominant community, and the one to which the concept of 'community' is assumed to refer, is defined geographically as the place where we live, and may have grown up. A further assumption is that this geographically-based focus is particularly relevant to poorer communities, given that residents in these areas are more likely to spend a greater proportion of their time within the communities in which they live and less likely to have the resources to be part of a large number of other communities.

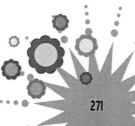

In this chapter we propose concepts of 'community' and 'mentally healthy communities' that would be applicable to communities of all types. Nevertheless, our particular interests lie with deprived urban communities and with developing a better understanding of approaches to turn around their fortunes. Our work in the GoWell research and learning programme (Egan *et al*, 2010; and see http://www.gowellonline.com/), which is examining the health impacts of urban regeneration in Glasgow, provides the basis for much of the material we will present.

In order to build a better understanding of what needs to happen to strengthen mental health within communities, five issues will be considered.

1. What is distinctive about taking a community approach to mental health? What does a community approach add to individual and population-wide approaches?

2. What do we know about the mental health of communities? And what more do we need to know?

3. What strengthens mental health within communities?

4. How are communities likely to change in the future?

5. What does this all mean for practice?

Taking a community approach to mental health

Although there are many types of community and important differences in the roles that communities play in people's lives, people have been found to largely agree about what a community is. Five core elements of community have been defined (MacQueen *et al*, 2001).

1. Locus: a sense of place, often referred to in terms of particular areas or settings.

2. Sharing: common interests and perspectives, including values, beliefs, activities, norms and characteristics such as religion, ethnicity and sexuality.

3. Joint action: a source of community cohesion and identity in the sense that a feeling of community can arise from joint actions/hanging out together.

4. Social ties: interpersonal relations including family, friends, neighbours, co-workers, and support groups. Characteristics of these relationships include trust, caring, socialising, and regular presence (sometimes in the background).

5. Diversity: social complexity, communities within communities, stratification, the presence of stigmatised, distrusted and hidden groups.

It follows that a community is far more than a group of people. Communities have their own physical and cultural contexts, interpersonal relationships and activities, and substructures. It is evident, however, that these will not necessarily promote good mental health, or protect the more vulnerable members of the community. For example, while social ties can bring love, they also bring heartbreak and pain and sharing can reduce isolation but also result in unhealthy peer pressure.

So what does a mentally healthy community look like? Hawe (2008) provided the following description:

> 'A mentally healthy community is a place where people report low levels of depression, suicidal thoughts, substance abuse, violence, discrimination and stress and high levels of quality of life, work satisfaction, economic security, social support, self-esteem and well-being. But it is more than that. It is a place where people's interdependence and mutuality is recognised, protected and valued.'

The final sentence is particularly significant for our purposes here.

Integral to most good public mental health strategies is a recognition of the need for action to support the determinants of good mental health (issues such as work satisfaction and economic security) and minimise those that undermine mental health (such as violence, exclusion and discrimination) across the population as a whole, in addition to focusing particular support on those most vulnerable or at risk. Such population-wide approaches are often universal, and may not be able to reflect the social complexities within particular communities. In other words, they have limited potential to impact on those core elements of community that determine the characteristics of relationships, and the prevailing values and beliefs. It is this gap above all that needs to be filled by community-based approaches.

Understanding community mental health

It is well established that mental health outcomes (usually measured in terms of mental health problems) and associated health-related behaviours, are worse in areas of low socio-economic status (SES), and that there are strong associations with levels of educational attainment, poverty, and employment across the population (see for example, Davidson *et al*, 2009; Hanlon *et al*, 2006). However, the mental health of a community can only be partly described as the sum of characteristics of individuals, and more is said about this in the 'measuring success chapter' of this handbook.

The measurement of social capital has been proposed as a helpful addition to individual and structural measures, and its relationship to mental health explored in several studies (McKenzie & Harpham, 2006). Community engagement activities can directly and indirectly affect mental health in the shorter and longer-terms, including through impacting on social capital and volunteering (National Institute for Health and Clinical Excellence, 2008). Further measures of community cohesion and social connectedness help to quantify people's sense of belonging, value and social support.

There is some evidence that people living in poverty are less likely to have supportive relationships (Kessler & McLeod, 1985) and a similar picture is found for community-level variables. As shown in table 1, findings from the most recent health and well-being survey, comprising a representative sample of the population of Greater Glasgow and Clyde (Traci Leven Research, 2010), demonstrate this association with deprivation across a range of dimensions of community health.

Against this backdrop, it is notable and surprising to find that mental well-being displays a slightly different pattern. Using the Warwick-Edinburgh Mental Well-being Scale (WEMWBS) (Tennant *et al*, 2007), we were able in 2008 to assess levels of positive mental health and well-being in 15 deprived communities in Glasgow undergoing major housing investment and area regeneration. All but one of the 15 study areas is in the 15% most deprived areas in Scotland on the SIMD. Scores on the WEMWBS scale are summed to give an aggregate score between 14 and 70. The mean scores across all the GoWell areas were 52.1 for men and 51.4 for women. These compare favourably to the Scottish Health Survey 2008 (Bromley *et al*, 2009) mean scores of 50.2 for men and 49.7 for women; and the 2008 Scottish national survey of attitudes to mental health and well-being (Davidson *et al*, 2009) which found mean scores of 51.1 for men and 50.2 for women. In other words, people in these deprived GoWell communities, experiencing a high degree of change as well as longstanding ill-health, neighbourhood problems and relative poverty, appear on average to have levels of wellbeing comparable to the Scottish population as a whole.

Table 1: Community-level variables – findings from NHS Greater Glasgow and Clyde health and well-being survey, 2008 [N = 8,278]	Respondents living in most deprived quintile of SIMD (%)	Respondents living in least deprived quintile of SIMD (%)	All respondents (%)
Generally, you can trust people in my local area	65%	83%	72%
Neighbours look out for one another	66%	79%	71%
Local people can influence decisions that affect neighbourhood	57%	74%	64%
Exchange small favours with neighbours	54%	67%	58%
Feel valued as a member of the community	51%	61%	55%
SIMD: Scottish Index of Multiple Deprivation			

Factors associated with mentally healthy communities

Taking these WEMWBS findings further, we have explored the factors associated with higher levels of well-being in the GoWell communities. To date we have been able to do this only on a cross-sectional basis, precluding conclusions about causality. Nevertheless, some important associations are evident, which have implications for actions to strengthen mental health in communities like these.

Figures 1–3 show associations between WEMWBS scores and community measures in the GoWell study areas. There are striking associations between mental well-being and:

1. perceptions that the neighbourhood in which the respondent is living makes them feel they are doing well in life; those strongly disagreeing that their neighbourhood makes them feel they are doing well in life having WEMWBS scores about 20% lower than those strongly agreeing

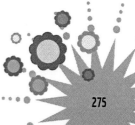

2. feeling that people in the local area can influence decisions, and that organisations are responsive to their views; those within the lowest quartile aggregate rating for these community empowerment measures having WEMWBS scores almost 20% lower than those within the highest quartile

3. interactions with neighbours: knowing them, talking to them, exchanging things with them, and so on; those reporting the lowest sense of neighbourliness in their communities had mental well-being scores about 10% lower than those reporting the highest levels of neighbourliness.

In further analyses, controlling for socio-demographic characteristics and physical health status, we have found strong associations between mental well-being and satisfaction with landlord and perceptions of personal progress, as well as with a number of aspects of housing (external appearance of the home and the front door, good insulation) and the attractiveness of the local environment (Bond *et al*, in preparation).

These findings add a new dimension to our understanding of how to strengthen mental health in communities. There is now a well-established literature on the wider causes of psychological well-being (Huppert, 2008) and on the effects of the physical environment (Cooper *et al*, 2008) and housing (Dunn, 2008). Collectively this reflects the need to be concerned not only with the physical design of neighbourhoods, but also with psychological, social and financial dimensions. There has been much less attention paid at a community level to factors associated with positive mental health than to mental health problems. As Huppert (2008) highlights, it cannot be assumed that the determinants of mental well-being will be the opposite of those associated with risk of mental ill-being. Our findings suggest that well-being may be less strongly linked to deprivation than other mental health indicators are, and that a number of dimensions of community life are very strongly associated with levels of well-being.

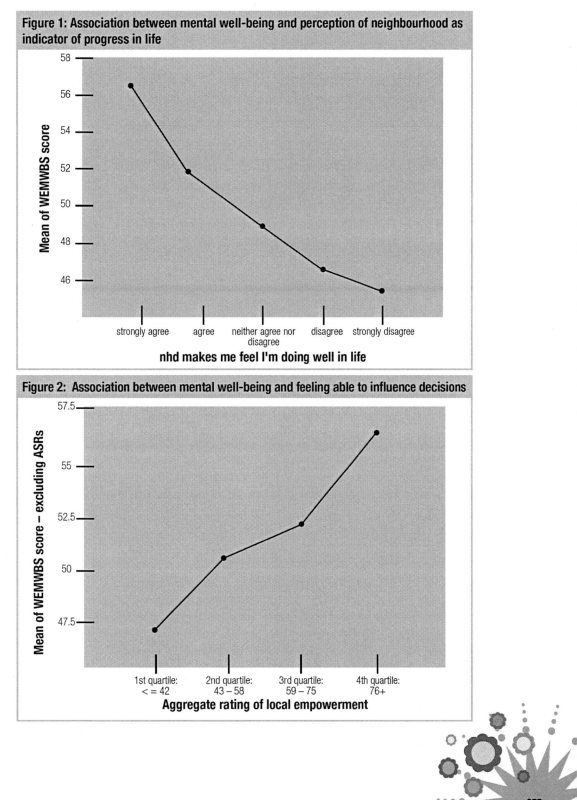

Figure 1: Association between mental well-being and perception of neighbourhood as indicator of progress in life

Mean of WEMWBS score (y-axis)

x-axis: strongly agree, agree, neither agree nor disagree, disagree, strongly disagree

nhd makes me feel I'm doing well in life

Figure 2: Association between mental well-being and feeling able to influence decisions

Mean of WEMWBS score – excluding ASRs (y-axis)

x-axis: 1st quartile: < = 42, 2nd quartile: 43 – 58, 3rd quartile: 59 – 75, 4th quartile: 76+

Aggregate rating of local empowerment

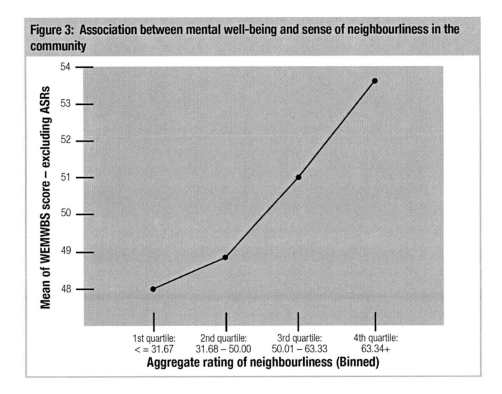

Figure 3: Association between mental well-being and sense of neighbourliness in the community

The changing nature of communities

Our considerations so far have been based on evidence and data from communities that exist, or at least that existed when the research was carried out. Communities are constantly changing, though, and new ones are being created. Sometimes this process is 'managed': a deliberate consequence of policy (as is the case, for example, in relation to the establishment of mixed tenure communities, bringing tenants of social rented housing closely alongside owner occupiers). In such cases, the implications for the community's mental health could be considered at the policy development stage. This would raise issues, in the mixed tenure policy example, as to what more would be required, over and above providing housing of different tenures, to facilitate joint actions, or social ties, in these mixed communities. Challenging as that would be, it is arguably a familiar process.

Much more challenging, and requiring the emergence of new solutions, are the changes to communities that will result from trends and processes resulting from factors external to policy: demographic change; climate change;

population migration; major events; urbanisation; technological developments; and so on. It is the way of things that the poorest, least healthy communities, will be the most vulnerable to the negative impacts of these trends, and the current economic climate magnifies that vulnerability.

The concept of resilient communities is helpful here. Resilience represents the ability to adapt positively when things change, and can to some extent mediate the effects of socioeconomic and material disadvantage. Friedli (2009) has summarised evidence on resilient places (those that over-perform in health terms, relative to their economic resources), resilient communities and resilient individuals. Resilient places, communities and individuals have a better than usual chance of sustaining mental health and well-being in the face of new challenges as well as old. A range of factors make resilience possible and 'these mostly have to do with the quality of human relationships, and with the quality of public service responses to people with problems' (Bartley, 2006).

Implications for policy and practice

Our concern with community-level action talks to everyone who feels part of a community, and specifically to those responsible for supporting disadvantaged communities. The holistic aims of community regeneration include more than the physical and economic regeneration of areas, and incorporate social and cultural regeneration, with processes of community empowerment underpinning all aspects. Experience to date shows some major improvements on the back of investment in physical regeneration, and progress in a number of other dimensions including satisfaction with services and sense of empowerment, but not in relation to the core elements of community cohesion, social capital and social ties (GoWell, 2010).

There is, of course, no straightforward prescription for strengthening mental health in communities. Klein (1969) was bold enough to itemise three steps, which resonate with the need to build resilience described above:

> '...we must first be concerned with strengthening the safety of the community and the sense of security of its inhabitants; second, we must support the caretaking agencies and institutions; third – and perhaps most important – we must enhance those aspects of community life which enable each citizen to possess significance and positive value in the eyes of others who are relevant to his life.'
> (Klein, 1969)

Drawing more widely on existing evidence, we would emphasise also the importance of the quality and aesthetics of the physical environment, including the quality of amenities such as social spaces and children's play areas therein. Consideration needs to be given upfront to 'designing in' for health so that features that foster well-being are maximised, and those that are risk factors for mental ill-health minimised, in the fabric of communities. Aspects to be considered in this regard include the provision of green space, the walkability of areas, low-rise rather than high-rise buildings, noise management, and well-lit areas.

These physical aspects of community regeneration need to be accompanied by equivalent attention to, and investment in, social regeneration. Of pre-eminent importance is the parent–child relationship as a fundamental determinant of mental well-being (see chapter 7 for further reading), and we have been struck by the infrequent mention made of children in regeneration policy and practice in Scotland. More routine emphasis also needs to be placed on community engagement, empowerment and control. There has been a positive shift in this regard, but much more is needed, and more often. For sustained community well-being, these processes also need to be sustained, and to move beyond ad-hoc consultations when new developments are proposed.

Lastly, there are implications for the delivery of services in developing beyond traditional individually-focused approaches. Social prescribing is one underutilised route whereby primary care services can contribute to increased social support and contact while providing support for vulnerable individuals (Friedli, 2005). More generally within and beyond the health sector, the provision of services for groups, buddying and mentoring in communities, can all contribute to reducing isolation and supporting social ties.

Summary

Communities are important to our well-being. The ways in which communities work, their norms, aesthetics, the interactions that take place, and the quality of services, have a strong influence on the mental health and well-being of those within them. In addition to population-wide strategies, and support for individuals, there is considerable scope for community-level action to improve mental health and well-being.

Considerations of the connection between well-being and ill-health have highlighted that the two concepts do not simply lie along the one continuum, but are perhaps best regarded in terms of two axes at right angles to, and crossing, each other (Downie *et al*, 1996, p21). As described in chapter 2 of this handbook, this framework has been further developed specifically in relation to mental health, as a dual continuum model which highlights, for example, that people with mental health problems may at the same time have positive mental health or well-being. Poorer communities experience worse mental health than the population as a whole but despite this, levels of mental well-being (as measured by WEMWBS) do not appear to be significantly lower. While continuing to emphasise the importance of policy action on the fundamental, structural determinants of mental ill-health (exclusion, discrimination, poverty, inequality, and so on) we suggest that there may be potential to support well-being in communities through routes that are distinct from these more established societal factors.

Against the background trends driving in the opposite direction (towards individualism, virtual networks, greater mobility, and family breakdown for example), community-level actions need to consciously prioritise and support social capital, interdependence, inclusion and mutuality. This sort of social regeneration is everybody's business, but as a result can end up as being nobody's business. It needs much more attention for the benefit of our collective well-being.

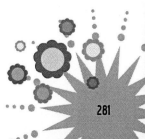

References

Bartley M (Ed) (2006) *Capability and Resilience: Beating the odds. ESRC Human Capability and Resilience Research Network London* [online]. UCL Department of Epidemiology and Public Health. Available at: http://www.ucl. ac.uk/capabilityandresilience/beatingtheoddsbook.pdf (accessed August 2010).

Bond L, Kearns A, Mason P, Tannahill C, Egan M & Whitely E (in preparation) *'It Ain't [Just] What You Do, It's the Way That You Do It': The contribution of regeneration to mental well-being in deprived areas.*

Bromley C, Bradshaw P & Given L (Eds) (2009) *The Scottish Health Survey, 2008.* Edinburgh: The Scottish Government.

Cooper R, Boyko C & Codinhoto R (2008) *The Effect of the Physical Environment on Mental Well-being.* State-of-Science Review: SR-DR2 produced for Foresight Mental Capital and Wellbeing Project. London: The Government Office for Science.

Davidson S, Sewel K, Tse D & O'Connor R (2009) *Well? What do you think? (2008) The fourth national Scottish survey of public attitudes to mental wellbeing and mental health problems* [online]. Scottish Government Social Research Available at: http://www.scotland.gov.uk/Resource/Doc/284594/0086432.pdf (accessed August 2010).

Downie RS, Tannahill C, & Tannahill A (1996) *Health Promotion: Models and values* (2nd ed). Oxford: Oxford University Press.

Dunn J (2008) *Housing as a Determinant of Mental Capital. State-of-Science Review: SR-E27 produced for Foresight Mental Capital and Wellbeing Project.* London: The Government Office for Science.

Egan M, Kearns A, Mason P, Tannahill C, Bond L, Coyle J, Beck S, Crawford F, Hanlon P, Lawson L, McLean J, Petticrew M, Sautkina E, Thomson H & Walsh D (2010) Protocol for a mixed methods study investigating the impact of investment in housing, regeneration and neighbourhood renewal on the health and well-being of residents: the GoWell programme. *BMC Medical Research Methodology* **10** 41.

Friedli L (2005) Private minds in public bodies: the public mental health role of primary care. *Primary Care Mental Health* **3** 41–46.

Friedli L (2009) *Mental Health, Resilience and Inequalities.* Copenhagen: WHO Europe.

GoWell (2010) *Progress for People and Places: Monitoring change in Glasgow's communities.* Evidence from the GoWell surveys 2006 and 2008. Glasgow: Glasgow Centre for Population Health, NHS Greater Glasgow and Clyde.

Hanlon P, Walsh D & Whyte B (2006) *Let Glasgow Flourish*. Glasgow: Glasgow Centre for Population Health.

Hawe P (2008) What makes for a mentally healthy community? In: Canadian Institute for Health Information (Ed) *Mentally Healthy Communities: A collection of papers* (pp19–24). Ottawa, Ontario: Canadian Institute for Health Information.

Huppert FA (2008) *Psychological Wellbeing: Evidence regarding its causes and consequences*. State-of-science review: SR-X2 produced for Foresight Mental Capital and Wellbeing Project. London: The Government Office for Science.

Kessler RC & McLeod JD (1985) Social support and mental health in community samples. In: S Cohen & SL Syme (Eds) *Social Support and Health*. London: Academic Press.

Klein DC (1969) The meaning of community in a preventive mental health program. *American Journal of Public Health* **59** (11) 2005–2012.

McKenzie K & Harpham T (2006) Meanings and uses of social capital in the mental health field. In: K McKenzie & T Harpham (Eds) *Meanings and Uses of Social Capital in the Mental Health Field* (pp11–23). London: Jessica Kingsley Publishers.

MacQueen KM, McLellan E, Metzger DS, Kegeles S, Strauss RP, Scotti R, Blanchard L & Trotter RT (2001) What is community? An evidence-based definition for participatory public health. *American Journal of Public Health* **91** (12) 1929–1938.

National Institute for Health and Clinical Excellence (2008) *Community Engagement to Improve Health. NICE public health guidance 9* [online]. Available at: (http://www.nice.org.uk/nicemedia/live/11929/39563/39563.pdf (accessed August 2010).

Tennant R, Hiller L, Fishwick R, Platt S, Joseph S, Weich S, Parkinson J, Secker J & Stewart-Brown S (2007) The Warwick-Edinburgh Mental Wellbeing Scale (WEMWBS): development and UK validation. *Health and Quality of Life Outcomes* **5** 63.

Traci Leven Research (2010) *NHS Greater Glasgow and Clyde 2008 Health and Wellbeing Survey*. Glasgow: NHS Greater Glasgow and Clyde.

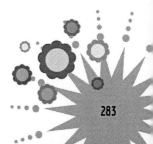

Chapter 19

The role of community development in tackling mental health inequalities

Neil Quinn

Introduction

There are significant inequalities in mental health, with mental health problems and poor mental health more common in areas of deprivation (Friedli, 2009). A key purpose of community development is to collectively bring about social change (Twelvetrees, 2008). This chapter explores how community development can be applied to tackling inequalities in mental health. It draws upon the author's experience of developing and evaluating a mental health equalities programme in East Glasgow, one of the areas of highest deprivation in the UK, over the last nine years. The model is illustrated for the public mental health practitioner by describing how the programme works with young people, older people, asylum seekers and refugees and in partnership with organisations such as housing, regeneration and the arts. Finally, the potential of this model for informing policy and practice is discussed.

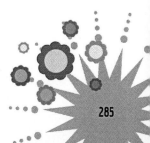

Mental health inequalities

There is a strong body of evidence that lower socio-economic status is associated with poorer mental health. Poverty increases the likelihood of developing mental health problems and experiencing a mental health problem can lead to an increased risk of poverty. Three key issues have been identified that assist in understanding the mental health impact of socio-economic inequalities.

▶ Social divisions – where mental health problems both reflect deprivation and contribute to it.

▶ Social drift – where the social and ecological impact of adversity, including the impact of physical health problems and the cycle of invisible barriers prevent or inhibit people from benefitting from opportunities.

▶ Social injuries – with mental distress an outcome of demoralisation and despair.

(Rogers & Pilgrim, 2003)

Higher levels of income inequality within society result in a higher prevalence of mental illness (Pickett *et al*, 2006). Relative deprivation creates physiological responses to chronic stress and low status can have a detrimental impact on social relationships (Wilkinson, 1996, 2005). There are a number of psycho-social dimensions of poverty, such as not being able to participate in the life of the community, feeling a lack of control of life choices and a lack of social capital (Thompson *et al*, 2007).

Community development

Before exploring the nature of community development, it is important to acknowledge that the term 'community' is an evolving concept. Definitions of community are elusive, imprecise, contradictory and controversial (Popple, 1995). It has been argued that when defining community, it is helpful to consider it in three different ways (Stepney & Popple, 2008).

The first involves looking backwards to an idealised view of community, which locates a golden age of clearly defined and secure neighbourhoods. This view represents community as a place of warmth, intimacy and social cohesion.

This view has sometimes been criticised by those on the radical left, who view community as an ideological construct used by the state, which hides the nature of divisions within society. Also, it is argued that more traditional views of communities have failed to recognise the ethnically diverse make-up of many neighbourhoods.

The second way is by looking forward to a period in which communities are living in harmony, where pluralism, solidarity and a shared identity are in the ascendancy. However, this similarly can be an idealised view, which is more of an aspiration than reality.

A third (and possibly more helpful) way of looking at community is to consider what it is like now. This view of community emanates from the fact that people have something in common, whether in terms of shared locality, a shared identity or a shared interest.

While acknowledging the contested nature of 'community', community development has been defined as 'the process of assisting people to improve their own communities by undertaking autonomous collective action' (Twelvetrees, 2008, p1). Community development can be described, first as a set of values and second as a set of approaches linked to these values. These values include social justice, respect, democracy, empowerment and getting a better deal for people who are collectively missing out (FCWTG, 1999). Within community development, there is an explicit concern to make the existing system work better for those in low income communities (Alinsky, 1972).

There are two broad approaches to community development. The first is to help support existing groups and help people form new ones, with community development workers working alongside people within a community, helping them to realise their collective goals. The second approach is to work directly with service providers to sensitise them to the needs of specific communities, assisting them to improve services or alter policies, often referred to as social planning.

Underlying the concept of community development is an analysis of power in which resources are not allocated on the basis of merit but on the basis of power. A community development worker's role is to promote empowerment, an enabling process through which individuals and communities take control over their lives and their environment (Rappaport, 1984). The underlying theory and philosophical framework for much community development comes from Brazilian educator, Paulo Freire (1970). Freire argued that through dialogue, individuals engage in critical reflection, or conscientisation, to analyse the social context for personal and community problems, and their own role in working on these problems. The goal of dialogue is praxis, or the ongoing interaction between reflection and the actions that people take to promote individual and community change.

Within the US, the term 'community organising' has often been used in place of community development, which is also seen as a process by which people are brought together to act in common self-interest. Community organising is seen as more radical and entails working with people to help them recognise that they face shared problems and to discover that by joining together they can fight to overcome these problems (Rubin & Rubin, 2008). Central to the ethos of community organising are the following concepts:

1. **Empowerment** – promoting a social action process whereby individuals, groups and communities gain mastery over their lives in the context of changing social, economic and political circumstances.

2. **Critical consciousness** – undertaking a social analysis of living conditions and people's roles in changing these conditions.

3. **Community capacity** – building the ability of communities to identify, mobilise, and address social and public health problems.

4. **Social capital** – developing the structures and relationships that facilitate co-ordination and co-operation for mutual benefit.

5. **Issue selection** – identifying winnable and specific targets of change that unify and build community strength.

6. **Participation and relevance** – ensuring that community organising starts where people are and engages community members as equals.

(adapted from Minkler & Wallerstein, 2006)

Community organisers enable social movements by building a base of concerned people and mobilising people to act. Building community is seen as a means to increase social justice and individual well-being, and reduce the negative impacts of being otherwise disconnected individuals.

Public Mental Health Today © Pavilion Publishing (Brighton) Ltd 2010

How can community development tackle mental health inequalities?

Community development promotes equity in two ways: first, by focusing on those experiencing multiple deprivation and second, by seeking to do this in an empowering way in partnership with members of that community. Given that the key principle of community development is about working collectively to bring about social change, the approach has a potentially important role in tackling mental health inequalities. These inequalities are issues of social justice, which require people with a common self-interest to come together in order to tackle them effectively.

Much of the focus of public mental health work is related to the concept of health gain approached through population-based initiatives, largely using social marketing approaches (Friedli *et al*, 2007). Population based health initiatives are often concerned with specific diseases, lifestyle behaviours, and public policies that influence health risks (Minkler & Wallerstein, 2006). However, these priorities may not be of concern to low income communities and may not contribute to tackling inequalities. There has been growing recognition within the public mental health field that there is a need to become more targeted and consider health equity rather than simply population health gain, if inequalities are to be addressed. A recent public health review argues that in order to reduce the steepness of the social gradient in health, actions must be universal, but with a scale and intensity that is proportionate to the level of disadvantage, referred to as 'proportionate universalism' (Marmot, 2010). Furthermore, it is argued that in order to achieve this, effective participatory decision-making is required at local level, which can only happen by empowering individuals and local communities. This provides an argument for community development approaches that allow us to shift the focus towards health equity that complements population-based public mental health initiatives.

Positive mental attitudes: a community development programme in an area of deprivation

In order to illustrate for the public mental health practitioner how to address mental health inequalities using a community development approach, the author will draw on personal experience of leading a mental health improvement programme in east Glasgow. East Glasgow is one of the areas of highest deprivation in the UK, with 52% of the adult population being economically inactive, 37% claiming Income Support, 58% without qualifications and 30% stating that they have a long-term limiting illness (NHS Health Scotland, 2004). These indicators are significantly above the Glasgow City and Scottish averages. Positive Mental Attitudes (PMA) is a mental health equalities programme that began in 2001 as a grass roots initiative by the local mental health service user forum but has now developed into a mainstream publicly funded programme. PMA is an integral part of the regeneration strategy and works closely with east Glasgow Community Planning Partnership, the lead regeneration agency in the area.

Community development principles underpin the work of PMA, specifically community participation and partnership working (Quinn & Knifton, 2005). A high degree of community participation is central to the design, planning and delivery of the programme, with local users of mental health services employed as project workers and playing a key role in the steering group. In relation to partnership working the programme has developed a broad coalition comprising over 50 partners from a range of sectors including housing, education, regeneration, arts and culture, planning agencies, who come together to support the programme.

PMA has applied these central principles to support the development of a wide range of programmes aimed at addressing inequalities in mental health. Working with a diverse range of partners means that the process for deciding how to select and prioritise programmes, often within the context of limited resources, is a complex one. Priorities can be contested and the process of prioritisation can be influenced by political considerations, such as the views of elected representatives or how much influence specific groups have in lobbying for extra resources.

Many programmes have been initiated by local service users, while others have arisen from the priorities of partner agencies or are directly funded by national programmes. To manage the differing perspectives and expectations from within the programme steering group, prioritisation has required careful consideration and negotiation. Some examples of these programmes are outlined below.

▶ **School Mental Health Curriculum pack** – Improving the health equity of young people in areas of deprivation is viewed as a key element in reducing inequalities. For this reason the Positive Mental Attitudes curriculum resource was developed, comprising 24 lessons, four per year group of secondary schooling, giving a focus to learning related to emotional well-being while challenging negative attitudes associated with mental health problems. Central to the development of this resource was the participation of young people in east Glasgow who shaped the content, including producing a DVD, which is a core component of the pack. Evaluation of the resource has shown that it appears to have had a significant positive impact upon pupils' attitudes to mental health and towards people experiencing mental health problems (Donnelly, 2009).

▶ **Equalities workshops** – An important factor of the inequalities experienced by people with mental health problems was in relation to the barriers they encountered in accessing services. A strategy to address this has been to develop mental health equalities workshops that could be delivered flexibly to significant numbers of workplace employees and community groups. These workshops were developed by a partnership of service users, community development staff, health workers and community planning staff who all brought unique skills and contributions, which collectively strengthened the workshop design. A key part of the training draws on the personal experiences of those with mental health problems. The workshops have been delivered in a range of settings including housing associations, benefits and welfare rights agencies, regeneration agencies, social care services, communication workforce and the NHS. Evaluation of the programme demonstrated that the workshops significantly improved participant knowledge. Attitude change was more complex with an overall significant improvement in attitudes, particularly in relation to unpredicatability and recovery. Service user narratives focusing on recovery were identified as the most valuable component of the intervention (Knifton *et al*, 2008).

▶ **Sanctuary** – Over recent years east Glasgow has hosted increasing numbers of asylum seekers and refugees. This changing demographic has meant that the mental health needs of this area have also changed and the importance of supporting this seldom-heard population has become apparent. The Sanctuary programme was developed by PMA and brought together national, regional and local partners. The main aims were to identify patterns of stigma and discrimination through action research and to consider how these attitudes and behaviours could be addressed in ways which were meaningful to the communities themselves. Peer-led research was undertaken with over 100 participants which found that pre-migration trauma as well as poverty, racism and the stress of the asylum process was impacting negatively upon people's mental health. In addition, significant levels of stigma and discrimination towards mental health problems were found within communities. This led to the development of a peer-led community education programme, known as 'community conversations', in which asylum seekers and refugees were trained to deliver workshops to community groups. Evaluation of this initiative indicated a reduction in stigma against people with mental health problems, particularly in relation to dangerousness, the promotion of recovery and improved help-seeking amongst asylum seeker and refugee communities (Shirjeel, 2010).

▶ **Later life peer education** – Mental health in later life has emerged as a key policy area in recent years and an important social justice issue. To address this, PMA developed a peer-led awareness programme on depression in later life later with the aim of promoting positive mental health, encouraging help-seeking, and addressing stigma and promoting recovery. This involved a needs assessment with over 60 older people, the development of a peer-led workshop on depression, and the development of a later life drama group with performances at the Scottish Mental Health Arts and Film Festival. One of the important outcomes from this programme has been to promote more openness in talking about mental health within later life community groups.

▶ **Housing, regeneration and well-being** – Quality of housing and physical environment have been identified as being central to levels of happiness within communities and as being important for good 'mental capital'. Evidence shows that poor housing can have a negative effect on mental health and well-being (Kirkwood *et al*, 2008). For this reason, PMA undertook a social action research project with housing and regeneration partners aimed at gaining the views of residents. These views helped to inform local agencies about how they can work together to address issues that negatively impact on community mental health and well-being. Within the study people raised a number of concerns about their neighbourhood and environment, such as lack of opportunities, services and support and antisocial behaviour. Residents felt that this contributed to feelings of isolation and how unhappy they felt living in the area. The study also found that these negative experiences reduced the bonds of community and the social networks, which can enhance and protect people's mental health and well-being. The learning from this programme has led to significant changes in local services. In addition, this has also helped to develop awareness amongst partner services of the importance of ensuring that the promotion of mental health and of tackling mental health inequalities is an integral part of housing and regeneration programmes (Stevenson & Biggs, 2010).

▶ **Community building through the arts** – There is a long history of the arts being used to give voice to communities, including community murals, guerrilla theatre, dance brigades, participatory video and even the use of graffiti to promote social change (McDonald *et al*, 2006). Within a health context, the arts can play a powerful role in tackling inequalities and because they tap into people's feelings, they have the potential to shape consciousness. PMA has developed visual arts, creative writing and drama groups to challenge stigma towards people with mental health problems. This has involved mental health service users coming together to produce exhibitions and performances and resulted in an arts festival each October, known as Headspace (part of the Scottish Mental Health Arts and Film Festival), where the PMA arts groups engage with thousands of community members. Evaluation demonstrated that events increased positive attitudes towards people with mental health problems, including positive representations of people's contributions, capabilities and potential to recover (Quinn *et al*, 2010).

▶ **Suicide prevention in an area of deprivation** – As a result of the link between high suicide rates and deprivation (Platt *et al*, 2007), PMA received funding to develop national demonstration activities in suicide prevention within east Glasgow. This has involved a range of initiatives including: training in suicide prevention with community gatekeepers (with a particular focus on those working with men, such as football coaches); the use of forum theatre with community activists to encourage peer support, reduce stigma and encourage help-seeking; the production of a film with young people to disseminate key suicide prevention messages amongst young people in east Glasgow; and workshops for mental health service staff to reduce stigmatising attitudes towards those who attempt suicide and self-harm. This innovative work is being carefully evaluated to assess its impact.

Further information on all the programmes can be found on the PMA's website (www.positivementalattitudes.org.uk).

Challenges

There are many challenges associated with using a community development approach to tackle mental health inequalities. One such challenge is building capacity amongst community partners to deliver a public mental health programme. While there has been engagement of a whole range of partners within the work of PMA, most did not have specific knowledge or experience of mental health issues. What they have offered is expertise in their particular area, for example, working with young people or the business community. PMA has combined this knowledge with the expertise offered by mental health service users, which has created a team approach where a mix of different but complementary skills can be drawn upon. This approach has helped to build capacity and significantly increased the outputs of the programme, however, this process has required skilled support and facilitation.

Another tension has been surrounding the ownership of the programme. PMA developed as a grassroots initiative but through its success had attracted mainstream NHS funding within east Glasgow. Furthermore, the success of the programme has resulted in many of the initiatives having a national profile and attracting national funding. While this has been positive for the programme's profile and in ensuring long-term funding, it has also resulted in a tension between national policy objectives and local priorities. This led to concerns that the programme was in danger of losing its community development ethos, which raises the question of whether it is possible for those in social change organisations to partner with or take funds from those in the establishment without losing their independence (Rubin & Rubin, 2008).

Another challenge has been in relation to the use of community and service user narratives. While these narratives have been one of the strongest elements of the programme, using these has presented huge challenges. It has been clear that it is important that support is available when people share their experiences and that they are aware of potential consequences of their stories being placed in the public domain. There is also inherent danger that a negative self-identity can be reinforced such as the label of being a 'service user' or being labelled as living in a low income area.

The potential of this model for informing policy and practice

The model presented here provides strong support for a community development approach to addressing mental health inequalities. An example of how this has been applied more widely is the development of a regional anti-stigma partnership, which involves more than a hundred organisations. This partnership is guided by the principles of community development modelled by PMA and the majority of these regional programmes have been led by PMA in recognition of their experience of working alongside communities. This has resulted in the development of a 'community of practice' in mental health equalities work (Wenger, 1998), which is based on constructivist principles, such as valuing community knowledge and service user narratives (Quinn & Knifton, 2009).

Some of the initiatives developed by PMA, such as the Sanctuary programme for asylum seekers and refugees and the school curriculum pack have now been adopted by national partners. These programmes, therefore, have the potential to be rolled out across Scotland and to influence future national policy. In addition, national partners are now investing in PMA to take forward a range of national initiatives at a community level. This has enhanced the profile of PMA and its contribution to tackling inequalities in east Glasgow.

Finally, the success of the work of PMA demonstrates that there is the potential for community development to play a greater role in government public mental health policy and to make a valuable contribution on a national level as well as a local level to addressing inequalities in mental health.

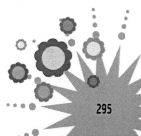

References

Alinsky SD (1972) *Rules for Radicals: A pragmatic primer for realistic radicals*. New York: Vintage Books.

Donnelly R (2009) *Exploring the impact of a mental health lesson on S3 pupils' attitudes to mental health and people experiencing mental health problems, 4th International Stigma Conference*. London, January 2009.

FCWTG (1999) *Defining Community Work*. Sheffield: FCWTG.

Freire P (1970) *Pedagogy of the Oppressed*. New York: Seabury Press.

Friedli L, Oliver C, Tidyman M & Ward G (2007) *Mental Health Improvement: Evidence-based messages to promote mental wellbeing*. Edinburgh: NHS Health Scotland.

Friedli L (2009) *Mental Health, Resilience and Inequalities*. Copenhagen and London: World Health Organization and Mental Health Foundation.

Kirkwood T, Bond J, May C, McKeith I & Teh M (2008) *Foresight Mental Capital and Wellbeing Project. Mental Capital Through Life: Future challenges*. London: The Government Office for Science.

Knifton L, Walker A & Quinn N (2008) Workplace interventions can reduce stigma. *Journal of Public Mental Health* **7** (4) 40–50.

Marmot M (2010) *Fair Society, Healthy Lives: Strategic review of health inequalities in England post 2010*. London: The Marmot Review.

McDonald M, Sarche J & Wang CC (2006) Using the arts in community organising and community building. In: M Minkler (Ed) *Community Organising and Community Building for Health*. New Jersey: Rutgers University Press.

Minkler M & Wallerstein N (2006) Improving health through community Organisation and Community Building: A health education perspective. In: M Minkler (Ed) *Community Organising and Community Building for Health*. New Jersey: Rutgers University Press.

NHS Health Scotland (2004) *Eastern Glasgow: A community health and well-being profile*. Edinburgh: NHS Health Scotland.

Pickett KE, James OW & Wilkinson RG (2006) Income inequality and the prevalence of mental illness: a preliminary international analysis. *Journal of Epidemiology and Community Health* **60** 646–647.

Platt S, Boyle P, Crombie I, Feng Z & Exeter D (2007) *The Epidemiology of Suicide in Scotland 1989–2004: An examination of temporal trends and risk factors at national and local levels*. Edinburgh: Scottish Executive.

Popple K (1995) *Analysing Community Work: Its theory and practice.* Buckingham: Open University Press.

Quinn N & Knifton L (2005) Promoting recovery and addressing stigma: mental health awareness through community development in a low-income area. *International Journal of Mental Health Promotion* **7** (4) 37–44.

Quinn N & Knifton L (2009) Addressing stigma and discrimination through community conversation. In: P Bywaters, E McLeod & L Napier (Eds) *Social Work and Global Health Inequalities: Policy and practice developments.* Bristol: Policy Press.

Quinn N, Shulman A, Knifton L & Byrne P (2010) The impact of a national mental health arts and film festival on stigma and recovery. *Acta Psychiatrica Scandinavica* [online] 20 May. Available at: http://www3.interscience.wiley.com/journal/123455046/abstract?CRETRY=1&SRETRY=0 (accessed July 2010).

Rappaport J (1984) Studies in empowerment: introduction to the issue. *Prevention in Human Services* **3** (2) 1–7.

Rogers A & Pilgrim D (2003) *Inequalities and Mental Health.* London: Palgrave Macmillan.

Rubin HJ & Rubin S (2008) *Community Organising and Development* (4th ed). Boston: Pearson.

Shirjeel S (2010) *Sanctuary Community Conversation Evaluation.* Glasgow: NHS Health Scotland.

Stevenson R & Biggs H (2010) *Sandyhills Community Mental Health and Wellbeing Consultation.* Edinburgh: Scottish Development Centre for Mental Health.

Stepney P & Popple K (2008) *Social Work and the Community.* Basingstoke: Palgrave Macmillan.

Thompson S, Abdallah S, Marks N, Simms A & Johnson V (2007) *The European Happy Planet Index: An index of carbon efficiency and wellbeing in the EU* [online]. London: New Economics Foundation. Available at: http://www.neweconomics.org/gen/z_sys_PublicationDetail.aspx?pid=242 (accessed July 2010).

Twelvetrees A (2008) *Community Work* (4th ed). Basingstoke: Palgrave Macmillan.

Wenger E (1998) *Communities of Practice: Learning, meaning and identity.* New York: Cambridge University Press.

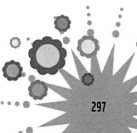

Wilkinson RG (1996) *Unhealthy Societies: The afflictions of inequality*. London: Routledge.

Wilkinson R (2005) *The Impact of Inequality: How to make sick societies healthier*. London: Routledge.

Chapter 20

Improving mental health through participatory arts

Jenny Secker

Introduction

There is a growing interest among policy-makers in the UK in the potential for arts participation to improve mental health. Equally, there is a growing body of evidence that investment in participatory arts will be repaid in terms of mental health benefits. This chapter provides an overview of the policy and practice context of participatory arts and mental health work, presents the research evidence and considers the processes through which arts participation 'works' to support mental health. The chapter begins by explaining how the terms 'mental health' and 'participatory arts' are defined in this context, and concludes by considering the strength of the evidence base.

Defining mental health and participatory arts

Although they may seem self-explanatory at first sight, the terms 'mental health' and 'participatory arts' do need some explanation, because both are open to different interpretations.

Taking mental health first, in much of the policy and practice discourse, the term mental health has become synonymous with mental ill health, or is seen as implying an absence of mental illness. In the fields of public health and health promotion, however, positive mental health, or mental well-being, is viewed as distinct from an absence of mental illness. As defined by the World Health Organization (2007), in this positive sense mental health is seen as:

'A state of well-being in which the individual realizes his or her own abilities, can cope with the normal stresses of life, can work productively and fruitfully, and is able to make a contribution to his or her community.'

An important corollary of this distinction is that people who need to use mental health services can nevertheless aspire to the state of mental well-being encompassed within the World Health Organization definition, in the same way that someone with a physical disability or long-term condition can nevertheless aspire to physical well-being.

The recognition that a diagnosis indicative of mental ill health does not preclude well-being accords with recent evidence that challenges clinical notions of recovery from mental ill health as necessarily involving the absence of symptoms. Instead, recovery can be understood as a social process of recovering a fulfilling life regardless of the presence or absence of symptoms (Shepherd *et al*, 2008), exactly the kind of life suggested by the World Health Organization definition.

In the context of this chapter, a positive definition of mental health is therefore adopted which includes the potential and aspirations of people using mental health services, as well as those of people struggling with low levels of well-being despite having no formal diagnosis indicative of ill health.

Turning to participatory arts, this term has been coined within the field of arts and health to distinguish active engagement in creative activities for their own sake from the many other ways in which the arts can play a part in health care, for example in the design of the health care environment. Arts therapies in particular, using music, drama or visual arts, can play an important part in enabling people to reflect on and move forward from experiences of distress, with a primary focus on art as a medium for therapy. The distinction between participatory arts and art therapy is not always as clear-cut as it may seem, because participatory arts, as we will see, can certainly be therapeutic and many art therapists also work in participatory art projects. The defining factor, however, is that the focus of participatory art is on the development of artistic skills and the creation of art – 'art for art's sake' – rather than on art as a therapeutic medium.

Policy context

In terms of interest at a health policy level, an overview provided by Clift *et al* (2009) of arts and health in England suggests a checkered history over the past decade, with flurries of high-level activity subsiding into apparent inactivity. In 2009, however, following a debate in the House of Lords and a speech from the [then] Secretary of State for Health calling for greater recognition of the health benefits of arts participation, Professor Louis Appleby, National Director for Mental Health in England, was appointed as joint lead on arts and health for the Department of Health. Although it remains to be seen what impact the recent change of UK government may have, the appointment promises a higher profile both for arts and health more generally and for arts and mental health work.

In Scotland, significant developments have also taken place in recent years, not least due to recognition within the Mental Health (Care and Treatment) (Scotland) Act 2003 of a wider role for services to promote well-being and social development, including provision of social, cultural and recreational activities. Further developments described by Goldie (2007) included the Scottish Executive's National Programme for Improving Mental Health and Well-being (2003–2008), which gave support to the role of the arts in mental health by working with the Scottish Arts Council to establish a time limited programme (ArtFull). The ArtFull programme was aimed at building partnerships between arts providers and public sector agencies including the NHS and local authorities across Scotland. ArtFull also worked to bring practitioners and academics together with the explicit aim of developing a research evidence base, which would demonstrate and promote the benefits of arts in relation to mental health and well-being (Goldie, 2007).

Alongside these health policy developments, an increasing emphasis across the UK on the need to combat social exclusion has been a further driver. The publication of the Social Exclusion Unit's report (SEU, 2004) on mental health and social exclusion focused attention on the extreme exclusion experienced by many people with mental health problems and the importance of community participation for combating exclusion, including participation in arts. One of the actions instigated by the SEU was an England-wide study, jointly commissioned by the Department of Health and the Department for Culture, Media and Sport, aimed at developing the evidence base for participatory arts and mental health work. A team from Anglia Ruskin University and the University of Central Lancashire (UCLan) carried out the research (Secker *et al*, 2007) and the results are drawn on in the following sections by way of illustration, alongside other relevant studies.

Practice context

Despite varying levels of interest at a policy level, in practice, as White (2009) illustrates, arts and health activity has burgeoned since its beginnings in community arts initiatives during the late 1960s and mental health has been a focus of much of that activity, whether explicitly or implicitly.

A survey of 102 arts and mental health projects in England carried out in 2005 as part of the national study referred to above (Secker *et al*, 2007) concluded that participatory arts and mental health activity was a vibrant strand within the wider mental health economy. The 102 responding projects were offering an impressive variety of arts activities to almost 4,000 people with mental health problems each week. The range of sources from which referrals were received and accepted was wide, with self-referral second only to specialist mental health services in frequency, suggesting a high degree of accessibility.

Many projects worked with people from the wider community as well as with people with identified mental health problems, in keeping with the inclusive approach to mental health promotion encompassed within the World Health Organization definition. In addition, the projects appeared to be succeeding in areas where other mental health providers struggle.

1. They reported reaching above average proportions of people from black and minority ethnic communities.

2. Levels of participant involvement in shaping the activities in which they engaged were reported to be high, as were levels of involvement in the running of projects.

A reliance on opportunistic, often short-term funding, was, however, identified as a problem for many projects, a situation also prevailing in Scotland, as Goldie (2007) reports. A reason commonly put forward for this, particularly within the health sector, is a lack of firm evidence that mental health benefits ensue from arts participation. The following section examines the available evidence in order to challenge that view.

Evidence for the mental health benefits of participatory arts

In their review of arts and health activity Clift *et al* (2009) note that retrospective qualitative evaluation is the most common approach to project evaluation. This approach seeks project participants' views of the benefits of participatory arts, based on their experiences, and was also the approach most commonly taken by the arts and mental health projects surveyed by Secker *et al* (2007). What is most striking about the results from across these studies is the extent of agreement about the specific mental health benefits of arts participation. Participants' testimonials consistently highlight:

1. reduced stress levels, associated with being able to relax and have time away from pressures

2. increased motivation

3. improved concentration

4. enhanced self-esteem and confidence

5. lifting of spirits, and in several cases reduced recurrence of depression

6. greater understanding of feelings and ability to express them

7. feeling valued and accepted as a person

8. decreased social isolation

9. enjoyment and pride in achievements.

Prospective approaches, where information is obtained before or at the beginning of participation and again after an interval of time, are currently less common but a number of studies have been reported. These include two strands of the national study reported by Secker *et al* (2007). The first was an analysis of data provided by two projects, Time Being on the Isle of Wight and Arts on Prescription in Stockport. Both projects worked with people with a range of mental health needs and the analysis of the data they provided demonstrated significant mental health gains, as case study 1 illustrates. In addition, the Anglia Ruskin/UCLan team carried out their own outcomes study (case study 2), which again revealed significant benefits for the 62 contributing participants.

Case study 1

Following on from their survey of arts and mental health projects in England, Secker *et al* (2007) carried out a retrospective analysis of data provided by two participating projects, Time Being on the Isle of Wight and Arts on Prescription in Stockport.

The outcomes measured at Time Being included mood, four symptoms of depression, 10 negative feelings or states, self-esteem, seven social anxiety situations and ease of talking to people. At follow-up participants were invited to respond to four additional open-ended questions about their experience of the project. The project was able to provide data for 107 participants.

Stockport Arts on Prescription had used a variety of outcome measures over a period of time. Sufficient data were available for analysis from three measures of depression; two completed by 10 women experiencing postnatal depression and the third by 17 other participants. Participants were invited to respond to two additional open-ended questions at follow-up about the benefits of the project.

Statistical analysis demonstrated significant improvements in Time Being participants' ratings of their mood, self-esteem and ease of talking to people. There were also significant improvements in one symptom of depression (difficulty falling asleep) and two negative feelings/states (sadness and anxiety). With very few exceptions, participants' responses to open ended questions included in the follow up questionnaire were positive and identified many benefits, including improvements in mental health and self-esteem, the opportunity for social contact, renewed motivation, decreased anxiety and interest in further arts activity.

At Arts on Prescription there were significant improvements in the levels of depression recorded for all participants. Participants' responses to open ended comments were unanimously positive and identified very similar benefits to those identified at Time Being.

Case study 2

As a further strand of their research Secker *et al* (2007) carried out an outcomes study, for which measures of empowerment, mental health and social inclusion were completed by 62 participants from 22 arts and mental health projects, on starting at their project, and six months later. The empowerment measure included scales assessing self-worth, self-efficacy, mutual aid and positive outlook. The mental health measure used was the Clinical Outcomes in Routine Evaluation (CORE), which includes scales assessing well-being, problems/symptoms, life functioning and risk to self or others. Scales on the social inclusion measure developed for the study assess social isolation, social relations and social acceptance.

Overall scores improved significantly on all three measures. On the empowerment measure, scores improved for self-efficacy and positive outlook. Improvements in self- worth scores were also close to statistical significance. There was little difference in mutual aid scores but the baseline scores had been at quite a high level already. On the CORE, scores improved significantly on the individual scales measuring problems/symptoms and well-being. Improvements for risk to self or others and life functioning were close to significance. On the social inclusion measure, scores improved significantly on all three scales.

Further questions included in the study asked about participants' levels of service use. At follow-up the proportion of participants identified as frequent and regular service users had decreased significantly.

Other local evaluations using prospective designs have also demonstrated significant benefits. One example is an evaluation of Open Arts in south Essex being carried out by the south Essex service user research group (Secker & Heydinrych, 2009). For this evaluation, participants were asked to complete a measure of well-being, the Warwick-Edinburgh Mental Wellbeing Scale (WEMWBS), and the social inclusion measure developed for the national study. Results from the first year of the study showed that participants' well-being scores had improved significantly, as had scores for social isolation and social acceptance on the social inclusion measure. Ratings of the Open Arts experience were very positive, with all participants indicating that they had enjoyed their course and over three-quarters reporting increases in confidence and motivation. Additional comments at the end of the follow-up questionnaire supported the gains in well-being and social inclusion found on the two measures.

While the studies reported so far have focused primarily on people of working age, Clift *et al* (2009, p16) provide an example of a local project evaluation focusing on older people, which also demonstrated significant benefits. Levels of mental health as measured by the 12-item version of the Short Form instrument (SF12) increased and levels of depression measured on the Geriatric Depression Scale decreased.

Experimental approaches to evaluation using 'control' groups of people not participating in arts alongside 'intervention' groups of arts participants are very much less common in the arts and health field, owing to the practical difficulties entailed as well as doubts in the arts and health field about the value of experimental designs in this context. No experimental evaluations of arts and mental health work appear to have been carried out, but both the national study reported by Secker *et al* (2007) and the Open Arts evaluation (SE-SURG *et al*, 2008) have attempted to use an alternative approach to assessing the confidence with which the benefits reported can be attributed to arts participation. This involves asking participants themselves to rate the extent to which they believe their arts participation has improved the various dimensions measured. Statistical tests are then used to assess correlations between participants' ratings and improvements in scores on the measures.

In the national study (case study 2), positive ratings of the impact of arts were significantly associated with improvement on all three measures, with the largest effect for empowerment. In the Open Arts evaluation there was a significant correlation between participants' ratings of the impact on well-being and changes in their well-being scores but no correlation between ratings of impact on social inclusion and changes in those scores. This method is at an early stage of development and needs further testing and refinement. However, obtaining qualitative testimonials in the form of open-ended comments alongside standard measures can also illuminate and support outcome study results, as the examples above illustrate.

Processes through which participating in arts activity supports mental health

While qualitative evaluation methods such as seeking participant testimonials add to the weight of outcome studies, they are also of central importance in their own right, since it is necessary to know not just whether mental health benefits ensue from arts participation, but also how those benefits come about. Addressing that question through a series of detailed case studies at six diverse arts and mental projects was a final strand of the national study reported by Secker *et al* (2007). Workshops with project workers aimed at identifying why they thought their project would benefit participants (their 'theories of change') were followed by in-depth interviews with participants at each project to test out and refine the resulting theories. The results indicated that eight processes were important to varying degrees, depending on the project context and participants' different needs. Case study 3 provides an overview of the eight processes.

While one study cannot be conclusive on its own, the similarities with results from other studies that have used qualitative methods are again striking. As was seen earlier, when participants are asked about their experience of arts participation, increased motivation, improved concentration, decreased isolation and enhanced self-esteem are consistent and common themes, as they were in the national study. Equally, participant testimonials often revolve around feeling more valued and accepted as a person as a result of producing art work that is appreciated by others, enabling participants to reclaim an identity other than that of 'a problem' or service user. Developing pride in one's own achievements and abilities and discovering ways of expressing feelings are further consistent themes across studies, along with the alleviation of stress and distress that comes from having time away from life's pressures.

Case study 3

The Anglia Ruskin/UCLan research team tested out the 'theories of change' held by workers at six projects through in-depth interviews with 34 project participants. Analysis of the interview data revealed eight processes through which benefits were achieved.

Three processes set in motion by arts participation were important for the majority of participants at all six projects.

1. Getting motivated inspired hope and reduced inactivity, and so improved mental well-being and decreased mental distress.

2. Focusing on art and the intense concentration involved provided relaxation and distraction, which again resulted in improved mental well-being and decreased mental distress.

3. Connecting with others in a supportive environment decreased social isolation and increased confidence to relate to others, thus combating social exclusion and mental distress.

Two processes were important for some participants at all six projects.

1. Rebuilding identities was associated with increased self-belief, external validation and moving beyond a service user identity, thus combating social exclusion and mental distress.

2. Expanding horizons led to wider aspirations and opportunities and to enhanced self-esteem, resulting in reduced social exclusion and improved mental well-being.

A further three processes were important for some people at some of the six projects.

1. Self-expression promoted catharsis and self-acceptance, and provided alternative ways of coping – benefits that decreased mental distress and reduced social exclusion

2. Connecting with abilities gave a sense of pride and achievement, which improved mental health/well-being

3. Having time out helped alleviate worries and responsibilities, thus decreasing mental distress.

Of the eight processes, rebuilding identities, expanding horizons and self-expression were particularly important for people with long experience of mental health problems and service use. Having time out was particularly important for people experiencing depression and anxiety stemming from the pressures they faced in their everyday lives.

Conclusion

As Clift *et al* (2009) point out, among some reviewers of arts and health research there is a tendency to conclude that a robust evidence base is lacking, largely on account of the dearth of experimental studies in this field. However, this chapter has demonstrated that while there may have been no experimental studies of arts and mental health work, the evaluations that are reported consistently demonstrate similar mental health gains, and similar processes through which these are achieved. In his contribution to a recent Voluntary Arts England publication, Professor Louis Appleby, joint arts and health lead for the Department of Health, writes:

'The more rigorous that we can be about the benefits of arts participation then the better it will be… However, the measurable benefits could come in different forms. I think it is much more difficult to do a randomised trial on arts in the same way that it is, for example, on a new drug treatment. The evidence will always look a little softer I suspect. On the other hand, if you have a mass of people saying that the sense of pleasure, the sense of creativity and the sense of emotional identification which comes with arts participation helps maintain their well-being or helps their recovery then that is bound to be a powerful influence.'
(In: Duval, 2009, p18)

Taken together, the retrospective evaluations summarised earlier draw on testimonials from several hundred arts participants. Add to those the 200 or so who have taken part in prospective evaluations to date and there is indeed a mass of people testifying to the benefits of participatory arts, and a growing body of outcomes evidence to add further weight. Although there is no doubt that further research is needed, including economic evaluation, on the basis even of the existing evidence-base it seems reasonable to conclude that support for arts and mental health work is justified by the benefits so many people have reported for their well-being and mental health.

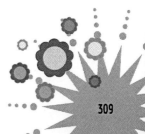

References

Clift S, Camic P, Chapman B, Clayton G, Daykin N, Eades G, Parkinson C, Secker J, Stickley Y & White M (2009) The state of arts and health in England. *Arts in Health* **1** (1) 6–35.

Duval P (2009) *Restoring the Balance: The effect of arts participation on wellbeing and health*. Newcastle upon Tyne: Voluntary Arts England.

Goldie I (2007) *Arts, Creativity and Mental Health Initiative: Participatory arts self-evaluation approach project report*. Glasgow: Mental Health Foundation.

Secker J, Hacking S, Spandler H, Kent M & Shenton J (2007) *Mental Health, Social Inclusion and Arts: Developing the evidence base. Final report* [online]. Available at: http://www.socialinclusion.org.uk/resources/index.php?subid=71 (accessed August 2010).

Secker J & Heydinrych K (2009) Open Arts: promoting well-being and social inclusion through art. *A Life in the Day* **13** (4) 20–24.

Shepherd G, Boardman J & Slade M (2008) *Making Recovery a Reality*. London: Sainsbury Centre for Mental Health.

Social Exclusion Unit (2004) *Mental Health and Social Inclusion*. London: Office of the Deputy Prime Minister.

South Essex Service User Research Group (SE-SURG), Secker J & Tebbs M (2008) Modernising day and employment services in the South East: the role of service user researchers. *A Life in the Day* **12** (3) 29–32.

White M (2009) *Arts Development in Community Health: A social tonic*. Oxford: Radcliffe Publishing.

World Health Organization (2007) *Mental Health: Strengthening mental health promotion. Fact sheet No.220* [online]. Available at: www.who.int/mediacentre/factsheets/fs220/en (accessed August 2010).

Chapter 21

Work and public mental health: welfare and well-being in and through employment

David Donald, Lee Knifton, John Hollingsworth and Rob Gründemann

Introduction

Throughout Europe there is widespread agreement that having a regular job is both good for the person employed and benefits the rest of the community. Jobs provide an income and make employment the main means of the distribution of the national income and the provision of the consumer purchasing power that drives a modern economy. The other side of the same coin is that being 'out of the labour force' means dependence on others for the production of desirable goods and services. Perhaps less immediately obvious, but nevertheless still widely acknowledged, are the benefits of appropriate regular work to physical and mental health (Waddell & Burton, 2006). Being 'out of work' has the potential to threaten mental well-being and to trigger vulnerabilities. All this has a special force in contemporary, commercially dominated, heavily urbanised societies that was not true in traditional societies. Being without work is more stigmatised in modernised societies; being in paid employment is widely accepted as 'the norm'.

This acceptance of the centrality of wage earning employment thus has had an important place for welfare and economic policy and practice since the end of the Second World War. However, when we move from general statements of intent to particular actions, a lack of agreement on the nature and effects of the possible types of intervention makes for a complex and sensitive policy area. If securing appropriate employment for all – or for as many people as possible – has considerable sociological and psychological significance as well as economic importance for both the community and the individual, then how should we go about ensuring an adequate supply of real and appropriate jobs? The terms of the debates to which that question gives rise to are 'essentially contested' (Gallie, 1956). The actors in the situation do not agree on definitions of what is good or bad, or feasible or impossible. They disagree on many things and, in particular, what it means to secure 'appropriate levels of employment' and how to achieve that. Public mental health practice has to take such fundamental disagreement into account. It needs to be a blend of art and evaluation, politics and science that attempts to secure some common agreement in contemporary circumstances.

The authors of this chapter are acutely aware that the issues are complicated. In this short chapter, we would ideally cover 'from Marx to marketing' to consider the promotion of mental health in mature capitalist society. In the event, we lower our horizons to suggest some concerns that continue to shape approaches to policy and raise some issues to be addressed in contemporary European society. First, we introduce some ideas that have had practical effects. Next, we look at practice and some feasible responses to present day implementation.

Why work? The general significance of work in employment to mental health

European social policy, and in particular health policy, is still engaged in a debate over some of the assumptions introduced in the immediate post-war period under the general mobilising slogan of 'the Welfare State'. The British were, in particular, influenced by the contentions of 'the father of the Welfare State' Sir William Beveridge. In his famous and influential reports (Beveridge 1942, 1944) he identified five 'giants' as obstacles to the welfare of the populace. For present purposes we are concerned with the one which he labelled (in rather Victorian terms) 'idleness' (an absence of regular work) and which he distinguished from 'want' (an absence of income). He said:

> '*Idleness is not the same as want, but a separate evil, which men do not escape by having an income. They must also have the chance of rendering useful service and of feeling that they are doing so.*'

And elsewhere:

> '*A person who has difficulty in buying the labour that he wants suffers inconvenience or reduction of profits. A person who cannot sell his labour is in effect told that he is of no use. The first difficulty causes annoyance or loss. The other is a personal catastrophe.*'

Beveridge wrote in the context of the Second World War with the prospect of returning military personnel. He had an acute awareness of the discontents and social problems of the Great Depression that had so disfigured social life in the immediate pre-war period. The Depression had promoted much consideration of the effects of unemployment. A seminal example of such work was the study of the Austrian industrial village of Marienthal and its unemployed workers by a team centred round the social psychologist Marie Jahoda and the sociologist Paul Lazarsfeld and published (in German) in 1932 as Marienthal: The sociography of an unemployed community (Jahoda *et al*, 1932,1972). The team documented the negative effects on individuals and the community of the loss of jobs. But what are the specific benefits of having a job? How does work in paid employment benefit our mental health? Some time after her pioneering study, Marie Jahoda developed a useful characterisation of Ideal Mental Health (Jahoda, 1958). We introduce it here because it has been influential and has led to a great deal of research and discussion. It is still useful to stimulate debate. The perfectly adjusted human being, she suggested, would be capable of, and exhibit, the following:

1. efficient self-perception
2. realistic self-esteem and acceptance
3. voluntary control of behaviour
4. true perception of the world
5. sustaining relationships and giving affection
6. self-direction and productivity.

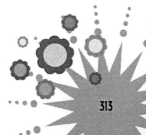

These are an ideal set – rarely achieved in their fullest expression and variable from time to time according to circumstance and predicament. In the real world, she suggested, we might get close to their fullest realisation and maintenance only if we were very well adjusted. Her contention was that these characteristics were most frequently promoted and sustained in the modern world through full-time, paid employment. The experience of the 1930s meant that both Beveridge and Jahoda thought that the state had a major role to play in ensuring that such work was available.

Debating work and mental health: politics

Beveridge and Jahoda contended that work roles, and thus their absence, framed people's felt and perceived status, identities, and in general shaped their social circumstances. In the contemporary western world the question 'what do you do?' remains very close to the question 'who are you?' But Beveridge was a Liberal greatly influenced by the Fabian ideas of the Webbs and Jahoda was a self-proclaimed socialist. The political positions they held are highly contentious. In the years since they wrote, no consensus has emerged over the formulation of the problems, let alone their solutions. Throughout Europe the post-war welfare state was an uneasy settlement with a range of reluctant participants – and both open and clandestine critics. However, the remnants of the post-war settlement remain both as ideas and as institutions and we must still acknowledge them. The critics came, and still come, from both left and right. Are there any areas of agreement?

Beveridge's central policy goal was very widely tolerated in the Keynesian influenced western world until the 1970s. It is proclaimed in the title of his book, *Full Employment in a Free Society* (1944). Full-employment was to a considerable extent approximated into the 1970s. However, especially from the 1980s onwards we have had to engage with the issues of less than full employment in a free market society. In the 'great capitalist restoration' of the last three decades, all ambition to centre policy on securing full employment was either dropped or diluted – especially in pursuit of anti-inflation policies. As we write, part-time employment is currently at a record high in the UK and a flexible labour force – in the sense of a high probability of job and career changes – is celebrated in the name of economic efficiency. Fluctuations in the level and stability of employment are assumed to be inevitable. These circumstances are presented as necessary and inescapable for efficiency and prosperity in an 'open globalised' economy. The social impact of these changes in policy, perspectives and predicaments are of significance for public health practice. But, even through this lens, an awareness of the psychological benefits of paid work and the value of the recognition of that occupation by others, are still widely acknowledged. Although unpaid volunteering is considered to be good for all concerned, the notion that 'being in work' is highly desirable has not become less important in contemporary circumstances. These views are shared across the political spectrum and including supporters of the current UK government. George Osborne used our opening quote from Beveridge in 2008 Annual Lecture to the Conservative supporting think tank the Centre for Policy Studies (Osborne, 2008; Nelson, 2008).

Work, working conditions, and the distribution of income determine the political, economic and social structures in which we live and operate. We cannot untangle the impact of unemployment, working conditions, salaries and taxation from poverty, social exclusion and inequality. Poverty, social exclusion and inequality remain at the forefront of recent public mental health discourse (Rogers & Pilgrim, 2003; Friedli 2009). But the public policy debate (if not all academic discourse) has moved away from discussions of socialism and redistribution. Health debates have instead tended to focus upon the impact of different forms of capitalist economies across Europe. In the United Kingdom the government is intent on a new order and a different ethic. The balance of the economy has to be shifted away from public employment to private enterprise and, within that, manufacturing has to be given a new priority. Private welfare services have to be further developed – to create more efficient and better directed care and to ease the pressures on taxation. Charitable and voluntary service has to be emphasised in the delivery of services and the pursuit of greater social cohesion. The roles of state institutions as direct service providers have to be diminished. Whether or not we agree with this, it is in this context that the promotion of mental health through, and in, employment must be pursued in the foreseeable future. This puts special emphasis on employers and their employment policies.

Workplaces as the locus of public mental health: specifics

Working with employers to improve mental health requires us to consider both the positive mental health of the whole workforce (Keyes, 2005) and, alongside, appropriate supports for people who experience mental health problems. And that means encouraging both progressive employment practices and the creation of positive workplace conditions. If work has the importance we have argued for, then influencing the circumstances of employment becomes very central to the promotion of mental health. Given that most people spend a significant proportion of their time and their lives in workplaces (Black, 2008), then they become a key setting through which to effectively engage large numbers of people. Only formal educational settings and the family are equivalent in significance.

How aware are employing organisations of the mental health dimensions of the jobs they provide? Work has 'manifest' and 'latent' functions and 'dysfunctions' (Merton, 1948; Berger, 1963). That is, some consequences are intended and some unintended. Employee health and mental health are mostly latent; they are by-products rather than the first order, intended consequences of most contemporary employers. Thus an organisation might promote practices for manifest purposes such as efficiency or cost minimisation and yet these might advantage the mental health of the worker. An obvious example is the time structuring of the working day where it is widely observed that 'the lack of a structured day' for people who are unemployed and other 'out of labour force' people is a challenge to mental health.

But this positive contribution is not always the case. Some employment is dysfunctional for both physical and (related) mental health. Studies indicate that the extent of poor mental health at work is significant (Grove, 2006). Over 15% of employees consistently report being very or extremely stressed by work. Anxiety, depression and stress result in more days off than any other cause, accounting for almost half of all absences in the UK (LFS, 2009). Sickness absence, staff turnover and lost productivity mean that the costs of mental health issues nears £30 billion each year (IDEA, 2010). Thus a challenge for public mental health is to understand and minimise the workplace conditions that inhibit mental health. Briefly, these include the following.

1. Unsafe working conditions leading to physical injury, chronic or life limiting illness. Physical illness is a predictor of poor mental health, and in the UK the 'social gradient' for disability-free life expectancy is even greater than the stark differences in mortality rates (Marmot, 2010).

2. Low pay and unequal incomes: diminishing mental health and increasing perceived exclusion. At a European level, manual and lower level employees fare worst (Anderson *et al*, 2009). Notably this is less so in countries with greater integration and cohesion – especially in Scandanavian countries where the social gradient is modest and the effect persists when accounting for GDP.

3. Workplace conditions of employment: creating stress and diminished mental health (eg. insecurity, low social support, bullying, repetitive work with little employee job control).

These factors are major structural and political issues, necessitating an ongoing role for public health in informing and enforcing legislative frameworks that protect against negative practice, while advocating social supports that ameliorate such effects. A central question that this raises is whether 'bad work is worse for health than no work'? Some current evidence from Australia suggests that 'bad work' (defined by the co-occurrence of a number of negative factors such as job strain, status and insecurity) has a similar, but not worse, health and well-being impact as unemployment (Broom *et al*, 2006). This leads us to assert that a mentally healthy society is one that maximises both employment rates and positive practice and working conditions. A key emphasis for public mental health practice is therefore to support employers to 'promote the positive'. How is this best approached?

A framework for supporting employers to promote mental health

An initial challenge is to devise a conceptual framework that can be understood by the public health practitioner and readily communicated to others including the health, voluntary and, especially, business sectors. This is rendered problematic by a lack of consistency across policy initiatives. Importantly, policy and practice in employability, health promotion and mental ill-health are often developed separately. A second issue is that the bulk of programmes (and therefore the evidence base) are concentrated around a limited number of areas, for example, stress management programmes. Examples of these can be found in the developing EU database of mental health promotion practice entitled Promenpol (BAUA, 2010).

Gründemann and Knifton led an EU public health funded project with the European Network for Workplace Health Promotion to develop a framework for promoting public mental health through workplaces (Knifton *et al*, 2009). The aim was to achieve agreement from agencies drawn from across EU countries with different social and economic systems and values. This required considerable compromises and efforts to understand contested and shared ideas that we have suggested are necessary for contemporary initiatives.

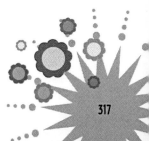

As we advocated in earlier sections of this paper, our framework adopts a broad perspective on mental health – ranging from promotion of positive mental health and well-being for all employees through to supporting recruitment for people who experience mental health problems. It is beyond the scope of this chapter to report this in full detail. Here we present four core elements.

1. **Positive recruitment**. From a public health perspective we see this as having two aspects. The first involves partnering with regeneration organisations to promote local recruitment in areas of low income with a primary objective of reducing the public mental health impact of concentrated, generational unemployment. The second focuses on working with people who are experiencing mental health problems to secure appropriate employment opportunities. Despite equalities legislation, people with enduring mental health problems have the lowest employment rates of almost all social groups at consistently under 20% compared to 43% of all people of working age who have a disability (Williams *et al*, 2008). Practical responses require employers to engage with employability organisations that use approaches that have the strongest evidence base such as supported employment and individual placement schemes (Schneider *et al*, 2003). Employers should also be encouraged to support anti-stigma campaigns. User-led research outlines complex and interlinked barriers to employment including significant levels of stigma from colleagues and employers in work and at recruitment stages (Faulkner & Layzell, 2000; Arthur *et al*, 2008).

2. **Retention**. Supporting the retention of people who experience mental health problems in work is a difficult public health challenge. Brown *et al* (2007) in a study in Scotland show that it becomes increasingly difficult for someone to return to work the longer they have been out of their post and on incapacity benefits. There is a strong public health, ethical and economic case for re-focusing resources from employability to retention. This means flexibility of support, adjustment to job specifications and conditions, and inter-agency working. Awareness through techniques such as mental health workshops, involving testimony from someone with experience of mental health problems, indicate positive effects on the attitudes and intentions of employees and colleagues to seek help and support one another (Pinfold *et al*, 2005; Knifton *et al*, 2008). Employers should also be made aware of the effectiveness and availability of brief therapies for employees experiencing common mental health problems (Seymour & Grove, 2005).

3. **Prevention**. Proactively preventing mental health problems and the minimisation of stress for all employees is increasingly practiced by

employers. There is strong evidence for the effectiveness of stress management programmes generally and for additional support for employees in high stress roles (Seymour & Grove, 2005). We have noted how poor mental health is unevenly distributed across and within organisations. With limited resources, priority should therefore be given to employment situations where there is low or unequal pay, where employees have job insecurity, high stress jobs, and to organisations who have fewer resources for personnel and development issues such as small businesses. At present, we risk achieving health gain at the expense of health equity.

4. **Promotion**. Promoting mental health is more complex when applied to positive mental health in workplaces. Many initiatives claim to promote positive mental health and well-being, yet in practice, merely target and measure stress and identify mental health problems. We have to decide how we measure positive mental health. Which dimensions of individuals should we consider? Self-esteem or confidence or one of the many other psychological states? Or is organisational well-being more than the sum of the well-being of the individuals? Should we instead assess organisational connectedness, networks, activities? While this cannot be resolved due to the contested nature of positive mental health, there is an emergent set of ideas, studies and interventions that indicate that we can improve workforce well-being and that this enhances organisational performance. How promotion is approached is highly contextual: tactics are best established through co-creation by employers and employees. Some promising areas outlined in a recent study include workplace culture, social capital, activities including exercise and creativity and resiliency programmes (Teixeira *et al*, 2010).

These ideas, and practical case study examples, are outlined fully in the resource *A Guide to Promoting Mental Health in the Workplace* (Knifton *et al*, 2009). This ongoing document, part of the European 'Work in Tune With Life' programme, will be updated and populated with case studies as a resource for practitioners into the future. It outlines the stages of developing mental health interventions in workplaces including issues of organisational buy in, empowering processes, ongoing evaluation common to public health practice. However, unless we are able to effectively engage with employers we will not be effective.

Engaging employers

The principles of social marketing, stemming from the commercial sector, remind us that we must understand the social environment and motivations of those we are targeting if we wish to influence their attitudes and behaviour (Hastings, 2007). We need to focus on specific objectives, and to design interventions and approaches to engagement that overcome the barriers to achieving the intended behaviour change.

On its own, legislation does not determine action. Engaging employers requires us to consider their particular environment and to identify factors that might motivate them to change their policies and practices. Taking advantage of cultural supports is important. It is useful to speculate about the relationships of employers and employment practices to civil society. We need to be clear about what we are asking them to do to promote mental health. Awareness is a starting point, but is rarely enough to initiate change.

In general, employers are, of course, attracted to changes that are good for business. The gains to be had from establishing a mentally healthy workforce and a supportive culture are significant but may not always be apparent. Valuable selling points include making an organisation more attractive to potential and existing employees, reducing absences, boosting organisational productivity, and enhancing and maintaining corporate reputation.

When engaging with employers we need to take into account the resources – people, time, premises, skills and knowledge that an employer has at its disposal. The size of an employer is a primary consideration as large organisations are more likely to have formal structures and procedures that shape communication with them. Smaller organisations may be less formal with a senior figure, such as the proprietor, taking responsibility for such organisational matters. Companies may be better approached through other companies or a trade association.

Companies are frequently aware that their reputations matter. 'Reputation management' is increasingly a concern. Although public mental health is not a central feature of their PR activities other public health and welfare issues have frequently been an issue and the well-being of employees has been a recurring theme. Although perhaps not quite as spectacular as the grand historical initiatives of firms such as Cadbury, some contemporary policies are encouraging and suggest directions that others might be persuaded to follow. BT, through their 'workfit' campaigns and, more recently Nestlé in their 'global corporate challenge', have sought publicity for schemes related to the promotion of mental health (Friedli *et al*, 2007; Cartwright, 2010). John Lewis have long promoted their partner's structure as linking the welfare and well-being of the workforce to their commercial success.

Conclusion

Our general argument is that, since 1945, the primary responsibility for securing and maintaining citizen public mental health has rested with the state. Legislation and interventions based in law with governments as agencies have been central. This remains the case but increasingly there is pressure for change – for good reasons and bad.

State services have often turned out to be bureaucratic and inflexible and left wing critics have sought more citizen participation, less central control and more successful outcomes. Right wing critics have suggested low efficiency and efficacy, poor value for money, and the erosion of freedom with the creation of dependency cultures. Both sets of criticisms have some force. Current circumstances – perhaps especially in the UK where the coalition government's Big Society initiative has prominence – oblige a greater reliance on the responsibilities of all the actors. Beveridge is being cited again and his tri-partite approach to securing a socially cohesive, high welfare community is being revisited. Government, private enterprise and voluntarism were the ingredients of his recipe. In his last major prescriptive work, Beveridge (1948) emphasised the importance of voluntary action, which he suggests can be paid or unpaid. He outlines what we might call the third sector. But it is the integration of state, commercial and this sector, which he advocates. Beveridge was quite clear that the dominance of commercial concerns would not produce a good society. In the current world, good corporate citizens will show prudent yet progressive attitudes to the way in which they create and manage employment. In addition to this, governments, and perhaps especially the European Union, will encourage and support firms who work well with the third sector.

In general, business has quite rightly, been given a privileged position by modernised states (Lindblom, 1977). This follows from their central significance to economic performance. But it is also an acknowledgment of their other public contributions and responsibilities (Donald & Hutton, 1998). As governments assert the imperatives of civic responsibilities they must apply their strictures widely and induce the commercial world to co-operate with the state and the third sector in the creation of a more integrated, civilised and democratic society. Public mental health should be high on the agenda and its practitioners vigilant in the defence and support of the interests of their fellow citizens.

References

Anderson R, Mikulia B, Vermeylen G, Lyly-Yrjanainen M & Zigante V (2009) *Second European Quality of Life Survey*. Dublin: European Foundation for the Improvement of Living and Working Conditions.

Arthur B, Knifton L, Park M & Doherty E (2008) Cutting the dash: experiences of mental health and employment. *Journal of Public Mental Health* **7** (4) 51–59.

BAUA (2010) *Promenpol – Practical approaches to the promotion and protection of mental health online database* [online]. Dortmund: BAUA. Available at: www.mentalhealthpromotion.net (accessed July 2010).

Berger P (1963) *Invitation to Sociology. A humanistic perspective*. New York: Anchor Books, Doubleday & Company, Inc.

Beveridge WHB (1942) *Social Insurance and Allied Services*. Cmd. 6404. London: HMSO.

Beveridge WHB (1944) *Full Employment in a Free Society*. London: Allen & Unwin.

Beveridge WHB (1948) *Voluntary Action*. London: Allen & Unwin.

Black C (2008) *Working for a Healthier Tomorrow*. London: TSO.

Broom D, D'Souza R, Strazdins L, Butterworth P, Parslow R & Rodgers B (2006) The lesser evil: bad jobs or unemployment? A survey of mid-aged Australians. *Social Science & Medicine* **63** (3) 575–586.

Brown J, Hanlon P, Webster D, Turok I, Arnott J & MacDonald E (2007) *Turning The Tap Off! Incapacity Benefit in Glasgow and Scotland – trends over the past five years*. Glasgow: Glasgow Centre for Population Health Briefing Papers.

Cartwright S (2010) *Outstanding Benefits of Exercise to Employees* [online]. Available at: www.lancs.ac.uk/shm/news/march_2010/exercise_good_for_workers/ (accessed July 2010).

Donald D & Hutton A (1998) Public purpose and private ownership. *Journal of Economic Issues* **32** (2) 457–464.

Faulkner A & Layzell S (2000) *Strategies for Living: A report of user-led research into people's strategies for living with mental distress*. London: Mental Health Foundation.

Friedli L, Oliver C, Tidyman M & Ward G (2007) *Mental Health Improvement: Evidence-based messages to promote mental wellbeing*. Edinburgh: NHS Health Scotland.

Friedli L (2009) *Mental Health, Resilience and Inequalities*. Copenhagen and London: World Health Organization and Mental Health Foundation.

Gallie WB (1956) Essentially contested concepts. *Proceedings of the Aristotelian Society* **56** 167–198.

Grove B (2006) Common mental health problems in the workplace: how can occupational physicians help? *Occupational Medicine* **56** (5) 291–293.

Hastings G (2007) *Social Marketing: Why should the devil have all the best tunes?* Oxford: Elsevier.

IDEA (2010) *Mental Health and Worklessness*. London: Improvement and Development Agency, Local Government Association.

Jahoda M, Lazarsfeld P & Zeisel H (1932, 1972) *Marienthal: The sociography of an unemployed community*. Translation from the German by the authors with John Reginall and Thomas Elsaesser. London: Tavistock Publications.

Jahoda M (1958) *Current Concepts of Positive Mental Health*. New York: Basic Books.

Keyes CLM (2005) Mental illness and/or mental health? Investigating axioms of the complete state model of health. *Journal of Consulting and Clinical Psychology* **73** (3) 539–548.

Knifton L, Walker A & Quinn N (2008) Workplace interventions can reduce stigma. *Journal of Public Mental Health* **7** (4) 40–50.

Knifton L, Watson V, Den Besten H, Gründemann R, & Dijkman A (2009) *A Guide to Promoting Mental Health in the Workplace*. Essen: BKK Bundesverband for the European Network for Workplace Health Promotion.

LFS (2009) Labour Force Survey 2008/09. UK: Office of National Statistics.

Lindblom CE (1977) *Politics and Markets: The world's political-economic systems*. New York: Basic Books.

Marmot Review (2010) *Fair Society, Healthy Lives: Strategic review of health inequalities in England post-2010*. London: Marmot Review.

Merton RK (1948) *Social Theory and Social Structure*. New York: The Free Press.

Nelson F (2008) *Tackling the Giant Evil of Idleness. Spectator Blog* [online], 7th December. Available at: www.spectator.co.uk/coffeehouse/3071651/tackling-the-giant-evil-of-idleness.thtml (accessed July 2010).

Osborne G (2008) Annual Lecture 2008. Available at: www.cps.org.uk/cps_catalog/Catalogue_Annual_Lecture_2008_614.html (accessed July 2010).

Pinfold V, Thornicroft G, Huxley P & Farmer P (2005) Active ingredients in anti-stigma programmes in mental health. *International Review of Psychiatry* **17** (2) 123–131.

Rogers A & Pilgrim D (2003) *Mental Health and Inequality*. Basingstoke: Palgrave.

Schneider J, Heyman A & Turton N (2003) *Employment for People with Mental Health Problems*. Leeds: National Institute for Mental Health England.

Seymour L & Grove B (2005) *Workplace Interventions for People with Common Mental Health Problems*. London: British Occupational Health Research Foundation.

Teixeira M, McGrory A & Knifton L (2010) *Pieces of a Jigsaw: Towards mentally healthy workplaces*. Glasgow: NHS Greater Glasgow and Clyde.

Waddell G & Burton AK (2006) *Is Work Good for your Health and Wellbeing?* London: TSO.

Williams B, Copestake P, Eversley J & Stafford B (2008) *Experiences and Expectations of Disabled People*. London: Office for Disability Issues, Department of Work and Pensions.

Chapter 22

Economics

David McDaid and A-La Park

Why think about economics and mental health?

As earlier chapters in this volume indicate there are many reasons for taking action, both to promote better mental well-being, and to help treat poor mental health in the population. While the key goal may be to improve quality of life across the population, there are also economic benefits for individuals and society as a whole. The adverse impacts of poor mental health can affect many aspects of life, often with startling economic consequences.

If resources were limitless it would therefore be straightforward to argue for investment in effective mental health promotion, disorder prevention, treatments and rehabilitation. Reality is somewhat different: resources are scarce and careful choices have to be made about their use. Decision makers want to know not only about the cost of different policy actions, but also their cost effectiveness. This information takes on an even greater resonance in the context of any economic downturn where budget holders may be under great pressure to demonstrate efficiency savings and, if necessary, cut services deemed to be of low priority (McDaid & Knapp, 2010).

In the case of mental health, having an understanding of these economic issues is of particular concern. It is critical to consider the many impacts that poor mental health can have for a range of budgets that go beyond health and social care, including employment, education, housing and criminal justice. Additional investment in mental health promoting services by one sector, for instance health, may generate substantial economic payoffs in one or more different sectors, for example, for employers and social security systems if there is a reduction in absenteeism and/or withdrawals from the labour market.

This chapter briefly highlights some of the economic consequences of poor mental health and potential benefits of improved well-being. It then looks at the role and appropriateness of economic evidence to help inform decisions on how to prioritise spending. We end with some illustrative examples where economic evidence has played an important role in supporting arguments for additional resources for actions intended to promote better mental health and well-being.

What are the economic consequences of poor mental health and mental well-being?

A starting point in building any case for investment in mental health involves quantifying the economic impacts of avoidable poor mental health. Much progress has been made in this regard and increased awareness of these costs has been cited as a key justification for action in national and pan-national mental health strategies and policy documents in the UK and abroad (HM Government, 2009; Commission of the European Communities, 2008; The Standing Senate Committee on Social Affairs, 2006).

Costs fall on many sectors. There are immediate costs arising from the need to treat and support people with mental health problems. These can include additional costs not only to the health and social care system, but also to social welfare services that may help provide financial support and accommodation, employment services who help promote reintegration into the workplace, education services that may be concerned with promoting better classroom behaviour and educational attainment, as well as to families who may give up their time to help support a loved one. This is to say nothing of the costs of suicides: each suicide on average can have a lifetime cost to society in the order of £1.5 million (McDaid & Kennelly, 2009). There are also longer-term consequences including the risk of discrimination in the labour and housing markets, reduced rates of utilisation of health services, potentially detrimental to physical health, and an increased risk of contact with the criminal justice system.

In England alone the annual costs of major child and adult mental problems have been estimated to be more than £52 billion; nearly 77% of these costs (excluding those for dementia) fell outside the health care sector, due largely to much lower rates of employment (McCrone *et al*, 2008). This is an enormous sum of money, equivalent to about half of what was spent on the National Health Service in England in 2009/2010, but it is also conservative. The authors acknowledged that non-healthcare costs have only been estimated for some mental health problems. The analysis also did not consider some further profound impacts on quality of life, which remain difficult to measure in monetary terms. These include the costs of discrimination and prejudice that people with mental health problems may experience on a daily basis.

While we know a lot about the costs of poor mental health, it remains the case that much less attention has been paid to the positive economic consequences of promoting positive mental well-being in the population. This imbalance is beginning to be addressed. Better mental well-being has been associated with better levels of cognitive functioning and openness to learning and development, improved productivity and lower rates of absenteeism in the workplace (Beddington *et al*, 2008). Better mental well-being can also help individuals increase their resilience to stress; there is some tentative evidence from the United States suggesting that individuals in a better state of well-being are less likely to experience future poor mental health (Keyes, 2007).

Using economics to help in priority setting

The chapters in this book have made many powerful arguments to support investment in mental health, but these aims will always be constrained by resources. No mental health system, even if it is perfectly designed and efficiently managed, can meet all mental health needs. Priority setting on the use of resources will thus be inevitable.

These choices are not restricted to mental health services alone – they affect all public expenditure decisions. One type of decision is concerned with setting priorities on how resources in an existing mental health system are allocated. Another choice may be about weighing up the relative merits of investing in mental health versus other health needs within a general health budget. Increasingly, choices need to be made on actions to promote health in all policies, for instance, policy-makers may wish to consider whether it is worth investing in support services to help small business implement workplace mental health promoting strategies, or actions in school to counter bullying or promote mental well-being.

It is essential that such prioritisation decisions are made on a transparent basis, in order to foster an environment where mental health needs are put on an equal footing with other claims on the use of resources. Economic evaluation can help inform this process. Widely used in informing health system policy and practice in many countries with publicly funded health care systems, including Australia, Belgium, England, Canada, Finland, the Netherlands, Scotland and Sweden, it allows for the comparative analysis of alternative courses of action in terms of both their costs and consequences.

Approaches to economic evaluation

There are several different approaches that may be used; all measure costs in monetary terms but differ in outcome measurement. The most widely used approach, cost-effectiveness analysis, measures outcomes using a natural (eg. mental health/illness specific) measure, for instance reporting costs per unit improvement on a clinical depression scale. While intuitively easy to understand, it cannot help compare the merits of potential investments in mental health with other areas of health care.

Cost-utility analysis theoretically overcomes this limitation by measuring all health outcomes using a common measure, the Quality Adjusted Life Year (QALY), so that cost effectiveness is reported in terms of cost per QALY gained. This approach weights the number of years of life gained to take account of the quality of life of those years, with one representing a year in perfect quality health and zero representing death.

The impacts of poor mental health on quality of life can be great indeed. For instance, living with severe depression has been estimated to have a QALY score of between 0.3 and 0.5. Two years lived in this state would be equivalent to obtaining 0.6 – 1 QALYs (Mann et al, 2009). This can then be compared to QALY scores for other health problems, for instance QALY scores ranging between 0.78 and 0.51 for mild to severe cardiovascular disease and 0.60 and 0.48 for people experiencing a relapse in schizophrenia (Briggs et al, 2008, Dyer et al, 2010).

Another alternative approach, cost-benefit analysis, measures both costs and benefits in monetary terms, allowing comparisons to be made between investments in health and other sectors such as education. A positive net benefit (ie. where the value of the benefits is greater than the costs incurred to achieve them) would merit investment. This approach would be particularly useful when looking at the case for interventions delivered outside the health sectors, such as mental health promotion in the workplace, where in addition to health benefits there may be gains in workplace productivity and staff morale. To date, however, its use has been very limited.

Limitations

While economic evaluation can be a powerful tool to inform any priority setting process, it should never be used in isolation. It is not free of value judgements. Unless a new intervention is both less costly and more effective than the existing situation policy-makers have to make a value judgement as to whether the additional benefits are worth the extra investment. While a cost per QALY gained of £30,000 is often considered the threshold for cost effectiveness in England, this may be considered too expensive in other jurisdictions where resources are more limited.

Perhaps of greater concern may be the reliance on clinical symptoms in cost effectiveness studies. These may fail to capture and convey broader benefits and economic payoffs that improved mental health and well-being can have, such as increased participation in employment and community activities. Without careful consideration of non-health system outcomes, potential investments in mental health services may be disadvantaged compared to investments in physical health that may be immediately seen to save lives.

This misperception may be particularly pertinent during a time of economic cutbacks; one survey in Germany asked 5,000 members of the public about services they wished to protect from health budget cuts (Matschinger & Angermeyer, 2004). Eighty-nine percent wanted to protect cancer services, 51% HIV services and 49% cardiovascular services. The three lowest priorities for protection were all in the mental health arena – only 10% of individuals felt that services for people with schizophrenia deserved protection, while only 7% and 6% of the survey sample wished to safeguard depression and alcohol related services.

Thus other key factors always need to be considered in any priority setting process. For instance what can be done to ensure that key target groups, such as those with mental health needs, actually make use of any new intervention? What views do potential service users and other stakeholders have about the appropriateness of interventions? Are there any ethical issues. For example, if a decision implies disbanding or reducing access to an existing service? In the case of mental health in particular, there may also be issues on social inclusion and human rights to consider. While the cost effectiveness of different strategies to improve the uptake of a new service by key population groups can be built into economic evaluation, most of these concerns will require different types of information gathering, eg. consultation and surveys of service users.

In saying this, despite its limitations, we argue that economic evidence remains an essential component of any priority setting process. Not weighing up the costs and benefits of different potential uses of resources can itself be unfair, as it may mean that resources are allocated in a non-transparent and ineffective manner, thus denying others the opportunity to benefit from help and support (Maynard & McDaid, 2003).

As we shall now illustrate, far from being a way of discriminating against people with mental health needs, input from economic analyses into the health policy decision-making process can be used to justify additional investment.

Making the case for investing in mental health: economics can make a difference

'Money talks' remains a reality of life. Better recognition of the costs of not taking action to promote mental health and well-being, coupled with a continued growth in studies demonstrating that effective interventions to prevent, as well as tackle, these problems can represent good value for money, are beginning to have an impact on resources being made available for mental health promotion, particularly when looking at developments in the early years of life and within workplaces. What is also significant is that these interventions are often both delivered and funded outside the health care sector, with economic payoffs falling on different budget holders.

There has been growth in economic analysis of mental health promotion and mental disorder prevention interventions targeted at children (Zechmeister *et al*, 2008, Kilian *et al*, 2010). Compelling data on the long-term adverse consequences of conduct disorders arising in childhood have provided a powerful argument for investing in early years interventions at home and in school. Information collated for the National Institute for Health and Clinical Excellence in England (NICE) have indicated that actions delivering modest improvements in emotional well-being may be highly cost effective at a cost per QALY gained of £5,500; there would also be additional benefits to the education sector from reduced classroom disruption (McCabe, 2008).

Another sector where actions have in part been driven by economic considerations concerns the labour market. The adverse consequences of poor mental health in the workplace fall both on employers, through a reduction in workplace performance, and on the public purse, through the need to contribute to the costs of sickness benefits. The long-term costs to the tax payer for those who drop out of work with mental health problems can be eye-watering. By 2007 in Great Britain 40% of all disability benefits were being paid out to claimants with mental health problems; this was more than the entire cost of paying out unemployment benefit.

Measures to encourage flexible workplaces, including opportunities for job change and career progression, as well as access to counselling and support to deal with stress and better risk management, are being fostered in both the public and private sectors. It is not insignificant that investment in these measures may reduce the costs of absenteeism and staff turnover to employers in England by 30% per annum, some £8 billion per annum (National Institute for Health and Clinical Excellence, 2009). One key argument advanced for government investment in the Individual Access to Psychological Therapies (IAPT) programme for the unemployed included the potential economic benefits that could be realised as a result of more individuals obtaining employment (Layard et al, 2007).

Clearly economic evidence can play a powerful role in helping to make the case for investment in mental health-related actions. Given that many actions will require investment outside the health care sector, where key priorities may be very different, such as in schools or in the workplace, it is important going forward that those involved in evaluating mental health related interventions, also put some emphasis on outcomes of direct relevance to these sectors, eg. improvement in educational attainment or workplace productivity. Such information could serve to strengthen further arguments for cross-sectoral investments in measures to improve and protect mental health and well-being.

References

Beddington J, Cooper CL, Field J, Goswami U, Huppert FA, Jenkins R, Jones HS, Kirkwood TB, Sahakian BJ & Thomas SM (2008) The mental wealth of nations. *Nature* **455** 1057–1060.

Briggs A, Wild D, Lees M, Reaney M, Dursun S, Parry D & Mukherjee J (2008) Impact of schizophrenia and schizophrenia treatment-related adverse events on quality of life: direct utility elicitation. *Health and Quality of Life Outcomes* **6** 105.

Commission of the European Communities (2008) *European Pact for Mental Health and Wellbeing* [online]. Brussels, Commission of the European Communities. Available at: http://ec.europa.eu/health/ph_determinants/life_style/mental/docs/pact_en.pdf (accessed August 2010).

Dyer MT, Goldsmith KA, Sharples LS & Buxton MJ (2010) A review of health utilities using the EQ-5D in studies of cardiovascular disease. *Health and Quality of Life Outcomes* **8** 13.

HM Government (2009) *New Horizons: A shared vision for mental health*. London: Department of Health.

Keyes CL (2007) Promoting and protecting mental health as flourishing: a complementary strategy for improving national mental health. *American Psychologist* **62** 95–108.

Kilian R, Losert C, Park A, McDaid D & Knapp M (2010) *Cost-effectiveness Analysis in Child and Adolescent Mental Health Problems: An updated review of literature*. Report for the CAMHEE project. Ulm: University of Ulm.

Layard R, Clark DM, Knapp M & Mayraz G (2007) Cost-benefit analysis of psychological therapy. *National Institute Economic Review* **202** 90–98.

Mann R, Gilbody S & Richards D (2009) Putting the 'Q' in depression QALYs: a comparison of utility measurement using EQ-5D and SF-6D health related quality of life measures. *Social Psychiatry and Psychiatric Epidemiology* **44** 569–578.

Matschinger H & Angermeyer MC (2004) The public's preferences concerning the allocation of financial resources to health care: results from a representative population survey in Germany. *European Psychiatry* **19** 478–482.

Maynard A & McDaid D (2003) Evaluating health interventions: exploiting the potential. *Health Policy* **63** 215–226.

McCabe C (2008) *Estimating the Short-term Cost Effectiveness of a Mental Health Promotion Intervention in Primary Schools*. London: National Institute for Health and Clinical Excellence.

McCrone P, Dhanasiri S, Patel A, Knapp M & Lawton-Smith S (2008) *Paying the Price: The cost of mental health care in England to 2026*. London: King's Fund.

McDaid & Kennelly B (2009) The case for suicide prevention: an economic perspective. In: D Wasserman & C Wasserman (Eds) *The Oxford Textbook of Suicidology – The five continents perspective*. Oxford: Oxford University Press.

McDaid D & Knapp M (2010) Black-skies planning? Prioritising mental health services in times of austerity. *British Journal of Psychiatry* **196** 423–424.

National Institute for Clinical Excellence (2009) *Promoting Mental Well-being Through Productive and Healthy Working Conditions: Guidance for employers* [online]. London: NICE. Available at: http://www.nice.org.uk (accessed August 2010).

The Standing Senate Committee on Social Affairs SAT (2006) *Out of the Shadows at Last: Transforming Mental Health, Mental Illness and Addiction Services in Canada*. Ottawa: The Senate.

Zechmeister I, Killian R & McDaid D (2008) Is it worth investing in mental health promotion and prevention of mental illness? A systematic review of the evidence from economic evaluations. *BMC Public Health* **8** 20.

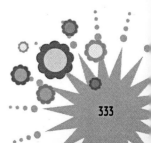